ACCOUNT

OF THE

RUSSIAN DISCOVERIES

BETWEEN

ASIA AND AMERICA

ACCOUNT

OF THE

RUSSIAN DISCOVERIES

BETWEEN

ASIA AND AMERICA

TO WHICH ARE ADDED

THE CONQUEST OF SIBERIA

AND

THE HISTORY OF THE TRANSACTIONS
AND COMMERCE BETWEEN RUSSIA AND CHINA

BY

WILLIAM COXE

THIRD EDITION

WITH SUPPLEMENT TO RUSSIAN DISCOVERIES

[1787]

AUGUSTUS M. KELLEY · PUBLISHERS

NEW YORK 1970

First Edition 1780
Third Edition 1787
(London: *Printed by* J. Nichols *for* T. Cadell
in the Strand, 1787)

REPRINTED 1970 BY
AUGUSTUS M. KELLEY · PUBLISHERS
REPRINTS OF ECONOMIC CLASSICS
New York New York 10001

. . . .

S B N *678-00626-1*
L C N *78-107912*

. . . .

PRINTED IN THE UNITED STATES OF AMERICA
by SENTRY PRESS, NEW YORK, N. Y. 10019

A C C O U N T

O F   T H E

RUSSIAN DISCOVERIES

B E T W E E N

ASIA AND AMERICA.

T O   W H I C H   A R E   A D D E D,

THE CONQUEST OF SIBERIA,

A N D

The HISTORY of the TRANSACTIONS and COMMERCE between RUSSIA and CHINA.

BY WILLIAM COXE, A.M. F.R.S.

One of the Senior Fellows of King's College, Cambridge; Member of the Imperial Œconomical Society at St. Peterfburg, of the Royal Academy of Sciences at Copenhagen; and Chaplain to his Grace the Duke of MARLBOROUGH.

THE THIRD EDITION, REVISED AND CORRECTED.

L O N D O N,

PRINTED BY J. NICHOLS,

FOR T. CADELL, IN THE STRAND

MDCCLXXXVII.

T O

JACOB BRYANT, ESQ.

AS A PUBLIC TESTIMONY

O F

THE HIGHEST RESPECT FOR

HIS DISTINGUISHED

LITERARY ABILITIES,

THE TRUEST ESTEEM FOR

HIS PRIVATE VIRTUES,

AND THE MOST GRATEFUL SENSE OF

MANY PERSONAL FAVOURS,

THE FOLLOWING PAGES ARE

INSCRIBED,

B Y

HIS FAITHFUL AND AFFECTIONATE

HUMBLE SERVANT,

WILLIAM COXE.

Cambridge,
March 27, 1780.

P R E F A C E.

THE late Ruffian Difcoveries between Afia and America have, for fome time, engaged the attention of the curious ; more efpecially fince Dr. Robertfon's admirable Hiftory of America has been in the hands of the public. In that valuable performance the elegant and ingenious author has communicated to the world, with an accuracy and judgement which fo eminently diftinguifh all his writings, the moft exact information at that time to be obtained, concerning thofe important difcoveries. During my ftay at Peterfburg, my inquiries were particularly directed to this interefting fubject, in order to learn if any new light had been thrown on an article of knowledge of fuch confequence to the hiftory of mankind. For this purpofe I endeavoured to collect the refpective journals of the feveral voyages fubfequent to the expedition of Beering and Tfchirikof in 1741, with which the celebrated Muller concludes his account of the firft Ruffian navigations.

During

During the courfe of my refearches I was informed, that a treatife in the German language, publifhed at Hamburg and Leipfic in 1776, contained a full and exact narrative of the Ruffian voyages, from 1745 to 1770 *.

As the author has not prefixed his name, I fhould have paid little attention to an anonymous publication, if I had not been affured, from very good authority, that the work in queftion was compiled from the original journals. Not refting however upon this intelligence, I took the liberty of applying to Mr. Muller himfelf, who, by order of the Emprefs, had arranged the fame journals, from which the anonymous author is faid to have drawn his materials. Previous to my application, Mr. Muller had compared the treatife with the original papers ; and he favoured me with the following ftrong teftimony to its exactnefs and authenticity : " Vous " ferès bien de traduire pour l'ufage de vos " compatriotes le petit livre fur les ifles " fitués entre le Kamtchatka et l'Amerique. " Il n'y a point de doute, que l'auteur n'ait

* The title of the book is, Neue Nachrichten von denen Neuendeckten Infuln in der See zwifchen Afia und Amerika aus mitgetheilten Urkunden und Aufzuegen verfaffet von J. L. S.

" eté

" eté pourvu de bons memoirs, et qu'il ne
" s'en foit fervi fidelement. J'ai confronté le
" livre avec les originaux." Supported therefore by this very refpectable authority, I confidered this treatife as a performance of the
higheft credit, and well worthy of being more
generally known and perufed. I have accordingly, in the firft part of the prefent publication, fubmitted a tranflation of it to the
reader's candour ; and added occafional notes
to fuch paffages as feemed to require an explanation. The original is divided into fec-
tions without any references. But as it feemed
to be more convenient to divide it into chapters ; and to accompany each chapter with a
fummary of the contents, and marginal references ; l have moulded it into that form,
without making however any alteration in the
order of the journals.

The additional intelligence which I procured at Peterfburg is thrown into a Second
Part : it confifts of fome new information, and
of three journals *, never before given to the
public. Amongft thefe I muft particularly
mention that of Krenitzin and Levafhef, which,

* The journal of Krenitzin and Levafhef, the fhort account of Synd's voyage, and the narrative of Shalaurof's expedition, Part II. Chapters I. VII. VIII.

together with the chart of their voyage, was
communicated to Dr. Robertſon, by order of
the Empreſs of Ruſſia ; and which that juſtly
admired hiſtorian has, in the politeſt and moſt
obliging manner, permitted me to make uſe
of in this collection.   This voyage, which re-
dounds greatly to the honour of the ſovereign
who planned it, confirms in general the authenticity of the treatiſe above-mentioned ;
and aſcertains the reality of the diſcoveries
made by the private merchants.

As a farther illuſtration of this ſubject, I
collected the beſt charts which could be procured at Peterſburg, and of which a liſt will
be given in the following advertiſement. From
all theſe circumſtances, I may venture, perhaps, to hope that the curious and inquiſitive
reader will not only find in the following pages
the moſt authentic and circumſtantial account
of the progreſs and extent of the Ruſſian diſcoveries, which has hitherto appeared in any
language ; but be enabled hereafter to compare them with thoſe more lately made by
that great and much to be regretted navigator, Captain Cooke, when his journal ſhall
be communicated to the public.

As

As all the furs which are brought from the New-difcovered Iflands are fold to the Chinefe, I was naturally led to make enquiries concerning the commerce between Ruffia and China; and finding this branch of traffic much more important than is commonly imagined, I thought that a general fketch of its prefent ftate, together with a fuccinct view of the tranfactions between the two nations, would not be unacceptable.

The conqueft of Siberia, as it firft opened a communication with China, and paved the way to all the interefting difcoveries related in the prefent attempt, will not appear unconnected, I truft, with its principal defign.

The materials of this fecond part, as alfo of the preliminary obfervations concerning Kamtchatka, and the commerce to the New-difcovered Iflands, are drawn from books of eftablifhed and undoubted reputation. Mr. Muller and Mr. Pallas, from whofe interefting works thefe hiftorical and commercial fubjects are chiefly compiled, are too well known in the literary world to require any other vouchers for their judgement, exactnefs,

and

and fidelity, than the bare mentioning of their names. I have only farther to apprize the reader, that, befides the intelligence extracted from thefe publications, he will find fome additional circumftances relative to the Ruffian commerce with China, which I collected during my continuance in Ruffia.

I CANNOT clofe this addrefs to the reader without embracing with peculiar fatisfaction the juft occafion, which the enfuing treatifes upon the Ruffian difcoveries and commerce afford me, of joining with every friend of fcience in the warmeft admiration of that enlarged and liberal fpirit, which fo ftrikingly marks the character of the prefent Emprefs of Ruffia. Since her acceffion to the throne, the inveftigation and difcovery of ufeful knowledge has been the conftant object of her generous encouragement. The authentic records of the Ruffian hiftory have, by her exprefs orders, been properly arranged ; and permiffion is readily granted of infpecting them. The moft diftant parts of her vaft dominions have, at her expence, been explored and defcribed by perfons of great abilities and extenfive learning ; by which means new and important lights have been thrown upon the geography and natural hiftory of thofe remote regions. In a word, this truly great princefs has contributed more, in the compafs of only a few years, towards civilizing and informing the minds of her fubjects, than had been effected by all the fovereigns her predeceffors fince the glorious æra of Peter the Great.

In

In order to prevent the frequent mention of the full title of the books referred to in the courfe of this performance, the following catalogue is fubjoined, with the abbreviations.

Müller's Samlung Ruffifcher Gefchichte, IX volumes, 8vo. printed at St. Peterfburg in 1732, and the following years; it is referred to in the following manner: S. R. G. with the volume and page annexed.

From this excellent collection I have made ufe of the following treatifes:

vol. II. p. 293, &c. Gefchichte der Gegenden an dem Fluffe Amur.

There is a French tranflation of this treatife, called Hiftoire du Fleuve Amur, 12mo, Amfterdam, 1776.

vol. III. p. 1, &c. Nachrichten von SeeReifen, &c.

There is an Englifh and a French tranflation of this work; the former is called " Voyages from Afia to America for completing the Difcoveries of the North Weft Coaft of America," 4to, London, 1764. The title of the latter is " Voyages et Decouvertes faites par les Ruffes," &c. 12mo, Amfterdam, 1766 p. 413. Nachrichten Von der Handlung in Sibirien.

Vol. VI. p. 109, Sibirifche Gefhichte.

Vol. VIII. p. 504, Nachricht Von der Ruffifchen Handlung nach China.

Pallas

Pallas Reife durch verchiedne Provinzen des Ruffifchen Reichs, in Three Parts, 4to, St. Peterfburg, 1771, 1773, and 1776, thus cited, Pallas Reife.

Georgi Bemerkungen einer Reife im Ruffifchen Reich in Jahre, 1772, III volumes, 4to, St. Petersburg, 1775, cited Georgi Reife.

Fifcher Sibirifche Gefchichte, 2 volumes, 8vo, St. Petersburg, cited Fif. Sib. Gef.

Gmelin Reife durch Sibirien, Tome IV. 8vo, Gottingen, 1752, cited Gmelin Reife.

There is a French tranflation of this work, called " Voyage en Siberie," &c. par Gmelin. Paris, 1767.

Neuefte Nachrichten von Kamtchatka aufgefetft im Junius des 1773sten Yahren von dem dafigen Befehls-haber Herrn Kapitain Smalew.

Aus dem abhandlungen der freyen Ruffifchen Gefellfchaft Mofkau.

In the journal of St. Petersburg, April, 1776— cited Journal of St. Petersburg.

Ex-

Explanation of fome Ruffian words made ufe
of in the following work.

Baidar, a fmall boat.

Guba, a bay.

Kamen, a rock.

Kotche, a veffel.

Krepoft, a regular fortrefs.

Nofs, a cape.

Oftrog, a fortrefs furrounded with palifadoes.

Oftroff, an ifland.

Oftrova, iflands.

Quafs, a fort of fermented liquor.

Reka, a river.

The Ruffians, in their proper names of perfons,
make ufe of patronymics; thefe patronymics are
formed in fome cafes by adding *Vitch* to the Chrif-
tian name of the father; in others *Off* or *Eff*: the
former termination is applied only to perfons of
condition; the latter to thofe of an inferior rank.
As, for inftance,

Among perfons of condition—— *Ivan Ivanovitch,* } Ivan the fon
of inferior rank, *Ivan Ivanoff,* } of Ivan.

Michael Alexievitch, } Michael the
Michael Alexeeff, } fon of Alexèy.

Sometimes a furname is added, *Ivan Ivanovitch
Romanoff.*

Table

Table of Ruffian Weights, Meafures of
Length, and Value of Money.

WEIGHT.

A pood weighs 40 Ruffian pounds = 36 Englifh.

MEASURES OF LENGTH.

16 verfhocks = an arfheen.

An arfheen = 28 inches.

Three arfheens, or feven feet, = a fathom *, or
fazfhen.

500 fazfhens = a verft.

A degree of longitude comprifes 104½ verfts = 69⅜
Englifh miles. A mile is therefore 1,515 parts
of a verft; two miles may then be eftimated
equal to three verfts, omitting a fmall fraction.

VALUE OF RUSSIAN MONEY.

A rouble = 100 copecs : Its value varies according
to the exchange from 3s. 8d. to 4s. 2d. Upon
an average, however, the value of a rouble is
reckoned at four fhillings.

* The fathom for meafuring the depth of water is the
fame as the Englifh fathom, = 6 feet.

ADVER-

ADVERTISEMENT,
To the Edition of 1780.

AS no aftronomical obfervations have been taken in the voyages related in this col-lection, the longitude and latitude afcribed to the New-difcovered Iflands in the journals and upon the charts cannot be abfolutely de-pended upon. Indeed the reader will perceive, that the pofition * of the Fox Iflands upon the general map of Ruffia is materially dif-ferent from that affigned to them upon the chart of Krenitzin and Levafhef. Without endeavouring to clear up any difficulties which may arife from this uncertainty, I thought it would be moft fatisfactory to have the beft charts engraved : the reader will then be able to compare them with each other, and with the feveral journals. Which reprefentation of the New-difcovered Iflands deferves the preference, will probably be afcertained upon the return of captain Clerke from his prefent expedition.

* See p. 383.

List

C O N-

[xix]

C O N T E N T S.

P A R T   I.

Containing Preliminary Observations con_
cerning KAMTCHATKA, and Account of
the NEW DISCOVERIES made by the RUS-
SIANS,   p. 3—16.

Chap. I. *First Discovery of* Kamtchatka.—
That Peninsula conquered and colonised by the
Russians—*Present State of* Kamtchatka—
Government—Population—Tribute—Volca-
nos,   p. 3.

Chap.

ACCOUNT

OF THE

RUSSIAN DISCOVERIES

BETWEEN

ASIA AND AMERICA.

ADVERTISEMENT

T O

THE THIRD EDITION.

THE author has, in this third edition, arranged the chapters in a more regular and connected manner than in the former impreffions; and has fubjoined a comparative View of the Ruffian Difcoveries with thofe made by Captains Cook and Clerke, which has lately appeared in a feparate publication.

May 30, 1787.

To

E R R A T A.

P. 11. l. 8. dele *having.*

P. 6. l. 7. for *are* read *were.*

P. 24. Note 2. for *Part II. Chap. I.* read *Appendix, No. I.*

P. 82. l. 18. for *turbot* read *halibuts.*

P. 124. l. 5. dele *right.*

P. 229. note 2. l. 2. for *chriſtatus* read *criſtatus.*

PART II.

Containing Supplementary Accounts of
the Russian Discoveries.

C O N T E N T S. xxvii

A P P E N D I X, Nº II.

A P P E N D I X, Nº III.

A P P E N D I X, Nº IV.

PART

PART I.

CONTAINING

I. PRELIMINARY OBSERVATIONS CONCERNING KAMTCHATKA.

AND

II. ACCOUNT OF THE NEW DISCOVERIES MADE BY THE RUSSIANS.

PRELIMINARY OBSERVATIONS

CONCERNING

ĶAMTCHATKA, &c.

CHAP. I.

First Discovery of Kamtchatka.—That Peninsula conquered and colonised by the Russians—Present State of Kamtchatka—Government—Population—Tribute—Volcanos.

THE Peninsula of Kamtchatka was not discovered by the Ruffians before the latter end of the laft century. The firft expedition towards thofe parts was made in 1696, by fixteen Coffacs, under the command of Lucas Semænof Morofko, who was fent againft the Koriacs of the river Opooka by Vlodimer Atlaffof commander of Anadirfk. Morofko continued his march until he came within four days journey of the river Kamt-

chatka,

chatka, and having rendered a Kamtchadel
village tributary, he returned to Anadirſk *.

The following year Atlaſſof himſelf, at the
head of a larger body of troops, penetrated
into the Peninſula; took poſſeſſion of the
river Kamtchatka by erecting a croſs upon its
banks; and built ſome huts upon the ſpot,
where Upper Kamtchatkoi Oſtrog now ſtands.

Theſe expeditions were continued during
the following years: Upper and Lower Kamtchatkoi Oſtrogs and Bolcheretſk were built;
the Southern diſtrict conquered and coloniſed;
and in 1711 the whole Peninſula was finally
reduced under the dominion of the Ruſſians.

During ſome years the poſſeſſion of Kamtchatka brought very little advantage to the
crown, excepting from the ſmall tribute of
furs exacted from the inhabitants. The Ruſſians indeed occaſionally hunted in that Peninſula foxes, wolves, ermines, ſables, and
other animals, whoſe valuable ſkins form an
extenſive article of commerce among the
Eaſtern nations. But the fur trade carried on
from thence was inconſiderable; until the
Ruſſians diſcovered the iſlands ſituated be-

* S. R. G. V. III. p. 72.

tween

tween Afia and America, in a feries of voyages; the journals of which will be exhibited in the fubfequent tranflation. Since thefe difcoveries, the variety of rich furs, which are procured from thofe iflands, has greatly encreafed the trade of Kamtchatka, and rendered it a very important branch of the Ruffian commerce.

The Peninfula of Kamtchatka lies between 51 and 62 degrees of North latitude, and 173 and 182 of longitude from the ifle of Fero. It is bounded on the Eaft and South by the fea of Kamtchatka, on the Weft by the feas of Okotfk and Penfhinfk, and on the North by the country of the Koriacs.

It is divided into four diftricts, Bolcherefk, Tigilfkaia Krepoft, Verchnei or Upper Kamtchatkoi Oftrog, and Nifhnei or Lower Kamtchatkoi Oftrog. The government is vefted in the chancery of Bolcheretfk, which depends upon, and is fubject to, the infpection of the chancery of Ochotfk. The whole Ruffian force, ftationed in the Peninfula, confifts of no more than three hundred men *.

The prefent population of Kamtchatka is very fmall, amounting to fcarce four thou-

* Journal of St. Peterfburg for April, 1777.

fand

fand fouls. Formerly the inhabitants were more numerous; but, in 1768, that country was greatly depopulated by the ravages of the fmall-pox, which diforder carried off five thoufand three hundred and fixty-eight per-fons. In 1776 there were only feven hundred and fix males in the whole Peninfula who are tributary, and an hundred and fourteen in the Kuril Ifles, which are fubjeƐt to Ruffia.

The fixed annual tribute confifts in 279 fables, 464 red foxes, 50 fea-otters with a dam, and 38 cub fea-otters. All furs export-ed from Kamtchatka pay a duty of 10 per cent. to the crown; the tenth of the cargoes brought from the new-difcovered iflands is alfo delivered into the cuftoms.

Many traces of volcanos have been obferved in this Peninfula; and there are fome mountains, which are at prefent in a burning ftate. The moft confiderable of thefe volcanos is fituated near the Lower Oftrog. In 1762 a great noife was heard iffuing from the infide of that mountain; and flames of fire were feen to burft from different parts. Thefe flames were immediately fucceeded by a large ftream of melted fnow-water, which flowed into the neighbouring valley, and drowned two Kamt-chadels,

chadels, who were at that time upon an hunting party. The afhes, and other combuftible matter, thrown from the mountain, fpread to the circumference of two hundred miles. In 1767 there was another difcharge, but lefs confiderable. Every night flames of fire were obferved ftreaming from the mountain ; and the eruption, which attended them, did no fmall damage to the inhabitants of the Lower Oftrog. Since that year no flames have been feen ; but the mountain emits a conftant fmoak. The fame phænomenon is alfo obferved upon another mountain, called Tabaetfhinfkian.

The face of the country throughout the Peninfula is chiefly mountainous. It produces in fome parts birch, poplars, alders, willows, underwood, and berries of different forts. Greens and other vegetables are raifed with great facility ; fuch as white cabbage, turneps, radifhes, beetroot, carrots, and fome cucumbers. Agriculture is in a very low ftate, which is chiefly owing to the nature of the foil and the fevere hoar frofts : for though fome trials have been made with refpect to the cultivation of oats, barley, and rye ; yet no crop has ever been procured fufficient in
quantity

quantity or quality to anfwer the pains and expence of raifing it. Hemp however has of late years been cultivated with great fuc-cefs *.

Every year a veffel, belonging to the crown, fails from Okotfk to Kamtchatka, laden with falt, provifions, corn, and Ruffian manufac-tures; and returns in June or July of the fol-lowing years with fkins and furs.

C H A P. II.

General idea of the commerce carried on to the New-difcovered Iflands—Equipment of the veffels—Rifks of the trade, profits, &c.

SINCE the conclufion of Beering's Voyage, which was made at the expence of the crown, the profecution of the New Difcove-ries begun by him has been almoft entirely carried on by individuals. Thefe perfons were principally merchants of Irkutfk, Ya-kutfk, and other natives of Siberia, who formed themfelves into fmall trading com-panies, and fitted out veffels at their joint expence.

* Journal of St. Peterfburg.

Moft

Moft of the veffels which are equipped for thefe expeditions are two-mafted ; are commonly built without iron, and in general fo badly conftructed, that it is wonderful how they can weather fo ftormy a fea. They are called in Ruffian *Shitiki*, or fewed veffels, becaufe the planksare fewed together with thongs of leather. Some few are built in the river of Kamtchatka ; but they are for the moft part conftructed at the haven of Okotfk. The largeft are manned with feventy men, and the fmalleft with forty. The crew generally confifts of an equal number of Ruffians and Kamtchadals. The latter occafion a confiderable faving, as their pay is fmall ; they alfo refift, more eafily than the former, the attack of the fcurvy. But as Ruffian mariners are more enterprifing, and more to be depended upon in time of danger than the others, fome are unavoidably neceffary.

The expences of building and fitting out the veffels are very confiderable : for there is nothing at Okotfk but timber for their conftruction. Accordingly cordage, fails, and fome provifions, muft be brought from Yakutfk upon horfes. The dearnefs of corn and flour, which muft be tranfported from the

diftricts

diftricts lying about the river Lena, renders it impoffible to lay-in any large quantity for the fubfiftence of the crew during a voyage, which commonly lafts three or four years. For this reafon no more is provided than is neceffary to fupply the Ruffian mariners with quafs and other fermented liquors.

From the exceffive fcarcity of cattle both at Okotfk and * Kamtchatka, very little provifion is laid in at either of thofe places : but the crew provide themfelves with a large ftore of the flefh of fea animals, which are caught and cured upon Beering's Ifland, where the veffels for the moft part winter.

After all expences are paid, the equipment of each veffel ordinarily cofts from 15,000 to 20,000 roubles : and fometimes the expences amount to 30,000. Every veffel is divided into a certain number of fhares, generally from thirty to fifty ; and each fhare is worth from 300 to 500 roubles.

The rifk of the trade is very great, as fhip-wrecks are common in the fea of Kamtchatka,

* In 1772, there were only 570 head of cattle upon the whole Peninfula. A cow fold from 50 to 60 roubles, an ox from 60 to 100. A pound of frefh beef fold upon an average for 12½ copecs. The exceffive dearnefs of this price will be eafily conceived, when it is known, that at Mofcow a pound of beef fells for about three copecs. Journ. St Peterfb.

which

which is full of rocks and very tempeſtuous. Beſides, the crews are frequently ſurpriſed and killed by the iſlanders, and the veſſels deſtroyed. In return the profits ariſing from theſe voyages are very conſiderable, and compenſate the inconveniencies and dangers attending them. For if a ſhip comes back after having an advantageous voyage, the gain at the moſt moderate computation amounts to cent. per cent. and frequently to as much more. Should the veſſel be capable of performing a ſecond expedition, the expences are conſiderably leſſened ; and the profits of courſe encreaſed.

Some notion of the general profits ariſing from this trade (when the voyage is ſucceſſful) may be deduced from the ſale of a rich cargo of furs, brought to Kamtchatka, on the 2d of June, 1772, from the New-diſcovered iſlands, in a veſſel belonging to Ivan Popof.

The tenth part of the ſkins being delivered to the cuſtoms, the remainder was diſtributed in fifty-five ſhares. Each ſhare conſiſted of twenty ſea-otters, ſixteen black and brown foxes, ten red foxes, three ſea-otter tails ; and ſuch a portion was ſold upon the ſpot from 800 to 1000 roubles : ſo that according to this

this price the whole lading was worth about 50,000 roubles *.

C H A P.   III.

Furs   and   skins procured   from Kamtchatka *and the New-discovered Islands.—Sea-Otters. —Different speices of Foxes.*

THE principal furs and skins procured from the Peninsula of Kamtchatka and the New-discovered Islands are sea-otters, foxes, sables, ermines, wolves, bears, &c.— These furs are transported to Okotsk by sea, and from thence carried to † Kiačta upon the frontiers of Siberia ; where the greatest part are sold to the Chinese at a very considerable profit.

Of all these furs the skins of the sea-otters are the richest and most valuable. Those animals resort in great numbers to the Aleütian and Fox Islands : they are called by the Russians *Bobri Morski*, or sea-beavers, and sometimes Kamtchadal beavers, on account of the resemblance of their fur to that of the com-

* Georgi Reise Tom. I. p. 23, & seq. Journal of St. Petersburg.

† See Part III. Chap. III.

mon

mon beaver. From thefe circumftances feveral authors have been led into a miftake,
and have fuppofed that this animal is of the
beaver fpecies ; whereas it is the true fea-otter *.

The female are called *Matka*, or dams ; and
the cubs till five months old *Medviedki*, or little bears, becaufe their coat refembles that of
a bear ; they lofe that coat after five months,
and then are called *Kofchloki*.

The fur of the fineft fort is thick and long,
of a dark colour, and a fine gloffy hue. The
methods of taking thefe fea-otters are, by
ftriking them with harpoons as they are fleep-
ing upon their backs in the fea ; by hunting
them down in boats ; by furprifing them in
caverns ; or taking them in nets.

Their fkins bear different prices, according
to their quality.

At Kamtchatka † the beft fell for
  per fkin from — — 30 to 40 roubles.
   Middle fort 20 to 30
   Worft fort 15 to 25

* S. R. G. III. p. 530. For a defcription of the fea-
otter, Lutra Marina, called by Linnæus Muftela Lutris,
fee Nov. Comm. Pet. Vol. II. p. 367, &c.
† Journal St. Peterfburg.

At

At Kiachta * the old and middle-
    aged fea-otter fkins are fold
    to the Chinefe per fkin from 80 to 140
        The worft fort 30 to 40

As thefe furs are fold at fo great a price to the Chinefe, they are feldom brought into Ruffia for fale: and feveral, which have been carried to Mofcow as a tribute, were purchafed for 30 roubles per fkin; and fent from thence to the Chinefe frontiers, where they were dif-pofed of at a very high intereft †.

There are feveral fpecies of Foxes, whofe fkins are fent from Kamtchatka into Siberia and Ruffia. Of thefe the principal are the black foxes, the *Petfi* or Arctic foxes, the red and ftone foxes.

The fineft black foxes are caught in dif-ferent parts of Siberia, and more commonly in the Northern regions between the Rivers Lena, Indigirka, and Kovyma: the black foxes found upon the remoteft Eaftern iflands dif-covered by the Ruffians, or the Lyffie Oftrova, are not fo valuable. They are very black and large; but the coat for the moft part is as coarfe as that of a wolf. The great difference in the finenefs of the fur, between thefe foxes

* Pallas Reife, Part III. p. 137.
† S. R. G. V. III. Pallas Reife.

and

and thofe of Siberia, arifes probably from the following circumftances. In thofe iflands the cold is not fo fevere as in Siberia; and, as there is no wood, the foxes live in holes and caverns of the rocks; whereas in the abovementioned parts of Siberia, there are large tracts of forefts in which they find fhelter. Some black foxes, however, are occafionally caught in the remoteft Eaftern Iflands, not wholly deftitute of wood, and thefe are of great value. In general the Chinefe, who pay the deareft for black furs, do not give more for the black foxes of the New-difcovered iflands than from 20 to 30 roubles per fkin.

The *Arctic* or ice foxes are very common upon fome of the New-difcovered Iflands. They are called *Petfi* by the Ruffians, and by the Germans blue foxes *. Their natural colour is of a bluifh-grey or afh colour; but they change their coat at different ages, and in different feafons of the year. In general they are born brown, are white in winter, and brown in fummer; and in fpring and autumn, as the hair gradually falls off, the coat is marked with different fpecks and croffes.

* Pennant's Synopfis.

At

At Kiaɛta * all the several varieties fell upon an average to the Chinefe per ſkin from 50 copecs to — —— — 2⅔ roubles.

Stone foxes at Kamtchatka per ſkin from ———— — 1 to 2½

Red foxes from 80 copecs to — 1 rouble, 80 copecs.

At Kiaɛta from 80 copecs to — 9 roubles.

Common wolves ſkins at per ſkin 2

Beſt ſort per ſkin from — 8 to 16

Sables per ditto ———— 2½ to 10

A pood of the beſt ſea-horſe teeth † ſells

At Yakutſk for —— 10 roubles.

Of the middling —— 8

Inferior ditto —— from 5 to 7.

Four, five, or ſix teeth generally weigh a pood, and ſometimes, but very rarely, three. They are ſold to the Chinefe, Monguls, and Calmucs.

* Pallas Reiſe.
† S. R. G. V. III.

CHAP.

ACCOUNT

OF THE

NEW DISCOVERIES

MADE BY THE

RUSSIANS

IN THE EASTERN OCEAN,

BETWEEN KAMTCHATKA AND AMERICA.

TRANSLATED FROM THE GERMAN.

WITH NOTES BY THE TRANSLATOR.

ACCOUNT

OF THE

RUSSIAN DISCOVERIES.

CHAP. I.

*Conquest of Siberia—Commencement of the New
Discoveries—Their Progress—The Empress
promotes all Attempts towards New Discoveries—Position of the New-discovered
Islands.*

A Thirst after riches was the chief motive which excited the Spaniards to
the discovery of America; and which turned
the attention of other maritime nations to
that quarter. The same passion for riches
occasioned, about the middle of the sixteenth
century, the discovery and conquest of
Northern Asia, a country, before that time
unknown to the Europeans. The first foundation of this conquest was laid by the celebrated Yermac *, at the head of a band of

* The reader will find an account of this conquest by
Yermac in Part III. Chap. I.

adven-

adventurers, lefs civilized, but at the fame
time not fo inhuman as the conquerors of
America. By the acceffion of this vaſt territory, now known by the name of Siberia,
the Ruffians have acquired an extent of empire
never before attained by any other nation.

The firſt project * for making difcoveries
in that tempeſtuous fea, which lies between
Kamtchatka and America, was conceived and
planned by Peter I. the greateſt fovereign who
ever fat upon the Ruffian throne, until it was
adorned by the prefent emprefs. The nature
and completion of this project under his immediate fucceffors are well known to the public
from the relation of the celebrated Muller.
No fooner had † Beering and Tfchirikof, in
the

* There feems a want of connection in this place, which
will be cleared up by confidering, that, by the conqueſt of
Siberia, the Ruffians advanced to the fhores of the Eaſtern
Ocean, the fcene of the difcoveries here alluded to.

† Beering had already made feveral expeditions in the
fea of Kamtchatka, by orders of the crown, before he
undertook the voyage mentioned in the text.
In 1728, he departed from the mouth of the Kamtchata
river, in company with Tfchirikof. The object of this voyage was to afcertain, whether the two Continents of Afia
and America were feparated, and Peter I. a fhort time before his death, had drawn up inftructions with his own
hand for that purpofe. Beering coaſted the Eaſtern fhore
of Siberia as high as latitude 67° 18′ ; but made no difcovery of the oppofite Continent.

the profecution of this plan, opened their way to iflands abounding in valuable furs, than private merchants immediately engaged with ardour in fimilar expeditions; and, within a period of ten years, more important difcoveries were made by thefe individuals, at their own private coft, than had been hitherto effected by all the expenfive efforts of the crown.

Soon after the return of Beering's crew from the ifland where he was fhipwrecked and died, and which is called after his name; the inhabitants of Kamtchatka ventured over to that ifland, to which the fea-otters and other fea-animals were accuftomed to refort in great numbers. *Mednoi Oftrof*, or Copper Ifland, which takes that appellation from large maffes of Native copper found upon the

In 1729, he fet fail again for the profecution of the fame defign; but this fecond attempt equally failed of fuccefs.

In 1741, Beering and Tfchirikof went out upon the celebrated expedition (alluded to in the text, and which is fo often mentioned in the courfe of this work) towards the coafts of America. This expedition led the way to all the important difcoveries fince made by the Ruffians.

Beering's veffel was wrecked in December of the fame year; and Tfchirikof landed at Kamtchatka on the 9th of October, 1742.

S. R. G. III. Nachrichten von See Reifen, &c. and Robertfon's Hiftory of America, Vol. I. p. 273, & feq.

beach,

beach, and which lies full in fight of Beering's Ifle, was an eafy and fpeedy difcovery.

Thefe two fmall uninhabited fpots were for fome time the only iflands that were known ; until a fcarcity of land and fea-animals, whofe numbers were greatly diminifhed by the Ruffian hunters, occafioned other expeditions. Several of the veffels which were fent out upon thefe voyages were driven by ftormy weather to the South-eaft ; by which means the Aleütian Ifles, fituated about the 195th * degree of longitude, and but moderately peopled, were difcovered.

From the year 1745, when it feems thefe iflands were firft vifited, until 1750, when the firft tribute of furs was brought from thence to Okotfk, the government appears not to have been fully informed of their difcovery. In the laft-mentioned year, one Lebedef was commander of Kamtchatka. From 1755 to 1760, Captain Theredof and Lieu-

* The author reckons, throughout this treatife, the longitude from the firft meridian of the ifle of Fero. The longitude and latitude, which he gives to the Fox Iflands, correfponds exactly with thofe in which they are laid down upon the General Map of Ruffia. The longitude of Beering's Copper Ifland, and of the Aleütian Ifles, are fomewhat different. See Advertifement relating to the Charts, and alfo Appendix Nº. II.

tenant

tenant Kafhkaref were his fucceffors. In
1760, Feodor Ivanovitch Soimonof, governor
of Tobolfk, turned his attention to the above-
mentioned iflands ; and, the fame year, Captain Rtiftfhef, at Okotfk, inftructed Lieutenant Shamalef, the fame who was afterwards commander in Kamtchatka, to promote and favour all expeditions in thofe feas.
Until this time, all the difcoveries fubfequent
to Beering's voyage were made, without the
interpofition of the court, by private merchants in fmall veffels fitted out at their own
expence.

The prefent Emprefs (to whom every circumftance which contributes to aggrandize
the Ruffian empire is an object of attention)
has given new life to thefe difcoveries. The
merchants who engaged in them have been
animated by recompences. The importance
and true pofition of the Ruffian iflands have
been afcertained by an expenfive voyage *,
made by order of the crown ; and much additional information will be derived from the

* The author here alludes to the fecret expedition of
Captain Krenitzin and Levafhef, whofe journal and chart
were fent, by order of the Emprefs of Ruffia, to Dr. Robertfon. See Robertfon's Hiftory of America, Vol. I. p. 276.
and 460. See Appendix, N°. I.

journals

journals and charts of the officers employed
in that expedition, whenever they fhall be
publifhed.

Meanwhile, we may reft aflured, that feveral modern geographers have erred in advancing America too much to the Weft, and
in queftioning the extent of Siberia Eaftwards, as laid down by the Ruffians. It appears, indeed, evident, that the accounts
and even conjectures of the celebrated Muller,
concerning the pofition of thofe diftant regions, are more and more confirmed by facts ;
in the fame manner as the juftnefs of his fuppofition concerning the form of the coaft of
the fea of Okotfk * has been lately eftablifhed.
With refpect to the extent of Siberia, it appears almoft beyond a doubt, from the moft
recent obfervations, that its Eaftern extremity
is fituated beyond † 200 degrees of longitude.
In regard to the Weftern coaft of America,
all the navigations to the New-difcovered
Iflands evidently fhew, that between 50 and
60 degrees of latitude, that Continent ad-

---

* Mr. Muller formerly conjectured, that the coaft of the
fea of Okotfk ftretched South-weft towards the river Ud ;
and from thence to the mouth of the Amoor South-eaft :
and the truth of this conjecture had been fince confirmed by
a coafting voyage made by Captain Synnd.

† Part II. Chap. I.

vances

vances no where nearer to Afia than the coafts touched at by Beering and Tfchirikof, or about 236 degrees of longitude.

As to the New-difcovered Iflands, no credit muft be given to a chart publifhed in the Geographical Calendar of St. Peterfburg for 1774; in which they are inaccurately laid down. Nor is the antient chart of the New Difcoveries, publifhed by the Imperial Academy, and which feems to have been drawn up from mere reports, more deferving of attention †.

The late navigators give a far different defcription of the Northern Archipelago. From their accounts we learn, that Beering's Ifland is fituated due Eaft from Kamtchatkoi Nofs, in the 185th degree of longitude. Near it is Copper Ifland; and, at fome diftance from them, Eaft-fouth-eaft, there are three fmall iflands, named by their inhabitants, Attak, Semitfhi, and Shemiya: thefe are properly the Aleütian Ifles; they ftretch from Weft-north-weft towards Eaft-fouth-eaft, in the fame direction as Beering's and Copper Iflands, in the longitude of 195, and latitude 54.

* Appendix, N° I.
† Appendix, N° II.

To

To the North-eaft of thefe, at the diftance of 600 or 800 verfts, lies another group of fix or more iflands, known by the name of the Andreanofffkie Oftrova.

South-eaft, or Eaft-fouth, of thefe, at the dif-tance of about fifteen degrees, and North by Eaft of the Aleütian, begins the chain of Lyfie Oftrova, or Fox Iflands : this chain of rocks and ifles ftretches Eaft-north-eaft between 56 and 61 degrees of North latitude *, from 211 degrees of longitude moft probably to the Con-tinent of America ; and in a line of direction, which croffes with that in which the Aleütian ifles lie. The largeft and moft remarkable of thefe iflands are Umnak, Aghunalafhka, or, as it is commonly fhortened, Unalafhka, Kadyak, and Alagfhak.

Of thefe and the Aleütian Ifles, the diftance and pofition are tolerably well afcertained by fhips reckonings, and latitudes taken by pi-lots. But the fituation of the Andreanoff-fky Ifles † is ftill fomewhat doubtful, though probably their direction is Eaft and Weft; and fome of them may unite with that part

* See p. 286.

† Thefe are the fame iflands which are called, by Mr. Stræhlin, Anadirfky Iflands, from their fuppofed vicinity to the river Anadyr.   See Part II. Chap. IV.

of the Fox iſlands which are moſt contiguous to the oppoſite Continent.

The main land of America has not been
touched at by any of the veſſels in the late
expeditions ; though poſſibly the time is not
far diſtant when ſome of the Ruſſian adventurers will fall in with that coaſt *. More
to the North perhaps, at leaſt as high as
70 degrees latitude, the Continent of America
may ſtretch out nearer to the coaſt of the
Tſchutſki ; and form a large promontory,
accompanied with iſlands, which have no
connection with any of the preceding ones.
That ſuch a promontory really exiſts, and
advances to within a very ſmall diſtance from
Tſchukotſkoi Noſs, can hardly be doubted ;
at leaſt it ſeems to be confirmed by all the
lateſt accounts which have been procured from
thoſe parts †. That prolongation, therefore, of America, which by Deliſle is made
to extend Weſtward, and is laid down juſt
oppoſite to Kamtchatka, between 50 and 60
degrees latitude, muſt be entirely removed ;
for many of the voyages related in this collection lay through that part of the ocean

* Part II. Chap. V.
† Ibid. Chap. VI.

where

where this imaginary Continent was marked down.

It is even more than probable, that the Aleütian, and fome of the Fox Iflands, now well known, are the very fame which Beering fell-in with upon his return ; though, from the unfteadinefs of his courfe, their true pofition could not be exactly laid down in the chart of that expedition *.

As the fea of Kamtchatka is now fo much frequented, thefe conjectures cannot remain long undecided ; and it is only to be wifhed, that fome expeditions were to be made North-eaft, in order to difcover the neareft coafts of America. For there is no reafon to ex-pect a fuccefsful voyage by taking any other direction ; as all the veffels, which have fteered a more foutherly courfe, have failed through an open fea, without meeting with any figns of land.

A very full and judicious account of all the difcoveries hitherto made in the Eaftern ocean

* This error is however fo fmall, and particularly with refpect to the more Eaftern coafts and iflands, as laid down in Beering's chart, fuch as Cape Hermogenes, Toomanoi, Shumaghin's Ifland, and mountain of St. Dolmat, that if they were to be placed upon the general map of Ruffia, which is prefixed to this work, they would coincide with the very chain of the Fox Iflands.

may

may be expected from the celebrated Mr.
Muller *. Meanwhile, I hope the following account, extracted from the original papers, and procured from the beft intelligence,
will be the more acceptable to the public ;
as it may prove an inducement to the Ruffians
to publifh fuller and more circumftantial
relations. Befides, the reader will find here
a narrative more authentic and accurate, than
what has been publifhed in the abovementioned calendar † ; and feveral miftakes in
that memoir are here corrected.

C H A P. II.

Voyages in 1745.—*Firft difcovery of the* Aleütian Ifles *by* Michael Nevodtfikof.

A Voyage made in the year 1745 by
Emilian Baffof is fcarce worth mentioning ; as he only reached Beering's Ifland,
and two fmaller ones, which lie South of the
former,

---

* Mr. Muller has already arranged and put in order feveral of the journals, and fent them to the board of ad-
miralty at St. Peterfburg, where they are at prefent kept,
together with the charts of the refpective voyages.

† A German copy of the treatife alluded to in the text,
was fent, by its author, Mr. Stræhlin, Counfellor of State
to the Emprefs of Ruffia, to the late Dr. Maty ; and it is
men-

former, and returned on the 31ft of July, 1746.

The firft voyage which is in any wife re-markable was undertaken in the year 1745. The veffel was a Shitik named Eudokia, fit-ted out at the expence of Aphanaffei Tfebaef-fkoi, Jacob Tfiuprof, and others ; fhe failed from the Kamtchatka river Sept. 19, under the command of Michael Nevodtfikof, a na-tive of Tobolfk. Having difcovered three un-known iflands, they wintered upon one of them, in order to kill fea-otters, of which there was a large quantity. Thefe iflands were undoubtedly the neareft * Aleütian Iflands : the language of the inhabitants was not underftood by an interpreter, whom they had brought with them from Kamtchatka. For the purpofe therefore of learning this language, they carried back with them one of the Iflanders ; and prefented him to the chancery of Bolcheretfk, with a falfe ac-

mentioned, in the Philofophical Tranfactions for 1774, un-der the following title : " A New Map and Preliminary Defcription of the New Archipelago in the North, dif-covered a few Years ago by the Ruffians in the N. E. beyond Kamtchatka." A tranflation of this treatife was publifhed the fame year by Heydinger.

* The fmall group of iflands lying S. E. of Beering's Ifland, are the real Aleütian ifles : they are fometimes called the Neareft Aleütian Iflands ; and the Fox Iflands, the Furtheft Aleütian Ifles.

count

count of their proceedings. This iflander was examined as foon as he had acquired a flight knowledge of the Ruffian language ; and, as it is faid, gave the following report. He was called Temnac, and the name of the ifland of which he was a native was Att. At fome diftance from thence lies a great ifland called Sabya, of which the inhabitants are denominated Kogii ; who, as the Ruffians underftood or thought they underftood him, made croffes, had books and fire arms, and navigated in baidars or leathern canoes. At no great diftance from the ifland where they wintered, there were two well-inhabited iflands : the firft lying E. S. E. and S. E. by South, the fecond Eaft and Eaft by South. The above-mentioned Iflander was baptifed under the name of Paul, and fent to Ok-otfk.

As the mifconduct of the fhip's crew towards the natives was fufpected, partly from the lofs of feveral men, and partly from the report of thofe Ruffians, who were not concerned in the diforderly conduct of their companions, a ftrict enquiry was inftituted ; in confequence of which the following circumftances were brought to light.

Ac-

According to the account of some of the crew, and particularly of the commander, after six days sailing they came in sight of the first island on the 24th of September, at mid-day. They passed it, and towards evening they discovered the second island ; where they lay at anchor until the next morning.

The 25th several inhabitants appeared on the coast, and the pilot was making towards shore in the small boat, with an intention of landing ; but, observing their numbers increase to about an hundred, he was afraid of venturing among them, although they beckoned to him. He contented himself therefore with flinging some needles amongst them : the islanders in return threw into the boat some sea-fowl of the cormorant kind. He endeavoured to hold a conversation with them by means of the interpreters, but no one could understand their language. And now the crew attempted to row the vessel out to sea ; but the wind being contrary, they were driven to the other side of the same island, where they cast anchor.

The 26th, Tsiuprof, having landed with some of the crew in order to look for water, met several inhabitants : he gave them some
tobacco

tobacco and fmall Chinefe pipes ; and received in return a prefent of a ftick, upon which
the head of a feal was carved. They endeavoured to wreft his hunting gun from
him ; but, upon his refufing to part with it
and retiring to the fmall boat, they ran after
him, and feized the rope by which the boat
was made faft to fhore. This violent attack
obliged Tfiuprof to fire ; and having wounded one perfon in the hand, they all let go
their hold ; and he rowed off to the fhip.
The Savages no fooner faw that their companion was hurt, than they threw off their
cloaths, carried the wounded perfon naked
into the fea, and wafhed him. In confequence of this encounter the fhip's crew
would not venture to winter at this place ;
but rowed back again to the other ifland,
where they came to an anchor.

The next morning Tfiuprof and one Shaffyrin landed with a more confiderable party :
they obferved feveral traces of inhabitants ;
but meeting none, they returned to the fhip,
and coafted along the ifland. The following
day the Coffac Shekurdin went on fhore,
accompanied by five failors : two he fent
back with a fupply of water ; and remained
                                        himfelf

himfelf with the others, in order to hunt fea-
otters. At night they came to fome dwellings inhabited by five families : upon their
approach the natives abandoned their huts
with precipitation, and hid themfelves among
the rocks. Shekurdin no fooner returned to
the fhip, than he was again fent on fhore with
a larger company, in order to look out for a
proper place to lay up the veffel during winter. In their way they obferved fifteen iflanders upon an height ; and threw them fome
fragments of dried fifh, in order to entice
them to approach nearer. But as this over-
ture did not fucceed, Tfiuprof, who was one
of the party, ordered fome of the crew to
mount the height, and to feize one of the
inhabitants, for the purpofe of learning their
language : this order was accordingly exe-
cuted, notwithftanding the refiftance which
the iflanders made with their bone-fpears ;
and the Ruffians immediately returned with
their prifoner to the fhip. They were foon
afterwards driven to fea by a violent ftorm,
and beat about from the 2d to the 9th of October, during which time they loft their
anchor and boat : at length they came back
to

to the fame ifland, where they paffed the winter.

Soon after their landing, they found in an adjacent hut the dead bodies of two of the inhabitants, who had probably been killed in the laft encounter. In their way the Ruffians were met by an old woman, who had been taken prifoner, and fet at liberty. She was accompanied with thirty-four iflanders of both fexes, who all came dancing to the found of a drum ; and brought with them a prefent of coloured earth. Pieces of cloth, thimbles, and needles, were diftributed among them in return ; and they parted amicably. Before the end of October, the fame perfons, together with the old woman and feveral children, returned dancing as before ; and brought birds, fifh, and other provifion. Having paffed the night with the Ruffians, they took their leave. Soon after their departure, Tfiuprof, Shaffyrin, and Nevodtfikof, accompanied with feven of the crew, went after them, and found them among the rocks. In this interview the natives behaved in the moft friendly manner ; and exchanged a baidar and fome fkins for two fhirts. They were obferved to have hatchets of fharpened ftone, stone, and needles made of bone: they lived upon the flesh of sea-otters, seals, and sea-lions, which they killed with clubs and bone-lances.

So early as the 24th of October, Tsiuprof had sent ten persons, under the command of Larion Belayef, upon a reconnoitring party. The latter treated the inhabitants in an hostile manner; upon which they defended themselves as well as they could with their bone-lances. This resistance gave him a pretext for firing; and accordingly he shot the whole number, amounting to fifteen men, in order to seize their wives.

Shekurdin, shocked at these cruel proceedings, retired unperceived to the ship, and brought an account of all that had passed. Tsiuprof, instead of punishing these cruelties as they deserved, was secretly pleased with them; for he himself was affronted at the islanders for having refused to give him an iron bolt, which he saw in their possession. He had, in consequence of their refusal, committed several acts of hostilities against them; and had even formed the horrid design of poisoning them with a mixture of corrosive sublimate. In order however to preserve appearances, he dispatched Shekurdin

din and Nevodtfikof to reproach Belayef for his diforderly conduct ; but fent him at the fame time, by the abovementioned perfons, more powder and ball.

The Ruffians continued upon this ifland, where they caught a large quantity of fea-otters, until the 14th of September, 1746 ; when, no longer thinking themfelves fecure, they put to fea with an intention of looking out for fome uninhabited iflands. Being however overtaken by a violent ftorm, they were driven about until the 30th of October, when their veffel ftruck upon a rocky fhore, and was fhipwrecked, with the lofs of almoft all the tackle, and the greateft part of the furs. Worn out at length with cold and fatigue, they ventured, the firft of November, to penetrate into the interior part of the country, which they found rocky and uneven. Upon their coming to fome huts, they were informed, that they were caft away upon the ifland of Karaga, the inhabitants of which were tributary to Ruffia, and of the Koriac tribe. The iflanders behaved to them with great kindnefs, until Belayef had the imprudence to make propofals to the wife of the chief. The woman gave

gave immediate intelligence to her hufband; and the natives were incenfed to fuch a degree, that they threatened the whole crew with immediate death : but means were found to pacify them, and they continued to live with the Ruffians upon the fame good terms as before.

The 30th of May, 1747, a party of Olo-torians made a defcent upon the ifland in three baidars, and attacked the natives ; but, after fome lofs on both fides, they went a-way. They returned foon after with a larger force, and were again compelled to retire. But as they threatened to come again in a fhort time, and to deftroy all the inhabi-tants who paid tribute, the latter advifed the Ruffians to retire from the ifland, and affifted them in building two baidars. With thefe they put to fea the 27th of June, and landed the 21ft of July at Kamtchatka, with the reft of their cargo, confifting of 320 fea-otters, of which they paid the tenth into the cuftoms. During this expedition twelve men were loft.

C H A P.

C H A P. III.

Succeſſive Voyages, from 1747 *to* 1753, *to* Beering's *and* Copper Iſland, *and to the* Aleütian Iſles.—*Voyage of* Emilian Yugof. —*Voyage of the* Boris *and* Glebb.—*Voyage of* Andrew Tolſtyk *to the* Aleütian Iſles, 1749.—*Voyage of* Vorobief, 1750.—*Voyage of* Novikof *and* Baccof *from* Anadyrſk.— *Shipwreck upon* Beering's Iſland.—*Voyage of* Durnef, *in the* St. Nicholas, 1754.— *Narrative of the Voyage.*—*Deſcription of the* Aleütian Iſles.—*Some account of the inhabitants.*

IN the year 1747 * two veſſels ſailed from the Kamtchatka river, according to a permiſſion granted by the chancery of Bolc-keretſk for hunting ſea-otters. One was fitted out by Andrew Wſevidof, and carried forty-ſix men, beſides eight Coſſacs : the

* It may be neceſſry to inform the reader, that, in this and the two following chapters, ſome circumſtances are occaſionally omitted, which are to be fcund in the original. Theſe omiſſions relate chiefly to the names of ſome of the partners engaged in the equipments, and to a detail of immaterial occurrences prior to the actual departure of the veſſels.

other

Other belonged to Feodor Kolodilof, Andrew Tolftyk, and company ; and had on board a crew, confifting of forty-one Ruffians and Kamtchadals, with fix Coffacs.

The latter veffel failed the 20th of October, and was forced, by ftrefs of weather and other accidents, to winter at Beering's Ifland. From thence they departed May the 31ft, 1748, and touched at another fmall ifland, in order to provide themfelves with water and other neceffaries. They then fteered S. E. for a confiderable way without dif-covering any new iflands ; and, being in great want of provifions, returned into Kamtchatka River, Auguft 14, with a cargo of 250 old fea-otter-fkins, above 100 young ones, and 148 *petfi* or arctic fox-fkins, which were all killed upon Beering's Ifland.

We have no fufficient account of Wfevi-dof's voyage. All that is known amounts only to this, that he returned the 25th of July, 1749, after having probably touched upon one of the neareft Aleütian Ifles which was uninhabited : his cargo confifted of the fkins of 1040 fea-otters, and 2000 arctic foxes.

Emilian

Emilian Yugof, a merchant of Yakutfk, obtained from the fenate of St. Peterfburg the permiffion of fitting out four veffels for himfelf and his affociates. He procured, at the fame time, the exclufive privilege of hunting fea-otters upon Beering's and Copper Ifland during thefe expeditions ; and for this monopoly he agreed to deliver to the cuftoms the third part of the furs.

October 6, 1750, he put to fea from Bol-cherefk, in the floop John, manned with twenty-five Ruffians and Kamtchadals, and two Coffacs : he was foon overtaken by a ftorm, and the veffel driven on fhore be-tween the mouths of the rivers Kronotfk and Tfchafminfk.

October 1751, he again fet fail. He had been commanded to take on board fome of-ficers of the Ruffian navy ; and, as he dif-obeyed this injunction, the chancery of Irkutfk iffued an order to confifcate his fhip and cargo upon his return. The fhip returned on the 22d of July, 1754, to New Kamt-chatkoi Oftrog, laden with the fkins of 755 old fea-otters, of 35 cub fea-otters, of 417 cubs of fea-bears, and of 7044 arctic fox-fkins : of the latter 2000 were white,

and

and 1765 black. Thefe furs were procured upon Beering's and Copper Ifland.
Yukof himfelf died upon the laft-mentioned ifland. The cargo of the fhip was,
according to the above-mentioned order,
fealed and properly fecured. But as it appeared that certain perfons had depofited
money in Yugof's hand, for the purpofe of
equipping a fecond veffel, the crown delivered
up the confifcated cargo, after referving the
third part according to the original ftipula-
tion.

This kind of charter-company, if it may
be fo called, being foon diffolved for mifconduct and want of fufficient ftock, other merchants were allowed the privilege of fitting
out veffels, even before the return of Yugof's
fhip ; and thefe perfons were more fortunate
in making new difcoveries than the above-
mentioned monopolift.

Nikiphor Trapefnikof, a merchant of Irkutfk, obtained the permiffion of fending
out a fhip, called the Boris and Glebb, upon
the condition of paying, befide the tribute
which might be exacted, the tenth of all the
furs. The Coffac Sila Sheffyrin went on
board

board this veffel for the purpofe of collecting
the tribute. They failed in Auguft, 1749,
from the Kamtchatka river; and re-entered
it the 16th of the fame month, 1753,
with a large cargo of furs. In the fpring of
the fame year, they had touched upon an unknown ifland, probably one of the Aleütians,
where feveral of the inhabitants were prevailed upon to pay a tribute of fea-otter
fkins. The names of the iflanders, who had
been made tributary, were Igya, Oeknu,
Ogogoektack, Shabukiauck, Alak, Tutun,
Ononufhan, Rotogei, Tfchinitu, Vatfch,
Afhagat, Avyjanifhaga, Unafhayupu, Lak,
Yanfhugalik, Umgalikan, Shati, Kyipago,
and Olofhkot * ; another Aleütian had contributed three fea-otters. They brought with
them 320 of the beft fea-otter fkins, 480 of
the fecond, and 400 of the third fort, 500
female and middle aged, and 220 medwedki
or young ones.

Andrew Tolftyk, a merchant of Selenginfk,
having obtained permiffion from the chancery
of Bolfheretfk, refitted the fame fhip which

* The author here remarks in a note, that the proper
names of the iflanders mentioned in this place, and in other
parts, bear a furprifing refemblance, both in their found
and termination, to thofe of the Greenlanders.

had

had made a former voyage; he failed from Kamtchatka Auguſt the 19th, 1749, and returned July the 3d, 1752.

According to the commander's account, the ſhip lay at anchor from the 6th of September, 1749, to the 20th of May, 1750, before Beering's Iſland, where they caught only 47 ſea-otters. From thence they made to thoſe Aleütian Iſlands, which were * firſt diſcovered by Nevodtſikof, and ſlew there 1662 old and middle-aged ſea-otters, and 119 cubs; beſide which, their cargo conſiſted of the ſkins of 720 blue foxes, and of 840 young ſea-bears.

The inhabitants of theſe iſlands appeared to have never before paid tribute; and ſeemed to be a-kin to the Tſchutſki tribe, their women being ornamented with different figures ſewed into the ſkin in the manner of that people, and of the Tunguſians of Siberia. They differed however from them, by having two ſmall holes cut through the bottom of their under-lips, through each of which they paſs a bit of the ſea-horſe tuſh, worked into the form of a tooth, with a ſmall button at one end, to keep it within the mouth when

* See Chap. II.

it

it is placed in the hole. They had killed, without being provoked, two of the Kamtchadals who belonged to the fhip. Upon the third Ifland fome inhabitants had payed tribute ; their names were reported to be Anitin, Altakukor, and Alefhkut, with his fon Atfchelap. The weapons of the whole ifland confifted of no more than twelve fpears and one dart of bone, all pointed with flint, and the Ruffians obferved in the poffeffion of the natives two figures carved in wood, refembling fea-lions.

Auguft 3, 1750, the veffel Simeon and John, fitted out by the above-mentioned Wfevidof, agent for the Ruffian merchant R. Rybenfkoi, and manned with fourteen Ruffians (who were partly merchants, and partly hunters), and thirty Kamtchadals, failed out for the difcovery of new iflands, under the command of the Coffac Vorobief. They were driven by a violent current and tempeftuous weather to a fmall defert ifland, the pofition whereof is not determined, but which was probably one of thofe that lie near Beering's Ifland. The fhip being fo fhattered by the ftorm, that it was no longer in a condition to keep the fea, Vorobief built
another

another fmall veffel with drift-wood, which he called Jeremiah; in which he arrived at Kamtchatka in autumn, 1752.

Upon the above-mentioned ifland were caught 700 old and 120 cub fea-otters, 1900 blue foxes, 5700 black fea-bears, and 1310 Kotiki, or cub fea-bears.

A voyage made about this time from Anadyrfk deferves to be mentioned.

Aug. 24, 1749, Simeon Novikof of Yakutfk and Ivan Baccof of Uftyug, agents for Ivan Shilkin, failed from Anadyrfk into the mouth of the Kamtchatka river. They affigned the infecurity of the roads, as their reafon for coming from Anadyrfk to Kamtchatka by fea : on this account, having determined to rifk all the dangers of a fea voyage, they built a veffel one hundred and thirty verfts above Anadyr, after having employed two years and five months in its conftruction.

The narrative of their expedition is as fol-lows. In 1748, they failed down the river Anadyr, and through two bays, called Kopeikina and Onemenfkaya, where they found many fand banks, but paffed round them without difficulty. From thence they fteered into the exterior gulph, and waited
for

for a favourable wind. Here they faw feveral Tfchutfki, who appeared upon the heights fingly and not in bodies, as if to reconnoitre ; which made them cautious. They had defcended the river and its bays in nine days. In paffing the large opening of the exterior bay, they fteered between the beach, that lies to the left, and a rock near it ; where, at about an hundred and twenty yards from the rock, the depth of water is from three to four fathoms. From the opening they fteered E. S. E. about 50 verfts, in about four fathom water ; then doubled a fandy point, which runs out directly againft the Tfchutfki coaft, and thus reached the open fea.

From the 10th of July to the 30th, they were driven by tempeftuous winds, at no great diftance from the mouth of the Anadyr; and ran up the fmall river Katirka, upon whofe banks dwell the Koriacs, a people tributary to Ruffia. The mouth of the river is from fixty to eighty yards broad, from three to four fathoms deep, and abounds in fifh. From thence they again put to fea ; and after having beat about for fome time, they at length reached Beering's Ifland. Here they lay at anchor from the 15th of

Septem-

September to the 30th of October, when a
violent storm drove the veffel upon the rocks,
and dafhed her to pieces. The crew however
being faved, they looked out for the remains of
Beering's wreck, in order to employ the materials for the purpofe of conftructing a boat.
They found indeed fome remaining materials,
but almoft entirely rotten, and the iron-
work corroded with ruft. Having felected
however the beft cables, and what iron-work
was immediately neceffary, and collected
drift-wood during the winter, they built with
difficulty a fmall boat, whofe keel was only
feventeen Ruffian ells and an half long, and
which they named Capiton. In this they
put to fea, and failed in fearch of an unknown ifland, which they thought they faw
lying North-eaft; but finding themfelves
miftaken, they tacked about, and ftood for
Copper Ifland : from thence they failed to
Kamtchatka, where they arrived at the time
above-mentioned.

The new-conftructed veffel was granted in
property to Ivan Shilkin as fome compenfa-
tion for his loffes, and with the privilege of
employing it in a future expedition to the
New difcovered Iflands. Accordingly he
                                      failed

failed therein on the 7th of October, 1757, with a crew of twenty Ruffians, and the fame number of Kamtchadals : he was accompanied by Studentzof a Coffac, who was fent to collect the tribute for the crown. An account of this expedition will be given hereafter *.

Auguft, 1754, Nikiphor Trapefnikof fitted out the Shitik St. Nicholas, which failed from Kamtchatka under the command of the Coffac Kodion Durnef. He firft touched at two of the Aleütian Ifles, and afterwards upon a third, which had not been yet difcovered. He returned to Kamtchatka in 1757. His cargo confifted of the fkins of 1220 fea-otters, of 410 female, and 665 cubs ; befide which, the crew had obtained in barter from the iflanders the fkins of 652 fea-otters, of 30 female ditto, and 50 cubs.

From an account delivered in the 3d of May, 1758, by Durnef and Sheffyrin, who was fent as collector of the tributes, it appears that they failed in ten days as far as Ataku, one of the Aleütian Iflands ; that they remained there until the year 1757, and lived upon amicable terms with the natives.

* See Chap. V.

The

The fecond ifland, which is neareft to Ataku, and which contains the greateft number of inhabitants, is called Agataku ; and the third Shemya : they lie from forty to fifty verfts afunder. Upon all the three iflands there are (exclufive of children) but fixty males, whom they made tributary. The inhabitants live upon roots which grow wild, and fea animals : they do not employ themfelves in catching fifh, although the rivers abound with all kinds of falmon, and the fea with turbot. Their cloaths are made of the fkins of birds and of fea-otters. The *Toigon* or chief of the firft ifland informed them, by means of a boy who underftood the Ruffian language, that Eaftward there are three large and well-peopled iflands, Ibiya, Kickfa, and Olas, whofe inhabitants fpeak a different language. Sheffyrin and Durnef found upon the ifland three round copper plates, with fome letters engraved upon them, and ornamented with foliage, which the waves had caft upon the fhore : they brought them, together with other trifling curiofities, which they had procured from the natives, to New Kamtchatkoi Oftrog.

Another

Another fhip built of larchwood by the fame Trapefnikof, which failed in 1752 under the conduct of Alexei Drufinin a merchant of Kurfk, had been wrecked at Beering's Ifland, where the crew conftructed another veffel out of the wreck, which they named Abraham. In this veffel they bore away for the more diftant iflands ; but being forced back by contrary winds to the fame ifland, and meeting with the St. Nicholas upon the point of failing for the Aleütian Ifles, they embarked on that fhip, after having left the new-conftructed veffel under the care of four of their own failors. The crew had flain upon Beering's Ifland five fea-otters, 1222 arctic foxes, and 2500 fea-bears : their fhare of the furs, during their expedition in the St. Nicholas, amounted to the fkins of 500 fea-otters, and of 300 cubs, exclufive of 200 fea-otters-fkins, which they procured by barter.

C H A P.

CHAP. IV.

Voyages from 1753 *to* 1756.

Kolodilof's *ſhip ſails from* Kamtchatka, 1753 -- *Departure of* Serebranikoff's *Veſſel.—Shipwrecked upon one of the more diſtant Iſlands. —Account of the Inhabitants.—The Crew conſtruct another Veſſel, and return to* Kamtchatka.—*Departure of* Kraſſilnikoff's *Veſſel. —Shipwrecked upon* Copper Iſland.—*The Crew reach* Beering's Iſland *in two Baidars.*

THREE veſſels were fitted out for the Iſlands in 1753, one by Kolodilof, a ſecond by Serebrenikof agent for the merchant Rybenſkoy, and the third by Ivan Kraſſilnikof a merchant of Kamtchatka.

Kolodilof's ſhip ſailed from Kamtchatka the 19th of Auguſt, the crew whereof conſiſted of thirty-four perſons ; and anchored the 28th before Beering's Iſland, where they propoſed to winter, in order to lay-in a ſtock of proviſions; but, as they were attempting to land, the boat overſet, and nine of the crew were drowned.

June

June 30, 1754, they ftood out to fea in queft of new difcoveries : the weather how-ever proving ftormy and foggy, and the fhip fpringing a leak, they were all in danger of perifhing ; but in this fituation they unex-pectedly reached one of the Aleütian Iflands, where they lay from the 15th of September until the 9th of July, 1755. In the autumn of 1754 they were joined by a Kamtchadal, and a Koriac : thefe perfons, together with four others, had deferted from Trapefnikof's crew ; and had remained upon the ifland in order to catch fea-otters for their own profit. Four of thefe deferters were killed by the iflanders for having feduced their wives : but, as the two perfons above-mentioned were not guilty of the fame diforderly conduct, the inhabitants fupplied them with women, and lived with them upon the beft terms. The crew killed upon this ifland above 1600 fea-otters, and came back fafe to Kamtchatka in autumn 1755.

Serebranikof's veffel failed in July 1753, manned alfo with thirty-four Ruffians and Kamtchadals : they difcovered feveral new iflands, whch were probably fome of the more diftant ones ; but were not fo fortunate

in

in hunting fea-otters as Kolodilof's crew.
They fteered S. E. and on the 17th of Auguft anchored under an unknown ifland;
whofe inhabitants fpoke a language they did
not underftand. Here they propofed looking out for a fafe harbour ; but were prevented by the coming on of a fudden ftorm,
which carried away their anchor. The fhip
being toft about for feveral days towards the
Eaft, they difcovered not far from the firft
ifland four others : ftill more to the Eaft
three other iflands appeared in fight ; but on
neither of thefe were they able to land.
The veffel continued driving until the 2d of
September, and was confiderably fhattered,
when they fortunately came near an ifland
and caft anchor before it : they were however again forced from this ftation ; the veffel
wrecked upon the coaft ; and the crew with
difficulty reached the fhore.

This ifland feemed to be oppofite to Katy-
fkoi Nofs in the peninfula of Kamtchatka,
and near it they faw three others. Towards
the end of September, Dmitri Trophin, accompanied with nine men, went out in the
boat upon an hunting and reconnoitring party : they were attacked by a large body of
in-

inhabitants, who hurled darts from a fmall wooden engine, and wounded one of the company. The firft fire however drove them back; and although they returned feveral times to the attack in numerous bodies, yet they were always repulfed without difficulty.

Thefe favages mark and colour their faces like the Iflanders above-mentioned; and alfo thruft pieces of bone through holes made in their under-lips.

Soon afterwards the Ruffians were joined in a friendly manner by ten iflanders, who brought the flefh of fea-animals and of fea-otters: a prefent the more welcome, as they had lived for fome time upon nothing but fmall fhell-fifh and roots, and had fuffered greatly from hunger. Several toys were in return diftributed among the favages. The Ruffians remained until June, 1754, upon this ifland: at that time they departed in a fmall veffel, conftructed from the remains of the wreck, and called the St. Peter and Paul; in which they landed at Katyrfkoi Nofs; where having collected 140 feahorfe teeth, they got fafe to the mouth of the Kamtchatka river.

During

During this voyage twelve Kamtchadals
deferted ; of whom fix were flain, together
with a female inhabitant, upon one of the
moft diftant iflands. The remainder, upon
their return to Kamtchatka, were examined ;
and from them the following circumftances
were collected. The ifland, where the fhip
was wrecked, is about 70 verfts long, and 20
broad. Around it lie twelve other iflands of
different fizes, from five to ten verfts diftant
from each other. Eight of them appear to be
no more than five verfts long. All thefe iflands
contain about a thoufand fouls. The dwellings of the inhabitants are provided with no
other furniture than benches, and mats of
platted grafs *. Their drefs confifts of a kind
of fhirt made of bird fkins, and of an upper
garment of inteftines ftitched together ;
they wear wooden caps, ornamented with a
fmall piece of board projecting forwards, as
it feemed, for a defence againft the arrows.
They are all provided with ftone knives, and
a few of them poffefs iron ones : their only
weapons are arrows with points of bone or
flint, which they fhoot from a wooden inftrument. There are no trees upon the ifland :

* Matten aus einem geviffen Kraut-geflochten.

it

it produces however the cow-parſnip *, which
grows at Kamtchatka. The climate is by
no means ſevere, for the ſnow does not lie
upon the ground above a month in the year.

Kraſſilnikof's veſſel ſailed in 1754, and
anchored on the 18th of October before
Beering's Iſland; where all the ſhips which
make to the New-diſcovered Iſlands are accuſtomed to winter, in order to procure a
ſtock of ſalted proviſions from the ſea-cows
and other amphibious animals, that are found
in great abundance. Here they refitted the
veſſel, which had been damaged by driving
upon her anchor; and, having laid in a ſufficient ſtore of all neceſſaries, weighed the 1ſt of
Auguſt, 1754 The 10th they were in ſight
of an iſland, the coaſt whereof was lined with
ſuch a number of inhabitants, that they durſt
not venture aſhore. Accordingly they ſtood
out to ſea, and being overtaken by a ſtorm,
they were reduced to great diſtreſs for want
of water : at length they were driven upon
Copper Iſland, where they landed ; and
having taken in wood and water, they again
ſet ſail. They were beat back however by
contrary winds, and dropped both their an-

* Heracleum.

chors

chors near the fhore ; but the ftorm increaf-
ing at night, both the cables were broken,
and the fhip dafhed to pieces upon the coaft.
All the crew were fortunately faved; and
means were found to get afhore the fhip's
tackle, ammunition, guns, and the remains
of the wreck : the provifions, however,
were moftly fpoiled. Here they were expofed to a variety of misfortunes ; three of
them were drowned on the 15th of October,
as they were going to hunt ; others almoft perifhed with hunger, having no nourifhment but
fmall fhell-fifh and roots. On the 29th of
December great part of the fhip's tackle, and
all the wood, which they had collected from
the wreck, was wafhed away during an high
fea. Notwithftanding their diftreffes, they
continued their hunting parties ; and caught
103 fea-otters, together with 1390 blue foxes.

In fpring they put to fea for Beering's
Ifland in two baidars, carrying with them all
the ammunition, fire-arms, and remaining
tackle. Having reached that ifland, they found
the fmall veffel Abraham, under the care of
the four failors who had been left afhore by
the crew of Trapefnikof's fhip * : but as that

* See the preceding chapter.

veffel

veſſel was not large enough to contain the whole number, together with their cargo of furs, they ſtaid until Serebranikof's and Tol-ſtyk's veſſels arrived. Theſe took in eleven of the crew, with their part of the furs. Twelve remained at Beering's Iſland, where they killed great numbers of arctic foxes, and returned to Kamtchatka in the Abraham, excepting two, who joined Shilkin's crew.

CHAP. V.

Voyages from 1756 to 1758.—Voyage of Andrean Tolſtyk in 1756 to the Aleütian Iſles.—Voyage of Ivan Shilkin in the Capiton, 1757.—Shipwrecked upon one of the Fox Iſlands.—The Crew conſtruct a ſmall Veſſel, and are again ſhip-wrecked.

SEPTEMBER 17, 1756, the veſſel Andrean and Natalia, fitted out by Andrean Tolſtyk, merchant of Selenginſk, and manned with thirty-eight Ruſſians and Kamtchadals, ſailed from the mouth of the Kamtchatka river. The autumnal ſtorms coming on, and a ſcarcity of proviſions enſuing, they made to Beering's Iſland, where they continued until the 14th of June, 1757. As no ſea-otters came on ſhore that

winter,

winter, they killed nothing but feals, fea-
lions, and fea-cows; whofe flefh ferved them
for provifion, and their fkins for the coverings of baidars.

June 13, 1757, they weighed anchor,
and after eleven days failing came to Ataku,
one of the Aleütian ifles difcovered by Nevodtfikof.   Here they found the inhabitants,
as well of that as of the other two iflands,
affembled ; thefe iflanders had juft taken
leave of the crew of Trapefnikof's veffel,
which had failed for Kamtchatka.   The Ruffians feized this opportunity of perfuading
them to pay tribute ; with this view they
beckoned the *Toigon*, whofe name was
Tunulgafen : the latter recollected one of the
crew, a Koriac, who had formerly been left
upon thefe iflands, and who knew fomewhat of
their language. A copper kettle, a fur and cloth
coat, a pair of breeches ftockings, and boots,
were beftowed upon this chief, who was prevailed upon by thefe prefents to pay tribute.
Upon his departure for his own ifland, he
left behind him three women and a boy, in
order to be taught the Ruffian language,
which the latter very foon learned.

The Ruffians wintered upon this Ifland,
and divided themfelves, as ufual, into dif-
                                        ferent

ferent hunting parties : they were compelled, by ftormy weather, to remain there until the 17th of June, 1758 : before they went
away, the above-mentioned chief returned
with his family, and paid a year's tribute.

This veffel brought to Kamtchatka the
moft circumftantial account of the Aleütian
ifles which had been yet received.

The two largeft contained at that time
about fifty males, with whom the Ruffians
had lived in great harmony. They heard of
a fourth ifland, lying at fome diftance from
the third, called by the natives Iviya, but
which they did not reach on account of the
tempeftuous weather.

The firft ifland is about an hundred verfts
long, and from five to twenty broad. They
eftimated the diftance from the firft to the
fecond, which lies Eaft by South, to be about
thirty verfts, and about forty from the latter
to the third, which ftands South Eaft. The
original drefs of the iflanders was made of
the fkins of birds, fea-otters, and feals, which
were tanned ; but the greateft part had procured from the Ruffians dog-fkin coats, and
under-garments of fheep-fkin, which they
were very fond of. They are reprefented as
naturally talkative, quick of apprehenfion,
and

and much attached to the Ruffians. Their
dwellings are hollowed in the ground, and
covered with wooden roofs refembling the
huts in the peninfula of Kamtchatka. Their
principal food is the flefh of fea animals,
which they harpoon with their bone-lances ;
they alfo feed upon feveral fpecies of roots
and berries : namely * cloud-berries, crake-
berries, bilberries, and fervices. The rivulets abound with falmon, and other fifh of
the trout kind fimilar to thofe of Kamtchatka ; and the fea with turbot, which are
caught with bone hooks.

Thefe iflands produce quantities of fmall
ofiers and underwood, but no large trees :
the fea however drives afhore fir and larch,
fufficient for the conftruction of their huts.
There are a great number of arctic foxes
upon the firft ifland, as well as fea-otters ;
and the fhores, during ftormy weather, are
covered with wild geefe and ducks.

The Ruffians, according to the order of
the chancery of Bolcheretfk, endeavoured to
perfuade the *Toigon* of thefe iflands to accompany them to Kamtchatka, but without
fuccefs : upon their departure they diftri-

* Rubus Chamæmorus — Empetrum — Myrtillus —
Sorbus.

buted

buted among the iflanders fome linen, and
thirteen nets for the purpofe of catching fea-
otters, which were very thankfully received.
This veffel brought to Kamtchatka the fkins
of 5030 old and young fea-otters, of 1040
old and young arctic foxes, and of 330 *Med-
wedki* or cubs of fea-otters.

In the year 1757, Ivan Nikiphorof, a
merchant of Mofcow, fitted out a veffel :
but we have no further account of this voyage, than that fhe failed to the Fox Iflands,
at leaft as far as Umnak.

The fmall veffel Capiton, the fame that
was built upon Beering's Ifland, and which
was given to the merchant * Ivan Shilkin,
put to fea September 26, 1757, carrying on
board the Coffac Ignatius Studentfof, who
has given the following account of the voyage.

They had not long failed, before they
were driven back to the fhore of Kamtchatka
by ftrefs of weather, and the veffel ftranded ;
by which accident they loft the rudder and
one of the crew. This misfortune prevented
them from putting to fea again until the following year, with thirty-nine of the original
crew, feveral perfons being left behind on

* See Chap. III.

account

account of ficknefs. They made directly to
Beering's Ifland, where they took up two
of Krafilnikof's crew *, who had been fhipwrecked. They again fet fail in Auguft of
the fame year, and touched at the neareft
Aleütian Ifles, after fuffering greatly from
ftorms. They then continued their courfe
toth e remoter iflands lying between Eaft and
South Eaft ; and, having paffed by the firft,
they anchored before the fecond. A boat
being immediately fent out towards the fhore,
the crew was attacked by a numerous body
of Iflanders in fo fudden a manner, that they
had fcarcely time to fecure themfelves by returning to the veffel. They had no fooner
got aboard, than a violent gale of wind
blowing from the fhore broke the cable, and
drove them out to fea. The weather became fuddenly thick and foggy ; and under
thefe circumftances the veffel was forced upon
a fmall ifland at no great diftance from the
other, and fhipwrecked. The crew got to
fhore with difficulty, and were able to fave
nothing but the fire arms and ammunition.

* See Chap. IV.

They

They had fcarcely landed before they were befet by a number of favages, rowing in baidars from the Weftern point of the ifland. This attack was the more to be dreaded, becaufe feveral of the Ruffians were difabled by cold and wet ; and there remained only fifteen capable of defending themfelves. They advanced however without hefitation to the iflanders ; and one Nicholas Tfiuprof (who had a flight knowledge of their language) accofted and endeavoured to footh them, but without fuccefs. For upon their approach the favages gave a fudden fhout, and, faluting them at the fame time with a volley of darts, wounded one perfon in the hand. Upon this the Ruffians fired, killed two of the affailants, and forced the remainder to retire ; and although a frefh body appeared in fight, as if they were coming to the affiftance of their companions, yet no new attack was made. Soon afterwards the favages left the ifland; and rowed acrofs the ftrait.

From the 6th of September to the 23d of April, they underwent all the extremities of famine : during that period their beft fare was fhell-fifh and roots ; and they were even at times reduced to ftill the cravings of their appetite with the leather which the waves
wafhed

washed ashore from the wreck. Seventeen died
of hunger ; and the rest would soon have followed their companions, if they had not fortunately discovered a dead whale, which the
sea had cast ashore.   They remained upon
this island another winter, where they killed
230 sea-otters ; and, having built a small
vessel out of the remains of the wreck, they
put to sea in the beginning of summer 1760.
They had scarcely reached one of the Aleütian islands, where Serebranikof's vessel lay
at anchor, when they were again shipwrecked, and lost all the remaining tackle and
furs.   Only thirteen of the crew now
remained, who returned on board the
above-mentioned vessel to Kamtchatka July
1751.

C H A P.

CHAP. VI.

Voyages in 1758, 1759, *and* 1760—*to the* Fox Iflands—*in the* St. Vlodimir, *fitted out by* Trapefnikof, *and commanded by* Paikof, 1758—*and in the* Gabriel, *by* Betfhevin— *The latter under the command of* Pufhkaref *fails to* Alakfu *or* Alachfkak, *one of the remoteft Eaftern Iflands hitherto vifited— Some account of its inhabitants and productions, which latter are different from thofe of the more Weftern Iflands.—Voyage of the* Peter *and* Paul *to the* Aleütian Iflands, 1759.

SEPTEMBER 1758, the merchant Simeon Krafilnikof and Nikiphor Trapefnikof fitted out two veffels for the purpofe of catching fea-otters. One of thefe veffels, called the St. Vlodimir, failed the 28th under the command of Dmetri Paikof, carrying on board the Coffac Sila Shaffyrin as collector of the tribute, and a crew of forty-five men. In twenty-four hours they reached Beering's Ifland, where they wintered. July 16, 1759, they fteered towards the South

in

in order to difcover land ; but, being difap-
pointed, they bore away to the North for
the Aleütian Ifles : being prevented however by contrary winds from reaching them,
they failed ftreight towards the diftant iflands,
which are known at prefent under the name
of Lyffie Oftrova, or the Fox Iflands. September 1, they reached the firft of thefe,
called by the natives Atchu, and by the Ruffians
Goreloi, or the Burnt Ifland : but, as the coafts
were very fteep and craggy, they made to Amlak, lying at a fmall diftance, where they determined to pafs the winter. They divided
themfelves accordingly into three parties :
the firft, at the head of which was Alexev
Drufinin, went over to a fmall ifland called
in the journal Sitkin ; the Coffac Shaffyrin
led the fecond, confifting of ten perfons, to
the ifland Atak ; and Simeon Polevoi remained aboard with the reft of the crew. All
thefe iflands were well peopled ; the men had
bones thruft through their ears, under the
lips, and griftle of their nofes ; and the
faces of the women were marked with blackifh
ftreaks made with a needle and thread in the
fkin, in the fame manner as a Coffac, one of
the

the crew, had obferved before upon fome of
the Tſchutſki. The inhabitants had no iron ;
the points of their darts and lances were tipped with bone and flint.

They at firſt imagined, that Amlak was
uninhabited ; but in one of their hunting
parties they found a boy of eight years old,
whom they brought with them : they gave
him the name of Hermolai, and taught him
the Ruſſian language, that he might ferve as
an interpreter. After penetrating further, they
difcovered an hut, wherein were two women,
four men, and as many boys, whom they
treated kindly, and employed in hunting,
fiſhing, and in digging roots. This kind
behaviour encouraged others to pay frequent
viſits, and to exchange fiſh and fleſh for
goats hair, horfes manes, and glafs beads.
They procured alfo four other iſlanders with
their wives, who dug roots for them : and
thus the winter paſſed away without any difturbance.

In the fpring the hunting parties returned ;
during thefe excurfions one man alone was killed upon the iſland Atak, and his fire-arms taken away by the natives. June 1760, the fame
parties were ſent again to the fame iſlands.
Shaffyrin, who headed one of the parties, was

foon afterwards killed, with eleven men, by the inhabitants of Atak, but for what reafon is not known. — Drufinin received the firſt information of this maſſacre from fome inhabitants of Sitkin, where he then was; and immediately fet out with the remaining hunters to join their companions, who were left on board. Although he fucceeded in regaining the veffel, their number was by this time fo confiderably reduced that their fituation appeared very dangerous: he was foon however relieved from his apprehenfions by the arrival of the merchat Betſhevin's veffel at the ifland of Atchu *. The two crews entered into partnerſhip: the St. Vlodimir received twenty-two men, and transferred eleven of her own to the other veffel. The former wintered at Amlak; and the latter continued at anchor before Atchu.

This veffel, fitted out at the expence of Betſhevin, a merchant of Irkhutſk, was called Gabriel; and put to fea from the mouth of the Bolſhaia Reka July 31ſt, 1760. She

* Atak and Atchu are two names for the fame ifland, called alfo by the Ruffians Goreloi, or Burnt Ifland. This ifland and Amlak are probably two of the Andreanoffsky Ifles. See Part II. Chap. IV.

was

was manned with forty Ruffians and twenty Kamtchadals, and carried on board Gabriel Puſhkaref, of the garriſon of Ochotſk, Andrew Shdanof, Jacob Sharypof, Prokopei Lobaſhkof, together with Nikiphor Golodof, and Aphanaſſei Oſkolof, Betſhevin's agents.

Having ſailed through the ſecond ſtrait of the Kurill Iſles, they reached the Aleütian Iſles on the 24th of Auguſt. They ſtood out from thence in order to make new diſcoveries among thoſe more remote iſlands which lie in one continued chain to the extent of 15 degrees of longitude.

September 25 they reached Atchu, or Burnt Iſland, and found the above-mentioned ſhip, the St. Vlodimir, lying twenty verſts from that iſland, before Amlak, in dange of being attacked by the iſlanders. They immediately joined crews, in order to enable the enfeebled company of the St. Vlodimir to continue hunting ; and, as is it uſual in ſuch caſes, entered into a contract for the diviſion of the profit. During that winter the two crews killed, partly upon Siguyam, about 800 ſea-otters of different ſizes, about 100 *med-wedki*

wedki or cubs, fome river otters, above 400 red, greyifh, and black foxes, and collected twelve pood of fea-horfe teeth.

In June, of the following year, the two crews were diftributed equally on board the two veffels : Kraffilnikof's remained at Am-lak, with an intention of returning to Kamt-chatka ; and Betfhevin's put to fea from Atchu, in queft of other iflands. They touch-ed firft at Umnak, where they met Niki-phorof's veffel. Here they took in wood and water, and repaired their fails : they then failed to the moft remote ifland Alakfu *, or Alakfhak, where, having laid up the fhip in a bay, they built huts, and made prepara-tions for wintering. This ifland was very well inhabited, and the natives behaved at firft in a very friendly manner, for they traf-ficked with the Ruffians, and even delivered up nine of their children as hoftages ; but fuch was the lawlefs and irregular behaviour of the crew, that the iflanders were foon ir-ritated and provoked to hoftilities.

In January 1762, Golodof and Pufhka-ref went with a party of twenty men along

---

* This is probably the fame ifland which is laid down in Krenitzin's chart under the name of Alaxa.

the fhore ; and, as they were attempting to violate fome girls upon the ifland Unyumga, were furprifed by a numerous body of the natives : Golodof and another Ruffian were killed, and three were wounded. Not long afterwards, the watch of the crew was fuddenly attacked by the iflanders ; four men were flain upon the fpot, as many wounded, and the huts reduced to afhes.

May 3, Lobafchkof and another Ruffian were killed, as they were going to bathe in the warm fprings, which lie about five verfts from the haven : upon which feven of the hoftages were put to death. The fame month the natives attempted to furprife the Ruffians in their huts ; but, being fortunately difcovered in time, were repulfed by means of the fire arms. At length the Ruffians, finding themfelves in continual danger from thefe attempts, weighed anchor, and failed for Umnak ; where they took up two inhabitants with their wives and children, in order to fhew them other iflands. They were prevented however by tempeftuous weather from reaching them ; and were driven out to fea Weftward with fuch violence, that all their fails were carried away : at length, on the 23d

of

of September, they ſtruck againſt land, which
they took for the peninſula of Kamtchatka ;
and they found it to be the diſtrict of Sto-
bolſkoi Oſtrog. Six men were immediately
diſpatched in the ſmall boat and two baidars
to land : they carried with them ſeveral girls
(who had been brought from the New-diſcovered iſlands) in order to gather berries.
Mean while the crew endeavoured to ply the
ſhip to the windward. When the boat returned, thoſe on board were ſcarcely able, on
account of the ſtorm, to row to the ſhip,
and to catch hold of a rope, which was flung
out to them. Two men remained with the
baidars ; and were afterwards carried by ſome
Kamtchadals to New Kamtchatkoi Oſtrog.
The ſhip without one ſail remaining was
driven along the coaſt of Kamtchatka towards Avatcha, and about ſeventy verſts
from that harbour ran into the bay of Ka-
latzoff on the 25th of September. Their
cargo conſiſted of the ſkins of 900 old and
young ſea-otters, and of 350 foxes.

Puſhkaref and his crew had during this
voyage behaved with ſuch inhumanity towards the iſlanders, that they were brought

to

to trial in the year 1764; and the above-
mentioned account is taken from the concur-
ring evidence of feveral witneffes. It appears alfo, that they brought away from
Atchu and Amleg two Aleütian men and
three boys, Ivan an Aleütian interpreter, and
above twenty women and girls whom they
feduced. Ivan, and one of the boys, whom
they called Mofes, were the only perfons
who arrived at Kamtchatka. Upon their
firft approach to that coaft, fourteen women
were fent afhore, to dig roots and to gather
berries. Of thefe, two ran away, and a
third was killed, as they were returning to
the fhip, by one Gorelin : upon this the
others in a fit of defpair leaped into the fea,
and were drowned. All the remaining
Aleütians, excepting the two perfons above-
mentioned, were immediately thrown over-
board by Pufhkaref's order. The account
which follows, although it is found in the
depofitions, does not deferve to be entirely
credited in all particulars.

The natives of the above-mentioned iflands
are very tall and ftrongly made, They
make their cloaths of the fkins of birds ;
and

and thruſt bones through their under-lips by way of ornament. They were ſaid to ſtrike their noſes until they bled, in order to ſuck the blood ; but we are informed from ſubſequent accounts, that the blood thus drawn from themſelves was intended for other purpoſes *. They were accuſed even of murdering their own children, in order to drink their blood ; but this is undoubtedly an invention of the criminals, who repreſented the iſlanders in the moſt hideous colours, in order to excuſe their own cruelties. Their dwellings under-ground are ſimilar to thoſe of the Kamtchadals ; and have ſeveral openings on the ſides, through which they make their eſcape when the principal entrance is beſet by an enemy. Their weapons conſiſt of arrows and lances pointed with bone, which they dart at a conſiderable diſtance.

The iſland Alakſu is ſaid to contain reindeer, bears, wild boars, wolves, otters, and a ſpecies of dogs with long ears, which are very fierce and wild. And as the greateſt part of theſe animals are not found upon

* It appears, in the laſt chapter of this tranſlation, that the iſlanders are accuſtomed to glue on the point of their darts with blood ; and that this was the real motive to the practice mentioned in the text.

thoſe

thofe Fox Iflands which lie nearer to the weft, this circumftance feems to prove that Alakfu is fituated at no great diftance from the Continent of America. As to red, black, and grey foxes, there is fo large a quantity, that they are feen in herds of ten or twenty at a time. Wood is driven upon the coaft in great abundance. The ifland produces no large trees, having only fome under-wood, and a great variety of bulbs, roots, and berries. The coafts are frequented by large flocks of feabirds, the fame which are obferved upon the fhore of the fea of Penfhinfk.

Auguft 4, 1759, the Peter and Paul, fitted out at the expence of the merchant Rybenfkoi by his agent Andrew Serebranikof, and manned with thirty-three perfons, fet fail from the mouth of the Kamtchatka river. They fteered fouthwards until the 20th of September without feeing any land, when they ftood for the Aleütian Ifles, one of which they reached the 27th of September. They remained there until the 24th of June, 1761; during which time they killed upon this and the two other iflands 1900 old and young fea-otters, and obtained 450 more by bartering

ing with the iflanders. The Coffac Minya-
chin, who was on board as collector of the
tribute, calls in his account the firft ifland by
the Ruffian name of Krugloi, or Round
Ifland, which he fuppofes to be about fixty
verfts in circumference : the largeft ifland
lies thirty verfts from thence, and is about an
hundred and fifty round ; the fmalleft is
about thirty verfts from the latter, and is
forty in circumference. Thefe three iflands
contain feveral high rocky mountains. The
number of inhabitants were computed to be
about forty-two men, without reckoning women and children.

C H A P.

C H A P. VII.

Voyage of Andrean Tolſtyk *in the* St. Andrean
and Natalia 1760—*Diſcovery of ſome new
Iſlands called* Andreanofskye Oſtrova—*De-
ſcription of ſix of thoſe Iſlands,* Ayugh,
Kanaga, Tſetchina, Tagalak, Atchu, *and*
Amlak ;—*Auccount of their inhabitants.—
The Veſſel wrecked upon the coaſt of* Kamt-
chatka.

THE moſt remarkable voyage hitherto
made is that of the St. Andrean and
Natalia, of which the following extract is
drawn from the Journals of the two Coſſacs,
Peter Waſyutinſkoi and Maxim Laſarof.
This veſſel, fitted out by the above-mentioned merchant Andrean Tolſtyk, weighed
from the mouth of the Kamtchatka river
September 27, 1760 ; ſtood out to ſea right
Eaſtwards ; and on the 29th reached Beering's Iſland. There ſhe lay at anchor in a
bay, from whence the crew brought all the
tackle and lading aſhore. Soon afterwards
they were driven upon the ſhore by a violent
autumnal ſtorm, without any other damage
than

than the lofs of an anchor. Here they paffed the winter; and, having refitted their
veffel, put to fea June 24, 1761 : they paffed by Copper Ifland, which lies about an
hundred and fifty verfts from the former ;
and fteered S. E. towards the Aleütian Ifles,
which they did not reach before the 6th of
Auguft. They caft anchor in an open bay
near Attak, in order to procure an interpreter
from the Toigon Tunulgafen ; but the latter
being dead, they fent prefents to the Toigon
Bakutun. As there were already three fhips
lying at anchor before this ifland, on the 19th
they again ftood out to fea in queft of the
more diftant iflands, for the purpofe of ex-
acting a tribute. They carried on board a
relation of the Toigon Bakutun, who had a
flight knowledge of the Ruffian language.
They fteered N. E. and N. E. by E. and were
driven, on the 28th, by an high gale of
wind towards an ifland, before which they
immediately caft anchor. The following
morning the two Coffacs, with a party of
eight perfons, went afhore to reconnoitre the
ifland ; but faw no inhabitants. Auguft
30, the veffel was brought into a fafe
bay.

bay. The next day fome of the crew were
fent afhore to procure wood, that the fhip
might be refitted ; but there were no large
trees to be met with upon the whole ifland·
Lafarof, who was one of the party, had been
there before in Serebranikof's veffel : he
called the ifland Ayagh or Kayaku ; and
another, which lay about the diftance of
twenty verfts, Kanaga. As they were returning to the fhip, they faw two iflanders
rowing in fmall canoes towards Kanaga,
one of whom had ferved as an interpreter,
and was known to Lafarof. The latter accordingly made them a prefent of fome frefh
provifion, which the others gratefully ac-
cepting continued their courfe acrofs the
ftrait to Kanaga. Soon afterwards Lafarof
and eight men rowed over to that ifland ;
and having invited the Toigon, who was a
relation of the above-mentioned intrepreter,
to pay them a vifit at Kayaku, they immediately returned to the fhip.

Near the place where they lay at anchor,
a rivulet falls into the bay ; it flows from a
lake that is about two or three verfts in circumference, and which is formed from a
number of fmall fprings. Its courfe is about
eight

eight verfts long ; and in fummer feveral
fpecies of falmon and other fifh, fimilar to
thofe which are found at Kamtchatka, afcend
the ftream as far as the lake.

Lafarof was employed in fifhing in this
rivulet, when the Toigon of Kanaga, accompanied with a confiderable number of
the natives in fifteen baidars, arrived at the
fhip : he was hofpitably entertained, and received feveral prefents. The Ruffians feized
this opportunity of perfuading the iflanders
to acknowledge themfelves fubjeＣt to the
Emprefs, and to pay a regular tribute ; to
which they made no great objeＣtion. By
means of the interpreter, the following information was obtained from the Toigon.
The natives chiefly fubfift upon dried fifh and
other fea animals. They catch * turbot of a
very large fize, and take feals by means of
harpoons, to which they faften bladders.
They fifh for cod with bone hooks, and lines
made of a long and tough fpecies of fea-weed,
which they dip in frefh water, and draw out
to the fize of a fine packthread.

As foon as the veffel was laid up in a fecure place, Tolftyk, Vaffyutin, and Lafarof,

* The author adds, that thefe turbot [paltus] weigh occafionally feven or eight pood.

with

with feveral others, went in four baidars to Kanaga. The firft remained upon that ifland; but the two others rowed in two baidars to Tfetchina, which is feparated from Kanaga by a ftrait about feven verfts in breadth : the iflanders received them amicably, and promifed to pay tribute. The feveral parties returned all fafe to Kayaku, without having procured any furs. Soon afterwards Tolftyk difpatched fome hunters in four baidars to Tagalak, Atchu, and Amlak, which lay to the Eaft of Kayaku : as none of thefe parties met with any oppofition from the natives ; they accordingly remained with great tranquillity upon thefe feveral iflands until the year 1764. Their fuccefs in hunting was not however very great ; for they caught no more than 1880 full grown fea-otters, 778 middle-aged, and 372 cubs.

The following is Lafarof's defcription of the above-mentioned fix iflands *, which lie in a chain fomewhat to the North Weft of the Fox Iflands, and muft not be blended with them. The firft certain account was

* Thefe are the fix Iflands defcribed by Mr. Stæhlin in his defcription of the New Archipelago. See Book II. Chap. IV.

brought

brought by this veffel, the St. Andrean and Natalia, from whence they are called the Andreanofskie Oftrova, or the Iflands of St. Andrean.

Ayagh is about an hundred and fifty verfts in circumference : it contains feveral high and rocky mountains, the intervals of which are bare heath and moor ground : not one foreft tree is to be found upon the whole ifland. The vegetables feem for the moft part like thofe which grow in Kamtchatka. Of berries there are found * crow or crake-berries and the larger fort of bilberries, but in fmall quantities. Of the roots of burnet and all kinds of fnake weed, there is fuch an abundance as to afford, in cafe of neceffity, a plentiful provifion for the inhabitants. The above-mentioned rivulet is the only one upon the ifland. The number of inhabitants cannot fufficiently be afcertained, becaufe the natives pafs continually from ifland to ifland in their baidars.

Kanaga ftands Weft from Ayagh, and is two hundred verfts in circumference. It contains an high volcano, where the natives find

* Empetrum, Vaccin. Uliginofum, Sanguiforba, & Biftorta.

fulphur

fulphur in fummer. At the foot of this
mountain are hot fprings, wherein they occafionally boil their provifion. There is no
rivulet upon this ifland : and the low grounds
are fimilar to thofe of Ayagh. The inhabitants are reckoned about two hundred fouls.

Tfetchina lies Eaftward about forty verfts
from Kanaga, and is about eighty in circumference. It is full of rocky mountains, of
which the *Bielaia Sopka*, or the White Peak,
is the higheft. In the valley there are alfo
fome warm fprings, but no rivulet abounding
in fifh : the ifland contains only four families.

Tagalak is forty verfts in circumference,
ten Eaft from Tfetchina : it contains a few
rocks, but neither rivulets with fifh, nor any
vegetable production fit for nourifhment.
The coafts are rocky, and dangerous to approach in baidars. This ifland is alfo inhabited
by no more than four families.

Atchu lies in the fame pofition forty verfts
diftant from Tagalak, and is about three
hundred in circumference : near it is an harbour, where fhips may ride fecurely at anchor. It contains many rocky mountains ;
and feveral fmall rivulets that fall into the

fea,

fea, and of which one running Eaftwards abounds in fifh. The roots which have juft before been mentioned, and bulbs of white lilies, are found there in plenty. Its inhabitants amount to about fixty fouls.

Amlak is a mountainous ifland ftanding to the Eaft more than feven verfts from Atchu, and is alfo three hundred in circumference. It contains the fame number of inhabitants as Atchu, has a commodious haven, and produces roots in abundance. Of feveral fmall rivulets there is one only, which flows towards the North, that contains any fifh. Befides thefe a clufter of other iflands were obferved ftretching farther to the Eaft, which were not touched upon.

The inhabitants of thefe fix iflands are tributary to Ruffia. They live in holes dug in the earth, in which they make no fires even in winter. Their clothes are made like fhirts, of the fkins of the * guillimot and puffin, which they catch with fpringes. Over thefe in rainy weather they wear an upper garment, made of the bladders and other dried inteftines of feals and fea-lions oiled and ftitched together. They catch cod

* Colymbus Troile, Alca Arctica.

and

and turbot with bone-hooks, and eat them raw. As they never collect a ftore of pro-vifion, they fuffer greatly from hunger in ftormy weather, when they cannot go out to fifh ; at which time they are reduced to live upon fmall fhell-fifh and fea-wrack, which they pick up upon the beach and eat raw. In May and June they kill fea-otters in the following manner : When the weather is calm, they row out to fea in feveral baidars : having found the animal, they ftrike him with harpoons, and follow him fo clofely, that he cannot eafily efcape. They take fea dogs in the fame manner. In the fevereft weather they make no addition to their ufual cloathing. In order to warm themfelves in winter, whenever it freezes very hard, they burn a heap of dry grafs, over which they ftand and catch the heat under their clothes. The clothes of the women and children are made of fea-otter fkins, in the fame form as thofe be-longing to the men. Whenever they pafs the night at a diftance from home, they dig a hole in the earth, and lay themfelves down in it, covered only with their clothes and matts of platted grafs. Regardlefs of every thing but the prefent moment, deftitute of

religion,

religion, and without the leaft appearance of decency, they feem but few degrees removed from brutes.

As foon as the feveral baidars fent out upon hunting parties were returned, and the veffel got ready for their departure, the Toigons of thefe iflands (excepting Kanaga) came in baidars to Tolftyk, accompanied with a confiderable number of the natives ; their names were Tfarkulini, Tfhunila, Kayugotfk and Mayatok. They brought with them a voluntary tribute, making prefents of pieces of dried falmon, and unanimoufly expreffing their fatisfaction upon the good conduct of the Ruffians. Tolftyk gave them in return fome toys and other trifles, and defired them to recommend to the inhabitants of the other iflands the like friendly behaviour towards the Ruffian merchants who fhould come amongft them, if they had a mind to be treated in the fame manner.

June 14, 1764, they failed for Kamtchatka, and anchored on the 19th before Shemiya, one of the Aleütian Iflands. The 21ft they were forced from their anchor by tempeftuous winds, and driven upon a rocky fhore. This

This accident obliged them to fend the lading afhore, and to draw the fhip upon land in order to repair the damage, which was performed with much difficulty. On the 18th of Auguft they ftood out to fea and made towards Atchu, which they reached on the 20th. Having fprung a leak, they again refitted the veflel ; and, after taking on board the crew of a fhip which had been lately caft away, they failed for Kamtchatka. On the 4th of September they came in fight of that peninfula near Tzafchminfkoi Oft-rog ; and on the 18th, as they were endeavouring to run into the mouth of the Kamtchatka river, they were forced by a ftorm upon the coaft. The veflel was deftroyed, and the greateft part of the cargo loft.

C H A P.

C H A P. VIII.

Voyage of the Zacharias *and* Elizabeth, *fitted out by* Kulkoff, *and commanded by* Drufinin, 1762—*They fail to* Umnak *and* Unalafhka, *and winter upon the latter ifland* —*The veffel deftroyed; and all the crew, except four, murdered by the iflanders—The adventures of thefe four* Ruffians, *and their wonderful efcape.*

I SHALL here barely mention that a veffel was fitted out in Auguft, 1760, at the expence of Terrenti Tfebaëffkoi; but I fhall have occafion to be very circumftantial in my accounts concerning feveral others, which failed during the following years : more copious information concerning the Fox Iflands having been procured from thefe voyages, although for the moft part unfortunate, than from all the preceding ones.

In 1762 four veffels failed for the Fox Iflands : of thefe only one returned fafe to Kamtchatka.

The firft was the Zacharias and Elizabeth, fitted out by Kulkof, a merchant of Vologda, and

and Company, under the command of Dru-finin, and manned by thirty-four Ruffians, and three Kamtchadals.

September the 6th, they weighed anchor from Okotfk, and arrived October the 11th in the haven of St. Peter and Paul, where they wintered. June the 24th, 1763, they again put to fea, and having reached, after eleven days failing, the neareft Aleütian Iflands, they anchored before Attak. They ftaid here about fourteen days, and took up feven Ruffians who had been fhipwrecked on this coaft. Among thefe was Korelin, who re-turned to Kamtchatka, and brought back the following account of the voyage.

July the 17th, they failed from Attak to-wards the more diftant iflands. In the fame month they landed upon an ifland, where the crew of the Andrean and Natalia was en-gaged in hunting; and, having laid in a pro-vifion of water, continued their voyage.

In the beginning of September they ar-rived at Umnak, one of the Fox Iflands; and caft anchor about a verft from the fhore. They found there Glottof's veffel, whofe voyage will be mentioned in a fucceeding

chapter

chapter *. Druſinin immediately diſpatched his firſt mate Maeſniſk and Korelin, with thirty-four of the crew, to land. They paſſed over to the eaſtern extremity of the iſland, which was diſtant about ſeventy verſts from the veſſel ; and retuned ſafe on the 12th of September. During this expedition, they ſaw ſeveral remains of fox-traps which had been ſet by the Ruſſians ; and met with ſeveral natives who ſhewed ſome tribute-quittances. The ſame day letters were brought by the iſlanders from Medvedef and Korovin †, who were juſt arrived at Umnak and Unalaſhſka in two veſſels fitted out by the merchants Protaſſof and Trapeſnikof. Anſwers were returned by the ſame meſſengers.

On the 22d, Druſinin ſailed to the Northern point of Unalaſhka, which lies about fifteen verſts from Umnak : the crew, having laid up the veſſel in a ſafe harbour, and brought the lading aſhore, made preparation to conſtruct an hut. Soon after their arrival, two Toigons of the neareſt village brought hoſtages of their own accord ; their example

* Chap. X.
† See the following chapter.

was

was immediately followed by feveral of the more diftant villages. Here they received information of an hunting party fent from Trapefnikof's fhip. Upon which Maefnifk alfo difpatched three companies upon the fame errand, one confifting of eleven men, among whom was Korelin, under the command of Peter Tfekalef; a fecond of the fame number, under Michael Kudyakof; and a third of nine men, under Yephim Kafkitfyn. Tfekalef's party was the only one of which we have received any circumftantial account : for not a fingle perfon of the other two, or of the crew remaining on board, ever returned to Kamtchatka.

Kafkitfyn remained near the haven, and the two other companies were difpatched to the Northern point of the ifland. Kudyakof ftopped at a place called Kalaktak, which contained about forty inhabitants : Tfekalef went on to Inalok, which lies about thirty verfts from Kalaktak. Having found there a dwelling with about feventy inhabitants, to whom he behaved with kindnefs, he built an hut for himfelf and his companions ; and kept a conftant watch.

December

December the 4th, fix of the party being difpatched to look after the pit-falls, there remained only the five following Ruffians, Peter Tfekalef, Stephen Korelin, Dmitri Bragin, Gregory Shaffyrin, and Ivan Kokovin : the iflanders therefore feized this opportunity of giving the firft proofs of their hoftile intentions, which they had hitherto concealed. As Tfekalef and Shaffyrin were upon a vifit to the iflanders, the latter fuddenly, and without any provocation, ftruck Tfekalef upon the head with a club, and afterwards ftabbed him with knives. They next fell upon Shaffyrin, who defended himfelf with an hatchet ; and, though defperately wounded, forced his way back to his companions. Bragin and Korelin, who remained in the hut, had immediate recourfe to their fire-arms ; but Kokovin, who was at a fmall diftance, was furrounded by the favages, and thrown down. They continued ftabbing him with knives and darts, until Korelin came to his affiftance ; who having wounded two iflanders, and driven away the others, brought his wounded companion half-dead to the hut.

Soon

Soon afterwards the natives furrounded the hut, which the Ruffians had taken the precaution to provide with fhooting holes. The fiege lafted four days without intermif-fion. The iflanders were prevented indeed by the fire-arms from ftorming the hut; but whenever the Ruffians made their appearance, darts were immediately fhot at them from all fides; fo that they could not venture to go out for water. At length, when Shaffyrin and Kokovin were a little recovered, they all fallied out upon the iflanders with their guns and lances; three perfons were killed upon the fpot, and feveral wounded; upon which the others fled away and difperfed. During the fiege the favages were feen at a little diftance bearing fome arms and caps, and holding them up in triumph: thefe things belonged to the fix Ruffians, who had been fent to the pit-falls; and had fallen a facrifice to the refentment of the natives.

The latter no fooner difappeared, than the Ruffians dragged the baidar into the fea, and rowed without moleftation out of the bay, which is about ten verfts broad. They next landed near a fmall habitation: finding it empty,

empty, they drew the baidar afhore, and
traverfed, with their fire-arms and lances,
the mountains towards Kalaktak, where they
had left Kudyakof's party. As they approached that place towards evening, they fired
from the heights ; but no fignal being returned, they concluded, as was really the
cafe, that this company had likewife been
maffacred by the inhabitants. They themfelves narrowly efcaped the fame fate; for,
immediately upon the report of the fire-
arms, numerous bodies of the iflanders made
their appearance, and clofely purfued the
Ruffians : darknefs however coming on, the
latter found means to efcape over the fandy
fhore of a bay to a rock, where they were
fheltered, and could defend themfelves. They
here made fo good a ufe of their arms, that
the iflanders thought proper to retire : the
fugitives, as foon as their purfuers were with-
drawn, feized the opportunity of proceeding
towards the haven, where their veffel lay
at anchor. They ran without interruption
during the whole night ; and at break of
day, when they were about three verfts from
the haven, they efpied a locker of the veffel
lying

lying on the fhore. Struck with aftonifh-
ment at this alarming difcovery, they retreated with precipitation to the mountains ;
from whence they defcried feveral iflanders
rowing in canoes, but no appearance of their
own veffel. During that day they kept themfelves clofely concealed, and durft not venture again towards the haven before the
evening. Upon their arrival they found the
veflel broken to pieces, and the dead bodies
of their companions mangled along the beach.
Having collected all the provifion which had
been untouched by the favages, they returned
to the mountains.

The following day they fcooped out a ca-
vity at the foot of a mountain fituated about
three verfts from the haven ; and covered it
with a piece of a fail. In the evening they
returned to the haven, and found there an
image of a faint and a prayer-book ; and all
the tackle and lading were taken away, excepting the facks for provifion. Thefe facks
were made of leather : the natives had ript
them up, probably to fee if they contained
any iron, and had left them, together with
the provifion, behind as ufelefs. The Ruffians collected all that remained ; and dragged

as much as they were able to carry into the mountains to their retreat, where they lived in a very wretched ftate from the 9th of December to the 2d of February, 1764.

Mean while they employed themfelves in making a little baidar, which they covered with the leather of the facks. Having drawn it at night from the mountains to the fea, they rowed without waiting for break of day along the Northern coaft of Unalafhka, in order to reach Trapefnikof's veffel, which, as they had reafon to think, lay at anchor fomewhere upon the coaft. They rowed at fome diftance from the fhore, and by that means paffed three habitations unperceived. The following day they obferved at fome diftance five iflanders in a baidar, who upon feeing them made to Makufhinfk, before which place the fugitives were obliged to pafs. Darknefs comingon, the Ruffians landed on a rock, and paffed the night afhore. Early in the morning difcovering the iflanders advancing towards them from the bay of Makufhinfk, they placed themfelves in an advantageous poft ; and prepared for defence.

The favages rowed clofe to the beach : part landing, and part remaining in their
baidars,

baidars, they commenced the affault by a
volley of darts ; and notwithftanding the
Ruffians did great execution with their fire-
arms, the fkirmifh continued the whole day.
Towards evening the enemy retired; and the
fugitives betook themfelves with their canoe
to an adjoining cavern. The attack was
again renewed during the night ; but the
Ruffians were fo advantageoufly pofted, that
they repulfed the affailants without much
difficulty. In this encounter Bragin was flightly wounded. They remained in this place three
days ; but the fea rifing at a fpring-tide into the rock, forced them to fally out towards
a neighbouring cavern, which they reached
without lofs, notwithftanding the oppofition
of the iflanders.

They were imprifoned in this cave five
weeks, and kept watch by turns. During
that time they feldom ventured twenty yards
from the entrance ; and were obliged to
quench their thirft with fnow-water, and
with the moifture dripping from the rock.
They fuffered alfo greatly from hunger, having no fuftenance but fmall fhell-fifh, which
they occafionlly found means to collect upon
the beach. Compelled at length by extreme
want, they one night ventured to draw their
baidar

baidar into the fea ; and were fortunate enough
to get off unperceived.

They continued rowing at night, but in the
day they hid themfelves on the fhore ; by this
means they efcaped unobferved from the bay
of Makufhinfk, and reached Trapefnikof's veffel the 30th of March, 1764. What hap-
pened to them afterwards in company with
the crew of this veffel will be mentioned in
the fucceeding chapter. Shaffyrin alone of
all the four died of ficknefs during the voyage ; but Korelin, Kokovin, and Bragin *,
returned fafe to Kamtchatka. The names
of thefe brave men deferve our admiration,
for the courage and perfeverance with which
they fupported and overcame fuch imminent
dangers.

* Thefe Ruffians were well known to feveral perfons of
credit, who have confirmed the authenticity of this relation. Among the reft, the celebrated naturalift Mr. Pallas
faw Bragin at Irkutfk : from him he had a narrative of
their adventures and efcape ; which, as he affured me,
perfectly tallied with the above account, which is drawn
from the journal of Korelin.

CHAP.

CHAP. IX.

Voyage of the veſſel called the Trinity, *under the command of* Korovin, 1762—*Sails to the* Fox Iſlands—*Winters at* Unalaſhka—*Puts to ſea the ſpring following—The veſſel is ſtranded in a bay of the iſland* Umnak, *and the crew attacked by the natives—Many of them killed—Others carried off by ſickneſs—They are reduced to great ſtreights—Relieved by* Glottof, *twelve of the whole company only remaining—Deſcription of* Umnak *and* Unalaſhka—*and account of the Inhabitants.*

THE ſecond veſſel which ſailed from Kamtchatka in the year 1762, was the Trinity, fitted out by the trading company of Nikiphor Trapeſnikof, merchant of Irkutſk, under the command of Ivan Korovin, and manned with thirty-eight Ruſſians and ſix Kamtchadals.

September 15, they ſailed down the Kamtchatka river, and ſtood out to ſea the 29th, when they were driven at large for ten days by contrary winds. At laſt upon the 8th of October

October they came in fight of Beering's and
Copper Ifland, where they caft anchor before
the South fide of the former. Here they
were refolved to winter on account of the
late feafon of the year. Accordingly they
laid up the veffel in a fecure harbour, and
brought all the lading afhore. They ftaid
here until the firft of Auguft, 1763; during
that time they killed about 500 arctic foxes
and 20 fea-otters; the latter animals reforted
lefs frequently to this ifland, in confequence of
the difturbance from the Ruffifian hunters.

Korovin, having collected a fufficient ftore
of provifion, feveral fkins of fea-cows for the
coverings of baidars, and fome iron which
remained from the wreck of Beering's fhip,
prepared for his departure. Upon his arrival at
Beering's Ifland the preceding autumn, he
found there a veffel fitted out by Jacob Protaffof, merchant of Tiumen, under the command of Dennis Medvedef *, with whom Korovin had entered into a formal contract for
the divifion of the furs. Here he took on board
ten of Medvedef's crew, and gave him feven
in return.

* This is the fourth veffel which failed in 1762. As the
whole crew was maffacred by the favages, we have no account of the voyage. Short mention of this maffacre is
occafionally made in this and the following chapters.

Auguft

Auguft 1, Korovin put to fea from Beering's Ifland with thirty-feven men, and Medvedef with forty-nine. They failed without
coming in fight of the Aleütian Ifles : on
the 15th, Korovin made Unalafhka, where
Glottof lay at anchor, and Medvedef reached
Umnak. Korovin received the news of the
latter's fafe arrival, firft by fome iflanders,
and afterwards by letters ; both veffels lay at
no greater diftance from each other than about
an hundred and fifty verfts, taking a ftreight
line from point to point acrofs the firth.

Korovin caft anchor in a convenient bay
at the diftance of fixty yards from the fhore.
On the 16th he landed with fourteen men ;
and having found nothing but an empty fhed,
he returned to the veffel. After having taken
a reinforcement, he again went afhore in
order to look for fome inhabitants. About
feven verfts from the haven, he came to two
habitations ; and faw three hundred perfons.
Among them were three Toigons, who recollected and accofted in a friendly manner
one Barnafhef, a native of Tobolfk, who had
been there before with Glottof: they fhewed
fome tribute-quittances, which they had lately

received

received from the Coffac Sabin Ponomaref. Two
of thefe Toigons gave each a boy of twelve
years of age as an hoftage, whom they paffed
for their children ; and the third delivered
his fon of about fifteen years of age, the
fame who had been Glottof's hoftage, and
whom Korovin called Alexèy. With thefe
hoftages he returned to the fhip, which he
laid up in the mouth of a river, after having
brought all the provifion and lading afhore.
Soon afterwards the three Toigons came to
fee the hoftages ; and informed Korovin,
that Medvedef's veffel rode fecurely at anchor
before Umnak.

September 15, when every thing was prepared for wintering, Korovin and Barnafhef
fet out in two baidars, each with nine men
and one of the hoftages, who had a flight
knowledge of the Ruffian language. They
went along the Northern coaft of the ifland,
towards its Weftern extremity, in order to
hunt, and to enquire after a certain interpreter called Kafhmak, who had been employed
by Glottof on a former occafion. Having
rowed about twenty verfts, they paffed by
a village ; and landed at another, which lay
about five verfts further. But as the number

ber of inhabitants feemed to amount to two hundred, they durſt not venture to the dwellings, but ſtayed by the baidar. Upon this the Toigon of the place came to them, with his wife and ſon : he ſhewed a tribute-quittance, and delivered his ſon, a boy of thirteen years of age, and whom Korovin called Stepanka, as an hoſtage, for which he received a preſent of corals.

They rowed now further to a third village, about fifteen verſts from the former, where they found the interpreter Kaſhmak ; the latter accompanied them to the two Toigons, who gave them a friendly reception, and ſhewed their tribute-quittances. A few natives only made their appearance; the others, as the Toigons pretended, were gone out to fiſh. The next morning each Toigon gave a boy as an hoſtage ; one of the boys Korovin called Gregory, and the other Alexèy. The Ruſſians were detained there two days by a violent ſtorm ; during which time a letter from Medvedef was brought by an Aleütian ; and an anſwer was returned by the ſame perſon. The ſtorm at length ſomewhat abating, they rowed back to the next village ; where
they

they continued two nights without any apprehenfions from the favages. At length
Korovin returned in fafety with the hoftages
to the crew.

In the beginning of October they built a
winter-hut, partly of wood, and partly of
feal-fkins ; and made all the neceffary preparations for hunting. On the 14th, two
companies, each confifting of eleven men,
were fent upon an hunting party to the
Eaftern point of the ifland ; and returned in
four days with hoftages. About fixty verfts
from the haven, they had met a party of
twenty-five Ruffians, commanded by Drufinin. About the fame time fome Toigons
brought a prefent of fturgeon and whale's
blubber ; and received in return fome beads
and provifion.

Korovin and his company now thought
themfelves fecure ; for which reafon twenty-
three men, under the command of the above-
mentioned Barnafhef, were difpatched in two
baidars upon an hunting party towards the
Weftern point of the ifland. Eight mufkets
were diftributed to each boat, a piftol and a
lance to each man, and alfo a fufficient
ftore of ammunition and provifion. The
follow-

following day two accounts were fent from
Barnafhef : and letters were alfo received from
the crew of Protaffof's veffel. From the 2d
of November to the 8th of December, the
Ruffians, who remained with Korovin, killed forty-eight dark-coloured foxes, together
with an hundred and feventeen of the common fort ; during this expedition one man
was loft. Some of the natives came occafionally in baidars ; and exchanged fea-otters
and fox-fkins for corals. On the 8th of December letters were. again brought from Barnafhef and alfo from the crew of Protaffof's
fhip. Anfwers were returned by the fame
meffengers.

After the departure of thefe meffengers,
the mother of Alexèy came with a meffage
from the Toigon her hufband, importing, that
a large number of iflanders were making
towards the fhip. Upon this Korovin ordered the men to arms ; and foon after feventy natives approached, and held up fome fea-
otter fkins. The Ruffians cried out, that no
more than ten at a time fhould come over the
brook towards their hut : upon which the iflanders left their fkins with Korovin, and returned

ed without attempting any hoftilities. Their
apprehenfions were now fomewhat quieted ;
but they were again raifed by the arrival of
three Kamtchadals belonging to Kulkof's fhip,
who flew for protection to Korovin : they
brought the account that the crew had been
killed by the favages, and the veffel deftroyed.
It was now certain, that the feventy iflanders
above-mentioned had come with hoftile intentions. This information fpread fuch a
fudden panic among the Ruffians ; that it
was even propofed to burn the veffel, and to
endeavour to find their companions, who
were gone upon hunting parties.

That day however paffed without any attack:
but, towards the evening of the 10th of December, the favages affembled in large bodies, and invefted the hut on all fides·
Four days and nights they never ceafed an-
noying the Ruffians with their darts ; two
of the latter were killed, and the furvivors
were nearly exhaufted by continual fatigue.
Upon the fifth day the iflanders took poft in
a neighbouring cavern, where they continued watching the Ruffians fo clofely during
a whole month, that none of the latter durft
venture

venture fifty paces from their dwelling·
Korovin, finding himfelf thus annoyed by
the natives, ordered the hut to be deftroyed ;
and then retired to his veffel, which was
brought for greater fecurity out of the mouth
of the rivulet to the diftance of an hundred
yards from the beach. There they lay at
anchor from the 5th of March to the 26th of
April, during which time they fuffered greatly
from want of provifion, and ftill more from
the fcurvy.

During this period they were attacked by
a large body of the natives, who advanced
in forty baidars with the hopes of furprifing the veffel. Korovin being warned of
their approach by two of the inhabitants,
one of whom was a relation of the interpreter Kafhmak, was prepared for their reception. As foon as the favages came near the
veffel, they brandifhed their darts, and prepared for the attack. Korovin however had
no fooner fired and killed one perfon, than
they were ftruck with a panic and rowed
away. They were fo incenfed at this failure
of fuccefs, that they immediarely put to
death the two good-natured natives, who
had betrayed their defign to the Ruffians.

Soon

Soon afterwards the father of Alexèy came and demanded his fon, who was reftored to him : and on the 30th of March Korovin and his three companions arrived as it is mentioned in the preceding chapter. By this reinforcement the number of the crew amounted to eighteen perfons.

April 26, Korovin put to fea from Unalafhka with the crew and eleven hoftages. The veffel was driven until the 28th by contray winds, and then ftranded in a bay of the ifland Umnak. The ammunition and fails, together with the fkins for the conftruction of baidars, were brought afhore with great difficulty. During the difembarkation one fick man was drowned ; another died as foon as he came to land ; and eight hoftages ran away amidft the general confufion. There ftill remained the faithful interpreter Kafhmak and three hoftages. The whole number of the Ruffians amounted to only fixteen perfons ; and of thefe three were fick of the fcurvy. Under thefe circumftances they fecured themfelves between their baidar and fome empty barrels, which they covered with feal-fkins, while the fails were fpread over them in form of a tent. Two Ruffians kept

.watch ;

watch; and there being no appearance of any iflanders, the others retired to fleep.

Before break of day, about an hundred favages advancing fecretly from the fea-fide, threw their darts at the diftance of twenty yards with fuch force, that many of them pierced through the baidar and the fkins ; others fell from above through the fails. By this difcharge, the two perfons who kept watch, together with the three hoftages, were killed on the fpot ; and all the Ruffians were wounded. The latter indeed were fo effectually furprifed, as to be prevented from having recourfe to their fire-arms. In this diftrefs Korovin fallied out, in company with four Ruffians, and attacked the enemy with lances : two of the favages were killed, and the others driven to flight. Korovin and his party were fo feverely wounded, that they had fcarcely ftrength fufficient to return to their tent.

During the night the ftorm increafed to fuch a degree, that the veffel was entirely dafhed to pieces. The greateft part of the wreck, which was caft on fhore by the fea, was carried away by the iflanders. They alfo

broke

broke to pieces the barrels of fat; emptied
the facks of provifion; and deftroyed moft
of the furs : having thus fatisfied their refentment, they went away; and did not
again make their appearance until the 30th
of April. Upon their retiring, the Ruffians
collected the wretched remains which had
been left untouched by the favages, or which
the waves had caft on fhore fince their departure.

April 30, a body of an hundred and fifty
natives advanced from the Eaftern point of
the ifland towards the tent; and, at the
diftance of an hundred yards, fhot at the Ruffians with fire-arms, but luckily without
execution. They alfo fet on fire the high
grafs, and the wind blew the flames towards
the tent; but the Ruffians by firing forced
the enemy to flight, and gained time to ex-
tinguifh the flames.

This was the laft attack which was made
upon Korovin; although ficknefs and mifery
detained him and his companions upon this
fpot until the 21ft of July. They then put
to fea in a baidar eight yards long, which
they had conftructed in order to make to Protaffof's veffel, with whofe fate they were as
yet

yet unacquainted. Their number was now reduced to twelve perfons, among whom were fix Kamtchadals.

After having rowed ten days, they landed upon the beach of the fame ifland Umnak : there they obferved the remains of a veffel which had been burnt, and faw fome clothes, fails, and ropes, torn to pieces. At a fmall diftance was an empty Ruffian dwelling, and near it a bath-room, in which they found, to their inexpreffible terror, twenty dead bodies in their clothes. Each of them had a thong of leather, or his own girdle, faftened about the neck, with which he had been dragged along. Korovin and his companions recollected them to have been fome of thofe who had failed in Protaffof's veffel ; and could diftinguifh among the reft the commander Medvedef. They difcovered no further traces of the remaining crew; and, as none ever appeared, we have no account of the circumftances with which this cataftrophe was attended.

After having buried his dead countrymen, Korovin and his companions began to build an hut ; but were prevented from finifhing it, by the unexpected arrival of Stephen

Glottof,

Glottof *, who came to them with a small party by land. Korovin and his companions accordingly joined Glottof, and rowed the next day to his veffel.

Soon afterwards Korovin was fent with a party of twenty men to coaft the ifland of Umnak, in order to difcover if any part of Medvedef's crew had made their efcape from the general maffacre : but his enquiries were without fuccefs. In the courfe of this expedition, as he lay at anchor, in September, before a fmall ifland fituated between Umnak and Unalafhka, fome favages rowed towards the Ruffians in two large baidars ; and having fhot at them with fire-arms, though without effect, inftantly retired. The fame evening Korovin entered a bay of the ifland Umnak, with an intention of paffing the night on fhore : but, as he came near the coaft, a large number of favages in an hundred baidars furrounded and faluted him with a volley of darts. Korovin fired, and having foon difperfed them made to a large baidar, which he faw at fome diftance, in hopes of finding fome Ruffians. He was however miftaken ;

* See the following chapter.

the

the iflanders who were aboard landed at his approach; and, after fhooting at him from their fire-arms, retired to the mountains. Korovin found there an empty baidar, which he knew to be the fame in which Barnafhef had failed, when he was fent upon a hunting party. Within were nothing but two hatchets and fome iron points for darts. Three women were feized at the fame time; and two natives, who refufed to furrender themfelves, were put to death. They then made to the dwelling, from which all the inhabitants had run away; and found therein pieces of Ruffian leather, blades of fmall knives, fhirts, and other things, which had belonged to the Ruffians. All the information which they could procure from the women whom they had taken prifoners, was, that the crew had been killed, and this booty taken away by the inhabitants, who had retired to the ifland Unalafhka. Korovin gave thefe women their liberty; and, being apprehenfive of frefh attacks, returned to the haven.

Towards winter Korovin, with a party of twenty-two men, was fent upon a hunting expedition to the Weftern point of Unalafhka: he

was

was accompanied by an Aleütian interpreter, called Ivan Glottof. Being informed by some islanders, that a Ruffian ship, under the command of Ivan Soloviof *, was then lying before Unalashka, he immediately rowed towards the haven where she was at anchor. On the way he had a sharp encounter with the natives, who endeavoured to prevent him from landing : of these, ten were killed upon the spot ; and the remainder fled away, leaving behind them some women and children.

Korovin staid three days aboard Soloviof's veffel ; and then returned to the place where he had been so lately attacked. The inhabitants however, for this time, made no oppofition to his landing ; on the contrary, they received him with kindnefs, and permitted him to hunt : they even delivered hoftages ; and entered into a friendly traffic, exchanging furs for beads. They were also prevailed upon to reftore feveral mufkets and other things, taken from the Ruffians who had been maffacred.

A short time before his departure, the inhabitants again shewed their hoftile inten-

* Chap. XI.

tions ;

tions ; for three of them came up to the Ruffian centinel, and fuddenly fell upon him with their knives. The centinel however difengaging himfelf, and retreating into the hut, they ran away. The Toigons of the village protefted ignorance of this treachery ; and the offenders were foon afterwards difcovered and punifhed. Korovin, as he was returning to Glottof, was forced to engage with the iflanders upon Unalafhka, and alfo upon Umnak, where they endeavoured to prevent him from landing. Before the end of the year a ftorm drove the baidar upon the beach of the latter ifland ; and the tempeftuous weather fetting in, they were detained there until the 6th of April, 1765. During this time they were reduced, from a fcarcity of provifion, to live chiefly upon fea-wrack and fmall fhell-fifh. On the 22d they returned to Glottof; and, as they had been unfuccefsful in hunting, their cargo of furs was very inconfiderable. Three days after his arrival, Korovin quitted Glottof, and went over with five other Ruffians to Soloviof, with whom he returned the following year to Kamtchatka. The fix Kamtchadals of Korovin's party joined Glottof.

Ac-

According to Korovin's account, the iflands Umnak and Unalafhka are fituated not much more Northwards than the mouth of the Kamtchatka river; and, according to the fhip's reckoning, about the diftance of 1700 verfts Eaftwards from the fame place. The circumference of Umnak is about two hundred and fifty verfts: Unalafhka is much larger. Both thefe iflands are wholly deftitute of trees; drift-wood is brought afhore in large quantities. There were five lakes upon the Northern coaft of Unalafhka, and but one upon Umnak, of which none were more than ten verfts in circumference. Thefe lakes give rife to feveral fmall rivulets, which flow only a few verfts before they empty themfelves into the fea: the fifh enter the rivulets in the middle of April; they afcend the lakes in July, and continue there until Auguft. Sea-otters and other fea-animals refort but feldom to thefe iflands; but there is great abundance of red and black foxes. North Eaftwards from Unalafhka two iflands appeared in fight, at the diftance of five or ten verfts; but Korovin did not touch at them.

The

The inhabitants of thefe iflands row in their fmall baidars from one ifland to the other. They are fo numerous, and their manner of life fo unfettled, that their number cannot exactly be determined. Their dwelling caves are made in the following manner. They firft dig a hole in the earth, proportioned to the fize of their intended habitation, of twenty, thirty, or forty yards in length, and from fix to ten broad. They then fet up poles of larch, firs, and afh, driven on the coaft by the fea. Acrofs the top of thefe poles they lay planks, which they cover with grafs and earth. They enter through holes in the top by means of ladders. Fifty, a hundred, and even a hundred and fifty perfons dwell together in fuch a cave. They light little or no fires within, for which reafon thefe dwellings are much cleaner than thofe of the Kamtchadals. When they want to warm themfelves in the winter, they make a fire of dry herbs, of which they have collected a large ftore in fummer, and ftand over it until they are fufficiently warmed. A few of thefe iflanders wear fur-ftockings in winter;

but

but the greateft part go bare-footed, and all
are without breeches. The fkins of cormorants, puffins, and fea-divers, ferve for the
mens cloathing ; and the women wear the
fkins of fea-bears, feals, and fea-otters. They
fleep upon thick mats, which they twift out
of a foft kind of grafs that grows upon the
fhore ; and have no other covering but their
ufual clothes. Many of the men have five or
fix wives ; and he that is the beft hunter or
fifher has the greateft number. The women
make their needles of the bones of birds
wings, and ufe finews for thread.

Their weapons are bows and arrows, lances and darts, which they throw like the
Greenlanders to the diftance of fixty yards by
means of a little hand-board. Both the darts
and arrows are feathered : the former are
about an ell and an half long ; the fhaft,
which is well made confidering their want
of inftruments, is often compofed of two
pieces that join into each other ; the point is
of flint, fharpened by beating it between two
ftones. Thefe darts as well as the lances
were formerly tipped with bone ; but at prefent the points are commonly made of the
iron which they procure from the Ruffians,
and

and out of which they ingenioufly form little hatchets and two-edged knives. They fhape the iron by rubbing it between two ftones, and whetting it frequently with feawater. With thefe inftruments and ftone hatchets they build their baidars. They have a ftrange cuftom of cutting holes in the under-lip and through the griftle of the nofe. They place in the former two little bones, wrought in the form of teeth, which project fome inches from the face. In the nofe a piece of bone is placed crofsways. The deceafed are buried with their boat, weapons, and clothes *.

* The author repeats here feveral circumftances which have been mentioned before, and many of them will occur again : but my office as a tranflator would not fuffer me to omit them.

C H A P.

C H A P. X.

Voyage of Stephen Glottof *in the* Andrean *and* Natalia, 1762—*He reaches the* Fox-Iſlands—*Sails beyond* Unalaſhka *to* Kadyak—*Winters upon that Iſland—Repeated attempts of the Natives to deſtroy the Crew—They are repulſed, reconciled, and prevailed upon to trade with the* Ruſſians—*Account of* Kadyak—*Its inhabitants—animals—productions—*Glottof *ſails back to* Umnak—*Winters there—Returns to* Kamtchatka—*Journal of his voyage.*

T H E following voyage, which extended further, and terminated more fortunately than the laſt mentioned expeditions, is one of the moſt memorable yet made.

Terenty Tſebaeffskoi and company, merchants of Lalſk, fitted out the Andrean and Natalia under the command of Stephen Glottof, an experienced and ſkilful ſeaman of Yarenſk. This veſſel ſailed from the bay of the river Kamtchatka the 1ſt of October, 1762,

1762, manned with thirty eight Ruffians and eight Kamtchadals. In eight days they reached Mednoi Oftrof, or Copper Ifland, where having fought out a convenient harbour, they unloaded and laid up the veffel for the winter. Their firft care was to fupply themfelves with provifions ; and they killed afterwards a quantity of ice-foxes, and a confiderable number of fea-otters.

For the benefit of the crown and their own ufe in cafe of need, they refolved to take on board all the remaining tackle and iron work of Beering's fhip, which had been left behind on Commander's Ifland and was buried in the beach. For this purpofe they difpatched, on the 27th of May, Jacob Malevinfkoy (who died foon after) with thirteen men in a baidar to that ifland, which was feventy verfts diftant. They brought back with them twenty-two pood of iron, ten of old cordage fit for caulkers' ufe, fome lead and copper, and feveral thoufand beads.

Copper Ifland has its name from the native copper found on the coaft, particularly at the Weftern point on its South fide. Of this native copper Malevinfkoy brought with him two large pieces, weighing together twelve
pounds,

pounds, which were picked up between a rock and the fea on a ftrand of about twelve yards in breadth. Amongft other floating bodies which the fea drives upon the fhores of this ifland, the true right camphor wood, and another fort of wood very white, foft, and fweet-fcented, are occafionally found.

Every preparation for continuing the voyage being made, they failed from Copper Ifland the 26th of July, 1763, and fteered for the iflands Umnak and Agunalafhka, where Glottof had formerly obferved great numbers of black foxes. On account of ftorms and contrary winds, they were thirty days before they fetched Umnak. Here they arrived the 24th of Auguft, and without dropping anchor or lofing any time, they refolved to fail further for the difcovery of new iflands : they paffed eight contiguous to each other and feparated by ftraits, which, according to their eftimation, were from twenty to an hundred verfts broad. Glottof however did not land till he reached the laft and moft Eaftward of thefe iflands, called by the inhabitants Kadyak ; from which the natives faid it was not far to the coaft of a wide-extended

tended woody continent. No land however was to be feen from a little ifland called by the natives Aktunak, which is fituated about thirty verfts more to the Eaft than Kadyak.

September 8th, the veffel ran up a creek, lying South Eaft of Aktunak, through which a rivulet empties itfelf into the fea; this rivulet comes from a lake fix verfts long, one broad, and about fifty fathoms deep. During the ebb of the tide the veffel was left aground ; but the return of the water fet her again afloat. Near the fhore were four large huts, fo crouded with people, that their number could fcarcely be counted : however, foon after Glottof's arrival, all thefe inhabitants quitted their dwellings, and retired with precipitation. The next day fome iflanders in baidars approached the veffel, and accofted the people on board : and as Ivan Glottof, the Aleütian interpreter, did not well underftand the language of thefe iflanders, they foon afterwards returned with a boy whom they had formerly taken prifoner from Ifanak, one of the iflands which lie to the Weft of Kadyak. Him the Aleütian interpreter perfectly underftood : and by his

his means every neceſſary explanation could be obtained from the iſlanders.

In this manner they converſed with the ſavages, and endeavoured to perſuade them to become tributary ; they uſed alſo every argument in their power to prevail upon them to give up the boy for an interpreter ; but all their entreaties were for the preſent without effect. The ſavages rowed back to the cliff called Aktalin, which lies about three verſts to the South of Kadyak, where they ſeemed to have habitations.

On the 6th of September Kaplin was ſent with thirteen men to the cliff, to treat peaceably with the iſlanders. He found there ten huts, from which about an hundred of the natives came out. They behaved ſeemingly in a friendly manner, and anſwered the interpreter by the boy, that they had nobody proper for an hoſtage ; that they would deliver the boy to the Ruſſians agreeably to their deſire. Kaplin received him very thankfully, and brought him on board, where he was properly taken care of : he afterwards accompanied Glottof to Kamtchatka, and was baptized by the name of Alexander Popof, being then about thirteen years of age.

For

For fome days after this conference the iflanders came off in companies of five, ten, twenty, and thirty : they were admitted on board in fmall numbers, and kindly received, but with a proper degree of circumfpectation.

On the 8th of September the veffel was brought further up the creek without unloading her cargo; and on the 9th Glottof with ten men proceeded to a village on the fhore about two hundred yards from the veffel, where the natives had begun to refide : it confifted of three fummer-huts covered only with long grafs ; they were from eight to ten yards broad, twelve long, and about four high. They faw there about an hundred men, but neither women nor children.

Finding it impoffible to perfuade the favages to give hoftages, Glottof refolved to let his people remain together, and to keep a ftrong guard.

Although the iflanders vifited them ftill in fmall bodies, yet it was more and more vifible that their intentions were hoftile. At laft on the 1ft of October, by day-break, a great number, having affembled together in the remote parts of the ifland, came unexpectedly

pectedly acrofs the country. They approached very near without being difcovered by the watch ; and feeing nobody on deck but thofe on duty, fhot fuddenly into the veffel with arrows. The watch found refuge behind the quarter boards, and gave the alarm without firing. Glottof immediately ordered a volley to be fired over their heads with fmall arms ; upon which they immediately retreated with great expedition. As foon as it was day, there was no enemy to be feen : but they difcovered a number of ladders, feveral bundles of hay in which the favages had put fulphur, likewife a quantity of birch-tree bark, which had been left behind in their precipitate flight.

They now found it very neceffary to be on their guard againft the attempts of thefe perfidious incendiaries. Their fufpicions were ftill further increafed by the fubfequent conduct of the natives : for though the latter came to the veffel in fmall bodies, yet it was obferved that they examined every thing, and more particularly the watch, with the ftricteft attention ; and they always returned without paying any regard to the friendly propofitions of the Ruffians.

On

On the 4th of October about two hundred
iflanders made their appearance, carrying
wooden fhields before them, and preparing
with bows and arrows for an attack. Glottof endeavoured at firft by perfuafion to prevail upon them to defift ; but obferving that
they ftill continued advancing, he refolved to
venture a fally. This intrepidity difconcer-
ted the iflanders, and they immediately retreated without making the leaft refiftance.

The 26th of October they ventured a third
attack, and advanced towards the veflel for
that purpofe by day-break : the watch however gave the alarm in due time, and the
whole crew were immediately under arms.
The approach of day-light difcovered to their
view different parties of the enemy advancing under the protection of wooden
fcreens. Of thefe moving breaft-works they
counted feven ; and behind each from thirty
to forty men armed with bone lances. Befide thefe a croud of armed men advanced
feparately to the attack, fome of them bearing whale jaw-bones, and others wooden
fhields. Diffuafion proving ineffectual, and
the arrows beginning to fall even aboard the
fhip,

fhip, Glottof gave orders to fire. The fhot from the fmall arms however not being of force enough to pierce the fcreens, the iflanders advanced under their protection with fteadinefs and intrepidity. Glottof neverthelefs determined to rifk a fally of his whole crew armed with mufkets and lances. The iflanders inftantly threw down their fcreens ; and fled with precipitation until they gained their boats, into which they threw themfelves and rowed off. They had about feventeen large baidars and a number of fmall canoes. The fkreens which they left behind were made of three rows of ftakes placed perpendicularly, and bound together with fea-weed and ofiers ; they were twelve feet broad, and above half a yard thick.

The iflanders now appearing to be fufficiently intimidated, the Ruffians began to build a winter hut of floated wood ; and waited the appearance of fpring without further annoyance. Although they faw none of the inhabitants before the 25th of December, yet Glottof kept his people together ; fending out occafionally fmall hunting and fifhing parties to the lake, which lay about five verfts from the creek. During the whole winter they

they caught in the lake feveral different fpeices of trout and falmon, foles, and herrings of a fpan and a half long, and even turbot and cod-fifh, which came up with the flood into the lake.

At laft, on the 25th of December, two iflanders came to the fhip; and converfed at a diftance by means of interpreters. Although propofals of peace and trade were held out to them in the moft friendly manner, yet they went off without feeming ro put much confidence in thefe offers; nor did any of them appear again before the 4th of April, 1764. Want of fufficient exercife in the mean time brought on a violent fcurvy among the crew, by which diforder nine perfons were carried off.

On the 4th of April four of the natives made their appearance, and feemed to pay more attention to the propofals : one of them at laft advanced, and offered to barter two fox-fkins for beads. They did not fet the leaft value upon other goods of various kinds, fuch as fhirts, linen, and nankeen ; but demanded glafs beads of different colours, for which they exchanged their fkins with plea-
fure.

fure. This friendly traffic, together with
Glottof's entreaties, operated fo powerfully,
that, after holding a confultation with their
countrymen, they returned with a folemn
declaration, that their brethren would in
future commit no hoftilities againft the Ruffians. From that time until their departure
a daily intercourfe was carried on with the
iflanders, who brought all forts of fox and
fea-otter fkins ; and received in exchange a
ftipulated number of beads. Some of them
were even perfuaded to pay a tribute of fkins,
for which receipts were given.

Amongft other wares the Ruffians procured two fmall carpets, worked or platted in
a curious manner, and on one fide fet clofe
with beaver-wool like velvet: they could
not however learn whether thefe carpets
were wrought by the iflanders. The latter
brought alfo for fale well-dreffed fea-otter
fkins, the hair of which was fhorn quite
fhort with fharp ftones, in fuch a manner,
that the remainder, which was of a yellowifh
brown colour, gliftened and appeared like
velvet. Their caps had furprifing and fometimes not ungracetul decorations, fome being
adorned on the forepart with manes like a
helmet ;

helmet; -others, feemingly pecular to the females, were made of inteftines ftitched together with rein-deer hair and finews in a moft elegant tafte, and ornamented on the crown with long ftreamers of hair died of a beautiful red. Of all thefe curiofities Glottof carried famples to Kamtchatka *.

The natives differ confiderably in drefs and language from the inhabitants of the other Fox Iflands : and feveral fpecies of animals were obferved upon Kadyak, which are not to be found upon the other iflands, viz. ermines, martens, beavers, river-otters, wolves, wild boars, and bears : the laft-mentioned animal was not indeed actually feen by the Ruffians, but the prints of its feet were traced. Some of the inhabitants had clothes made of the fkins of rein-deer and jevras; the latter of which is a fort of fmall marmofet. Both thefe fkins were probably

* Thefe and feveral other ornaments of a fimilar kind are preferved in a cabinet of curiofities at the Academy of Sciences of St. Peterfburg : a cabinet which well merits the attention of the curious traveller ; for it contains a large collection of the dreffes of the Eaftern nations. Amongft the reft, one compartment is entirely filled with the dreffes, arms, and implements, brought from the New-difcovered iflands.

pro-

procured from the continent of America *
Black, brown, and red foxes, were feen in
great number; and the coaft abounds with
fea-dogs, fea-bears, fea-lions, and fea-otters.
The birds are cranes, geefe, ducks, gulls,
ptarmigans, crows, and magpies ; but no uncommon fpecies was difcovered. The vegetable productions are bilberries, cranberries,
wortleberries, and wild lily-roots. Kadyak
likewife yields willows and alders, which
circumftance affords the ftrongeft proof that
it lies at no great diftance from the continent
of America. The extent of Kadyak cannot be exactly afcertained ; as the Ruffians,
through apprehenfion of the natives, did not
venture to explore the country.

The inhabitants, like thofe of the Aleütian
and nearer iflands, make holes in the under-
lips and through the griftle of the nofe, in
which they infert the bones of birds and animals worked into the form of teeth. Their
clothes are made of the fkins of birds, foxes,
fea-otters, young rein-deer, and marmofets ;

* Although this conjecture is probable, yet, when the
reader recollects that the ifland Alakfu is faid to contain
rein-deer, he will perceive that the inhabitants of Kadyak
might have been fupplied with the fkins of that animal from
thence. See p. 76.

they

they few them together with finews. They
wear alfo fur-ftockings of rein-deer fkins,
but no breeches. Their arms are bows, arrows, and lances, whofe points, as well as
their fmall hatchets, are of fharp flint : fome
few make knives and lance points of rein-
deer bones. Their wooden fhields are called
kuyaky, which amongft the Greenlanders
fignifies a fmall canoe. Their manners are
altogether rude. They have not the leaft difpofition to give a courteous reception to ftrangers : nor does there appear amongft themfelves any kind of deference or fubmiffion
from one to another.

Their canoes are fome of them fo fmall as
to contain only one or two perfons ; others
are large baidars fimilar to the women's boats
of the Greenlanders. Their food confifts
chiefly of raw and dried fifh, partly caught
at fea with bone hooks, and partly in rivulets,
in bag-nets made of finews platted together.
They call themfelves Kanagift, a name that
has no fmall refemblance to Karalit ; by
which appellation, the Greenlanders and Efquimaux on the coaft of Labradore diftinguifh themfelves : the difference between
thefe two denominations is occafioned perhaps

haps by a change of pronunciation, or by a
miftake of the Ruffian failors, who may have
given it this variation. Their numbers feem
very confiderable on that part of the ifland
where they had their fixed habitations.

The ifland Kadyak * makes, with Aghunalafhka, Umnak, and the fmall iflands lying between them, a continued Archipelago,
extending N. E. and E. N. E. towards America; it lies by the fhips's reckoning in 230
degrees of longitude; fo that it cannot be far
diftant from that part of the American coaft
which Beering formerly touched at.

The large ifland Alakfu, lying Northward from Kadyak where Pufhkaref † wintered, muft be ftill nearer the continent: and
the account given by its inhabitants of a great
promontory, called Ataktak, ftretching from
the continent N. E. of Alakfu, is not at all
improbable.

Although the conduct of the iflanders appeared more friendly; yet on account of their
numbers Glottof, refolving not to pafs another
winter upon Kadyak, prepared for his de-

* Kadyak is not laid down upon any chart of the New-
difcovered iflands : for we have no chart of Glottof's voyage; and no other Ruffian navigator touched at that ifland.
† See Chap. VI.

parture.

parture. He wanted hoops for repairing his water-casks; and being told by the natives that there were trees on the island at no great distance from the bay, he difpatched, on the 25th of April, Lukas Ftorulkin with eleven men, for the purpofe of felling wood. Ftorulkin returned the fame day with the following intelligence: that after rowing along the South coaft of the ifland forty or fifty verfts from the haven, he obferved, about half a verft from the fhore, a confiderable number of alders, fimilar to thofe found in Kamtchatka, growing in vallies between the rocks. The largeft trunks were from four to feven inches in diameter. Of this wood he felled as much as he had occafion for; and returned without having met with either iflander or habitation.

They brought the veffel down the creek in May; and, after taking in all the peltry and ftores, left Kadyak on the 24th. Contrary winds retarded their voyage, and drove them near the ifland Alakfu, which they paffed; their water being nearly exhaufted, they afterwards landed upon another ifland, called Saktunak, in order to procure a frefh ftock. At laft on the 3d of July, they arrived again at Umnak, and anchored in a bay which Glottof had

had formerly vifited. He immediately went
afhore in a baidar, and foon found out his
former hut, which was in ruins : near it he
obferved another Ruffian dwelling, that had
been built in his abfence ; in which lay a
murdered Ruffian, but whofe face none of
them knew. Refolving to procure further
information, he went acrofs the ifland the
5th of July, accompanied by fixteen of his
crew, and difcovered the remains of a burnt
veffel, fome prayer-books, images, &c. ; all
the iron work and cordage were carried off.
Near the fpot he found likewife a bathing
room filled with murdered Ruffians in their
clothes. From fome marks, he concluded
that this was the veffel fitted out by Protaffof ; nor was he miftaken in his conjectures.

Alarmed at the fate of his countrymen,
Glottof returned to the fhip, and held a confultation upon the meafures neceffary to be
taken ; and it was unanimoufly refolved that
they fhould endeavour to procure more intelligence concerning the veffel. In the mean
time feven iflanders advanced in baidars, and
pretended that they wanted to trade. They
fhewed fea-otter fkins at a diftance, but would
not

not venture on board; and by the interpreter defired Glottof and two of his people to come on fhore and barter. Glottof, however, having fufficient caufe to diftruft the favages, refufed to comply with their demands : upon this they immediately landed, and fhot from the fhore with fire-arms, but without doing any execution. They were even bold enough to get into their canoes a fecond time, and to row near the veffel. In order if poffible to procure intelligence from them, every me. thod of perfuading them to peace was tried by means of the interpreters ; and at laft one of them approached the fhip, and demanded victuals ; which being thrown to him, he came on board. He then related the fate of the above-mentioned veffel, of which the iflanders had made themfelves mafters; and gave likewife fome intelligence concerning the remaining fmall body of fugitives under the command of Korovin. He alfo confeffed, that their defign was to entice Glottof on fhore, and then to kill him ; for which purpofe more than thirty iflanders were pofted in ambufh behind the neareft rocks. After cutting off the leader, they imagined it would be an eafy matter to feize upon the fhip.

Upon

Upon this information Glottof detained the iflander on board, and landing with a ftrong party attacked the favages : the latter fhot with arrows, as well as from the mufkets which they had feized, but without effect, and were foon forced to retire to their canoes.

July the 14th a violent ftorm arofe, in which Glottof's veffel parted her cable ; and was forced on fhore without any other lofs than that of an anchor. The crew likewife, through want of frefh provifions, began to grow fo fickly, that they were almoft in a defence-lefs ftate. Glottof however, with ten men, fet out the 28th of July for that part of the ifland, where according to information they expected to find Korovin. They dif-covered only parts of the wreck, but none of the crew, fo that they now gave them up for loft. But on the 2d of Auguft, as Glottof was on his way back, five iflanders approached him in canoes, and afked why the baidar had been out ; to which a falfe an-fwer being given, they told him, that on the other fide of the ifland he would find Ko-rovin with his people, who were building a hut on the fide of the rivulet. Upon re-

ceiving

ceiving this intelligence, Glottof and his companions went over land to the place pointed out by the iflanders, and found every thing agreeable to their information : in this Kovorin had not the leaſt ſhare, not having been made privy to the tranſaction. The circumſtances of his joining, and afterwards ſeparating from Glottof, have already been mentioned *

Glottof now reſolved to winter upon Umnak, and accordingly laid up his veſſel for that purpoſe. On the 2d of September Korovin, as is before related, was at his own defire difpatched with a hunting party in two baidars. On his return, in May 1765, they received the firſt intelligence of the arrival of Soloviof's veſſel, which lay before Unalaſhka, and of which an account ſhall be given †. None of the iflanders appeared near the harbour during the winter, and there were none probably at that time upon Umnak ; for Glottof made excurſions on all ſides, and went once round the iſland. He likewiſe looked into the habitations of the iflanders, and found them empty : he examined the country, and

* See the preceding chapter.
† Chap. XI.

caufed

cauſed a ſtrict ſearch to be made after the remains of the plundered veſſel.

According to his account, Umnak is about
300 verſts in circumference. It contains feveral ſmall rivulets, which take their riſe
from lakes, and fall into the ſea after a very
ſhort courſe. No trees were obſerved upon
the iſland, and the vegetables were the ſame
as thoſe of Kamtchatka.

The following ſummer ſmall parties of the
inhabitants were ſeen ; but they immediately
fled upon the approach of the Ruſſians.
Some of them, however, were at laſt per-
ſuaded to a friendly intercourſe, and to pay a
tribute : by theſe means they got back part
of the arms, anchors, and iron work, of the
plundered veſſel. They continued to barter
with the natives during the ſummer of 1765,
exchanging beads for the ſkins of foxes and
ſea-otters.

The following winter hunting parties were
ſent out in Umnak as well as to Unalaſhka ;
and in July 1766 Glottof, without meeting
with any more difficulties, began his voyage homewards. We ſhall here conclude
with a copy of the journal kept on board
Glottof's veſſel, the Andrean and Natalia ;
from

from which inferences with regard to the
fituation of the iflands may be drawn.

Journal of Glottof, on board of the Andrean and Natalia.

1762.

Oct. 1. Sailed from Kamtchtka Bay.

2. Wind Southerly, fteered between
E. and S. E. three hours.

3. Wind S. E. worked at N. E. courfe,
16 hours.

4. From midnight failed Eaft with a
fair wind, 18 hours.

5. At fix o'clock A. M. difcovered
Beering's Ifland diftant about 18
verfts.

6. At 1 o'clock came to anchor on the
South Eaft point of Copper Ifland.

7. At 8 A. M. failed to the South fide
of the Ifland, anchored there at 10
o'clock.

1763.

July 26. Sailed from Copper Ifland at 5
P. M.

27. Sailed with a fair S. S. W. wind,
17 hours.

28. Made little way.

July

July   29. Drove—wind E. N. E.

30. Ditto.

31. Ditto.

Aug.   1. Ditto.

2. At 11 A. M. wind N. E. fteered E.

3. Wind W. S. W. failed 8 knots an hour, 250 verfts.

4. Wind South—failed 150 verfts.

5. Wind ditto—failed 126 verfts.

6. Wind ditto, 3 knots, 45 verfts.

7. Calm.

8. During the night gentle S. E. wind, fteered N. E. at 2½ knots.

9. Forenoon calm. At 2 o'clock P. M. gentle N. E. wind, fteered between E. N. E. and S. E. at the rate of three knots.

10. Morning, wind E. N. E. afterwards S.S.W. with which fteered N. E.

11. At 5 o'clock the wind S. S. E. fteered E. N. E. at the rate of three knots.

12. Wind S. fteered E. 2½ knots, failed 50 verfts.

13. Wind S. S. E. fteered E. at 4½ knots, failed 90 verfts.

14.

Aug.

14. Wind W. N. W. at 2 knots, failed
30 verfts.

15. The wind freſhened, at 4 knots,
failed 60 verfts.

16. Wind N. N. E. ſteered E. S. E.
at 3 knots, failed 30 verfts.

17. Wind E. S. E. and S. E. light
breezes and changeable.

18. Wind S. E. ſteered N. E. at 3¼
knots, failed in 12 hours 22 verfts.

19. Wind S. and light breezes, ſteered
E. at 3 knots, failed in 8 hours
11 verfts.

20. Before day-break calm ; three
hours after ſun-riſe a breeze ſprung
up at S. E. ſteered E. N. E. at 3
knots, and failed 20 verfts.

22. Calm.

23. Wind S. S. E. during the night,
the ſhip failed at the rate of two
knots ; the wind afterwards came
round to the S. S. W. and the
ſhip failed at 5 to 6 knots theſe
24 hours 150 verfts.

24. Saw land at day-break, at 3 knots,
failed 45 verfts.

25.

Auguſt

25. Wind W. S. W. ſailed along the
coaſt theſe 24 hours 50 verſts.

26. Wind N. W. ſteered N. E. at 5½
knots, 100 verſts.

27. Wind E. N. E. the ſhip drove towards land, on which diſcovered
a high mountain.

28. Wind N. E. and ſtormy, the ſhip
drove.

29. Wind N. W. ſteered E. N. E. at
the rate of 3 knots.

30. Wind S. S. E. at 6 knots, ſteer-
ing again towards land.

31. A violent ſtorm, wind weſt.

Sept.   1. Wind Weſt, ſteered N. E. at the
rate of 3 knots towards land.

2. Wind S. W. ſteered N. E. towards land at 5 knots.

3. Wind S. W. drove N. N. E. along
the coaſt.

4. Wind W. N. W. ſteered N. E. at
4 knots, ſailed 100 verſts.

5. Wind N. W. ſteered E. N. E. at
3 knots, and towards evening
came to anchor off the Iſland
Kadyak.

1764.

1764.

May 24. Sailed from Kadyak.

25. Wind N. W. and made but little way W. S. W.

26. Wind W. ſhip drove towards S. E.

27. Wind W. S. W. ſhip drove E. S. E. The ſame day the wind came round to the S. when ſteered a-gain towards Kadyak.

28. Wind E. S. E. fell in with the iſland Alaſka or Alakſu.

29. Wind S. W. ſteered N. W.

30. Wind W. N. W. the ſhip drove under the foreſail.

31. Wind W. drove to the South-ward.

June 1. Wind W. S. W. landed on the Iſland Saktunak, for a ſupply of water.

2. Wind S. E. ſteered S. W. along the iſland at 3 knots.

3. Wind N. E. ſteered W. S. W. at the rate of 3 to 4 knots, ſailing in theſe 24 hours 100 verſts.

4. Calm.

5. At Eight o'clock A. M. a ſmall breeze S. E.

June

June   6. Wind E. afterwards calm. Towards evening the Wind S. E.
steered S. W. at 3 knots, and unexpectedly discovered land ahead,
which kept clear of with difficulty.

From the 7th to the 10th at anchor
off a small cliff.

10. A hard gale at S. the ship drove
foul of the anchor, stood out to
sea steering E.

11. Anchored again at a small distance from land.

13. Wind S. S. W. stood out to sea
and steered E. S. E.

14. Wind W. S. W. steered S. S. E.
at the rate of 1 knot.

15. Calm.

16. Wind S. steered W. at 1 knot,
the ship drove a little to the Northward.

17. Wind S. S. E. steered W. S. W. at
3 knots.

18. Calm.

19. Ditto.

20. Wind N. E. steered S. W. and
sailed this day about 87 versts.

                                    June

June 21. The wind blowing right ahead, came to anchor off an unknown ifland, where continued till the

25. When ftood out to fea early in the morning.

26. Wind W. N. W. afterwards W. fteered S. E.

27. Calm, in the night a fmall but favourable breeze.

28. Wind N. W. continued the courfe, at the rate of 2 to 3 knots *.

29. Wind N. E. fteered W. at 3 to 4 knots, and faw land.

30. Wind N. E. fteered S. W. at the rate of 7 knots.

July 1. With the fame wind and courfe, at the rate of 5 knots, failed 200 verfts.

2. Fell in with the ifland Umnak, and came to an anchor under a fmall ifland until next day; when brought the fhip into the harbour, and laid her up.

1766.

June 13. Brought the fhip into the harbour,

* Lief man bey nordweft wind auf den ours zu 2 bis 3 knoten.

and

and continued at anchor there until the 3d of July.

July   3. Got under way.

4. Wind E.

5. A South Weft wind drove the fhip
about 50 verfts N. E.

6. Wind S. failed about 60 verfts W.

7. Wind W. S. W. the fhip drove to
the Northward.

8. Wind N. W. fteered S. at the
rate of one knot.

9. Wind N. W. fteered the whole
day W. S. W.

10. Wind S. S. W. failed about 40
verfts W. N. W.

11. Wind S. W. continued the fame
courfe, failing only 5 verfts.

12. Continued the fame courfe, and
failed 55 verfts.

13. For the moft part calm.

14. Wind W. N. W. and ftormy,
the fhip drove under the forefail.

15. Wind S. failed on the proper
courfe 100 verfts.

16. Wind E. S. E. failed W. S. W. at
the rate of 6 knots, 100 verfts.

July

July 17. Wind N. N. W. failed S. W. at
the rate of 2 knots, 30 verfts.

18. Wind S. fteered W. at the rate of
5 knots, and failed 130 verfts.

19. Wind S. W. the fhip drove under
the forefail.

20. Wind E. N. E. fteered W. N. W.
at the rate of 3 knots.

21. Wind E. N. E. at the rate of 4
to 5 knots, failed 200 verfts.

22. Wind N.E. at 4½ knots, 150 verfts.

23. Wind E. N. E. fteered W. at 3
knots, 100 verfts.

24. Wind E. fteered W. at the rate of
3 knots, 50 verfts.

25. Wind N. E. fteered W. at 5 knots
100 verfts.

26. The wind continued N. E. and
frefhened, fteered W. at the rate
of 7 knots, 200 verfts.

27. A fmall breeze N. N. W. with
which however failed 150 verfts.

28. Wind being W. S. W. drove 24
hours under bare-poles.

29. Wind South, fteered W. at the
rate of 2 knots, 48 verfts—this
day faw land.

July

July 30. Wind S. S. E. failed, at the rate of four knots, 96 verfts, and approached the land, which found to be the ifland Karaga.

From the 1ft to the 13th of Auguft, continued our voyage towards the mouth of Kamtchatka river, fometimes plying to windward, fometimes driving, and at laft arrived happily with a rich cargo.

CHAP. XI.

Voyage of Soloviof *in the* St. Peter *and* Paul, 1764—*he reaches* Unalafhka, *and paffes two winters upon that ifland—relation of what paffed there—fruitlefs attempts of the natives to deftroy the crew—Return of* Soloviof *to* Kamtchatka—*journal of his voyage in returning—defcription of the iflands* Umnak *and* Unalafhka—*productions—inhabitants— their manners—cuftoms,* &c. &c.

IN the year 1764, Jacob Ulednikof, merchant of Irkutfk, and company, fitted out a fhip called the Holy Apoftles Peter and Paul, under the command of Ivan Soloviof: fhe

fhe failed from the mouth of Kamtchatka river the 25th of Auguft. The crew confifted of fifty-five men, amongft whom were fome of the owners, and thirteen Kamtchadals.

They fteered at firft S. E. with the wind at N. W. but on its coming foutherly they afterwards fhaped their courfe E. N. E. The 27th one of the Ruffian failors died off Kamtchatka point ; the 31ft they made Beering's Ifland, which they paffed on their left. The 1ft and 2d of September they were becalmed, and afterwards the wind fpringing up at W. S. W. they continued their former courfe : until the 5th they failed on with the wind at South ; but on the 5th and 6th, from changeable breezes and dead calms, made no progrefs ; from the 7th to the 13th, they failed E. S. E. with Southerly and Wefterly winds ; and from that time to the 15th Eaft, with the wind at Weft.

September 16, they made the ifland Umnak, where Soloviof had formerly been in Nikiphorof's veffel. As they failed along the Northern coaft, three iflanders came to them in baidars ; but, the crew having no

in-

interpreter, would not truft themfelves on board. As they found no good bay on that fhore, they proceeded through a ftrait of about a verft broad, which feparates Umnak from Unalafhka. They lay-to during the night; and early on the 17th dropped anchor at the diftance of about two hundred yards from the fhore, in a bay on the North fide of the laft mentioned ifland.

From thence the captain difpatched Gregory Korenof at the head of twenty men in a baidar, with orders to land; reconnoitre the country; find out the neareft habitations; and report the difpofition of the people. Korenof returned the fame day, with an account that he had difcovered one of the dwelling-caves of the favages, but abandoned and demolifhed, in which he had found traces of Ruffians, viz. a written legend, and a broken mufket-ftock. In confequence of this intelligence, they brought the fhip near the coaft, and endeavoured to get into the mouth of a river called by the natives Tfikanok, and by the Ruffians Ofernia, but were prevented by fhallow water. They landed however their tackle and lading. No natives made

made their appearance until the 22d, when two of them came of their own accord, and welcomed the Ruffians on their arrival. They told their names, and were recognized by Soloviof : he had known them on a former expedition, when Agiak, one of the two, had ferved as an interpreter ; the other, whofe name was Kafhmak, had voluntarily continued fome time with the crew on the fame occafion.

Thefe two perfons recounted the particular circumftances which attended the lofs of Kulkof's, Protaffof's, and Trapefnikof's veffels ; from the laft of which Kafhmak had, with great hazard of his life, efcaped by flight. Agiak had ferved as interpreter to Protaffof's company ; and related that the iflanders, after murdering the hunting detachments of the Ruffians, came to the harbour, and entered the fhip under the moft friendly appearances. Finding the crew in perfect fecurity, they fuddenly attacked and flew them, together with their commander. He added, that he had hid himfelf under a bench until the murderers were gone : that fince that time, he, as well as Kafhmak, had lived as fugitives ;

tives; and in the courfe of their wanderings
had learned the following intelligence from the
girls who were gathering berries in the fields.
The Toigons of Umnak, Akutan, and Tofh-
ko, with their relations of Unalafhka, had
formed a confederacy. They agreed not to
difturb any Ruffians on their firft landing,
but to let them go out on different hunting
excurfions : being thus feparated and weakened, the intention of the Toigons was to
attack and cut them off at the fame time, fo
that no one party fhould have affiftance from
any of the others. They acquainted him alfo
with Glottof's arrival at Umnak.

Thefe unfavourable reports filled Soloviof
with anxiety : he accordingly doubled his
watch ; and ufed every precaution in his
power againft attacks from the favages. But
wanting wood to repair his veffel, and wifh-
ing for more particular information concerning the fituation of the ifland, he difpatched,
the 29th, a party of thirty men, with the
above-mentioned interpreter, to its weftern
extremity. In three or four hours they rowed
to Ankonom, a point of land, where they
faw a village, confifting of two large caves,
and over againft it a little ifland at no great
distance.

diftance. The moment the inhabitants faw them approaching, they got into their baidars, and put out to fea, leaving their dwellings empty. The Ruffians found therein feveral fkeletons, which, in the interpreter's opinion, were the remains of ten murdered failors of Trapefnikof's company. With much perfuafion the interpreter prevailed on the iflanders to return to the place which they had juft quitted : they kept however at a wary diftance, and were armed for whatever might occur.

Soloviof attempting to cut off their retreat, in order to fecure fome hoftages, they took the alarm, and began themfelves the attack. Upon this the Ruffians fired upon and purfued them ; four were killed, and feven taken prifoners, among whom was the Toigon of the little ifland Sedak. Thefe prifoners, being bound and examined, confeffed that a number of Korovin's crew had been murdered in this place ; and the Toigon fent people to bring in a number of mufkets, fome kettles and tackle, which the natives had taken upon that occafion. They alfo brought intelligence that Korovin, with a party in two baidars,

dars, had taken fhelter at a place called Inalga.
Upon this information, letters were immediately fent to Korovin ; upon the receipt of
which he joined them the 2d of October.

At the time of Korovin's arrival, the favages made another attack on Soloviof's watch
with knives ; which obliged the latter to fire,
and fix of the affailants were left dead on the
fpot. The captive Toigon excufed this attempt of his people, by afcribing it to their
fears, left Korovin out of revenge fhould put
all the prifoners to death ; on which account
this effort was made to refcue them. Soloviof,
for the greater fecurity, fent the prifoners
by land to the haven ; while Korovin and his
party went to the fame place by fea. The
Toigon however was treated kindly ; and
even permitted to return home on condition
of leaving his fon as an hoftage. In confequence of this kind behaviour, the inhabitants
of three other villages, Agulak, Kutchlok,
and Makufki, prefented hoftages of their own
accord.

From the remaining timber of the old
dwelling the Ruffians built a new hut ; and
on the fourteenth they laid up the veffel. Koronof was then fent upon a reconnoitring
party

party to the Southern fide of the ifland, which in that part was not more than five or fix verfts broad : he proceeded on with his companions, fometimes rowing in canoes, fometimes travelling by land and dragging them after. He returned the twentieth, and reported that he had found upon the coaft on the further fide of the ifland an empty habitation ; that he rowed from thence Eaftward along the fhore, and behind the firft point of land came to an ifland in the next bay ; where he found about forty iflanders of both fexes lodged under their baidars, who by his friendly behaviour had been induced to give three hoftages. Thefe people afterwards fettled in the above-mentioned empty hut, and came frequently to the harbour.

On the 28th of October, Soloviof himfelf went alfo upon a reconnoitring party along the North coaft, towards the North-Eaft end of the ifland. He rowed from the firft promontory acrofs a bay ; and found on the oppofite point of land a dwelling place called Agulok, which lies about four hours row from the harbour. He found there thirteen men and about forty women and children, who

who delivered up feveral gun-barrels and fhip-
ftores, and likewife informed him of two of
Korovin's crew who had been murdered.

November 5, they proceeded further ; and
after five or fix hours rowing, they faw on a
point of land another dwelling called Ikutch-
lok, beyond which the interpreter fhewed
them the haven, where Korovin's fhip had
been at anchor. This was called Makufhin-
fky Bay ; and on an ifland within it they
found two Toigons, called Itchadak and Kagumaga, with about an hundred and eighty
people of both fexes employed in hunting
fea-bears. Thefe natives not being in the
leaft hoftile, Soloviof endeavoured to eftablifh
and confirm a friendly intercourfe with them.
He remained there until the 10th, when the
Toigons invited him to their winter quarters,
which lay about five hours fail further Eaft :
there he found two dwelling caves, each of
forty yards fquare, near a rivulet abounding
with fifh which fell from a lake into a little
bay. In the neighbourhood of this village is
a hot fpring below the fea mark, which is
only to be feen at ebb tide. From thence he
departed the 25th, but was forced back by
                                    ftorms,

ſtorms, and detained there until the 6th of December.

Kagumaga then accompanied him to another village called Totchikala; both the Toigon and the interpreter adviſed him to be on his guard againſt the natives, whom they repreſented as very ſavage, ſworn enemies to the Ruſſians, and the murderers of nine of Kulkof's crew. For theſe reaſons Soloviof paſſed the night on the open coaſt, and next morning ſent the Toigon before to inſpire the natives with more friendly ſentiments. Some of them liſtened to his repreſentations; but the greateſt part fled upon Soloviof's approach; ſo that he found the place conſiſting of four large dwelling caves almoſt empty, in which he ſecured himſelf with ſuitable precaution. Here he found three hundred darts and ten bows with arrows, all which he deſtroyed, only reſerving one bow and ſeventeen arrows as ſpecimens of their arms. By the moſt friendly arguments he urged the few natives who remained to lay aſide their enmity, and to perſuade their leaders and relations to return to their habitations, and live on terms of amity and friendſhip.

On

On the 10th about an hundred men and a
ftill greater number of women returned. But
the faireft fpeeches had no effect on thefe favages, who kept aloof and prepared for hoftilities, which they began on the 17th by an
open attack. Nineteen of them were killed, amongft whom was Inlogufak one of
their leaders, and the moft inveterate fomen-
ter of hoftilities againft the Ruffians. The
other leader Aguladock being taken confeffed,
that, on receiving the firft news of Soloviof's
arrival, they had refolved to attack the crew,
and burn the fhip. Notwithftanding this
confeffion, no injury was offered to him ; in
confequence of this kind ufage, he was prevailed upon to give his fon as an hoftage, and
to order his people to live on friendly terms
with the Ruffians. During the month of
January, the natives delivered in three anchors,
and a quantity of tackle, which had been
faved from a veffel formerly wrecked on that
coaft ; and at the fame time they brought
three boys and two young girls as hoftages
and pledges of their future fidelity.

January, 25, Soloviof fet out for the haven
where his fhip lay : before his departure the
Toigons

Toigons of Makufhinfk paid of their own accord a double tribute.

February 1, Kagumaga of Makufhinfk, Agidalok of Totzikala, and Imaginak of Ugamitzi, Toigons of Unalafhka, with a great number of their relations, came to Soloviof, and acquainted him with the arrival of a Ruffian fhip at Unimak, the fixth ifland to the Eaft of Agunalafhka ; adding, that they knew none of the crew excepting a Kamtchadal named Kirilko, who had been there on a former occafion. They likewife informed him, that the natives, after having cut off part of the crew who had been fent out in two baidars, had found means to overpower the remainder, and to deftroy the veffel. From the name of the Kamtchadal, they concluded that this muft have been another veffel fitted out by Nikiphor Trapefnikof and company, of which no farther intelligence was ever received. Willing to procure farther intelligence, they endeavoured to perfuade the Toigons to fend a party of their people to the abovementioned ifland ; but the latter excufed themfelves, on account of the great diftance and their dread of the iflanders.

Fe-

February 16, Soloviof set out a second time for the West end of the island, where they had formerly taken prisoner, and afterwards set at liberty, the Toigon of Sedak. From thence he proceeded to Ikolga, which lies on the bay, and consists of only one hut. On the 26th he came to Takamitka, where there is likewise only one hut on a point of land by the side of a rivulet, which falls from the mountains into the sea. Here he met with Korovin, in whose company he cut the blubber of a whale, which the waves had cast on shore : after this Korovin went across the gulph to Umnak; and he proceeded to Ikaltshinsk, where on the 9th one of his party was carried off by sickness.

March 15, he returned to the haven, having met with no opposition from the islanders during this excursion. On his return he found one of the crew dead, and a dreadful scurvy raging amongst the rest ; of which distemper five Russians died in March, eight and a Kamtchadal in April, and six more in May. About this time the islanders were observed to pay frequent visits to the hostages ; and upon inquiring privately into the reason,

reafon, fome of the latter difcovered, that
the inhabitants of Makufhinfk had formed
the defign of cutting off the crew, and making themfelves mafters of the veffel. Soloviof had now great reafons to be apprehenfive ; for the crew were afflicted with the
fcurvy to fuch a violent degree, that only
twelve perfons were capable of defending
themfelves. Thefe circumftances did not
efcape the obfervation of the natives ; and
they were accordingly infpired with frefh
courage to renew their hoftilities.

On the 27th of May the Ruffians perceived the Toigon of Itchadak, who had formerly paid a voluntary tribute, near the fhore :
he was accompanied by feveral iflanders in
three baidars. Soloviof calling to him by
the interpreter, he came on fhore, but kept
at a diftance, defiring a conference with fome
of his relations. Soloviof gave orders to feize
him ; and they were lucky enough to take
him prifoner, together with two of his companions. He immediately confeffed, that he
had come with a view of inquiring of the
hoftages how many Ruffians were ftill remaining : having procured the neceffary intelligence,

ligence, his intention was to surprife the watch
at a convenient feafon, and afterwards to fet
fire to the fhip. As they faw feveral iflanders row paft the harbour at the fame time,
and the Toigon likewife informed them that
they were affembling to execute the above-
mentioned defign ; Soloviof refolved to be
much upon his guard. They feparated, however, without a tempting any hoftilities.

June 5, Glottof arrived at the harbour on
a vifit, and returned on the 8th to his fhip.
The captive Toigon was now fet at liberty,
after being ferioufly exhorted to defift from
hoftilities. In the courfe of this month two
more of the crew died ; fo that the arrival
of Korovin, who joined them about this
time, with two of his own and two of Kulkof's crew, was of courfe a very agreeable
circumftance. The fick likewife began to
recover by degrees.

July 22, Soloviof, with a party of his
people, in two baidars, made another excurfion Northwards ; he paffed by the places
formerly mentioned as far as Igonok, which
lies ten verfts beyond Totzikala. Igonok
confifts of one dwelling cave on the fide of a
rivulet, which falls from the mountains,
and

and empties itfelf into the fea. The inhabitants amounted to about thirty men, who
dwelt there with their wives and children.
From thence Soloviof proceeded along the
fhore into a bay ; five verfts further he found
another rivulet, which has its fource among
the hills, and flows through a plain.

Upon the fhore of the fame bay, oppofite
to the mouth of this rivulet, lay two villages, one of which only was inhabited ; it
was called Ukunadok, and confifted of fix
dwelling caves. About thirty-five of the inhabitants were at that time employed in catching falmon in the rivulet. Kulkof's fhip had
lain at anchor about two miles from thence ;
but there were no remains of her to be found.
After coming out of the bay, he went forwards to the fummer village Umgaina, diftant
about feven or eight leagues, and fituated on
the fide of a rivulet, which takes its rife in
a lake abounding with falmon. Here he found
the Toigon Amaganak, with about ten of the
natives, employed in fifhing. Fifteen verfts
further along the fhore they found another
fummer village called Kalaktak, where there
was likewife another rivulet, which came
from

from the hills. The inhabitants were sixty
men and an hundred and seventy women and
children : they gave Soloviof a very friendly reception ; and delivered two hostages, who
were brought from the neighbouring island
Akutan ; with these he set out on his return,
and on the 6th of August joined his crew.

On the 11th, he went over to the island
Umnak, accompanied by Korovin, to bring
off some ships stores left there by the latter ;
and returned to the haven on the 27th. On
the 31st Shaffyrin died, the same person
whose adventures have been already related *.

Sept. 19, Koronof being sent northwards
upon an hunting party, returned the 30th of
January, 1766. Although the Russians who
remained at the haven met with no molesta-
tion from the natives during his absence ; yet
he and his companions were repeatedly attacked. Having distributed to the inhabitants
of the several villages through which he passed nets for the purpose of catching sea-otters,
he went to the East part of the island as far
as Kalaktak, with an intention of hunting.
Upon his arrival at that place, on the 31st of
October, the inhabitants fled with precipi-

* Chap. VIII.

tation ;

tation ; and as all his efforts to conciliate their affections were ineffectual, he found it requifite to be upon his guard. Nor was this precaution unneceffary ; for on the following day they returned in a confiderable body, armed with lances, made with the iron of the plundered veffels. Korenof, however, and his companions, who were prepared to receive them, killed twenty-fix, and took feveral prifoners ; upon which the others be. came more tractable.

Nov. 19, Korenof, upon his return to the haven, came to Makufhinfk, where he was kindly received by a Toigon named Kulumaga ; but with regard to Itchadak, it was plain that his defigns were ftill hoftile. Inftead of giving an account of the nets which had been left with him, he withdrew privately : and on the 19th of January, accompanied by a numerous body of iflanders, made an attempt to furprife the Ruffians. Victory, however, again declared for Korenof; and fifteen of the affailants, amongft whom was Itchadak himfelf, remained dead upon the fpot. Kulumaga affured them, in the ftrongeft manner, that the defign had been carried on

without

without his knowledge ; and protefted, that he had often prevented his friend from committing hoftilities againft the Ruffians.

Korenof returned to the haven on the 30th of January ; and on the 4th of February he went upon another hunting expedition toward the Weftern point of the ifland. During this excurfion he met with a party, fent out by Glottof, at a place called Takamitka ; he then rowed over to Umnak, where he collected a fmall tribute, and returned on the 3d of March. During his abfence Kyginik, Kulumaga's fon, paid a vifit to the Ruffians, and requefted that he might be baptized, and be permitted to go aboard the veffel ; his demand was immediately complied with.

May 13th, Korovin went, with fourteen men, to Umnak, to bring off an anchor, which was buried in the fand. On his return preparations were made for their departure. Before the arrival of Korovin the hunters had killed 150 black and brown foxes, and the fame number of old and young feaotters ; fince his arrival they had caught 350 black foxes, the fame number of common foxes, and 150 fea-otters of different fizes.

This

This cargo being put on board, the interpreter Kafhmak fet at liberty, with a certificate of, and prefents for, his fidelity, and the hoftages delivered up to the Toigons and their relations, who had affembled at the haven, Soloviof put to fea on the 1ft of June, with an Eafterly wind. Before his departure he received a letter from Glottof, informing him that he was likewife preparing for his return.

June   2. The wind being contrary, they got but a fmall way from land.

      5. Steered again towards the fhore, came to an anchor, and fent a boat for a fupply of water, which returned without having feen any body.

      6. Weighed and fteered W. with a S. E. wind.

      7. Favourable wind at N. E. and in the afternoon at N.

      8. Wind at N. W. and ftormy, the fhip drove under the forefail.

9 & 10. Sailed Northwards, with a Wefterly wind.

    11. Calm till noon ; afterwards breeze fprung up at S. with which they
fteered

steered W. till next day at noon ;
when the wind coming round to
the Weſt, they changed their
courſe, and ſteered N. W.

June   12. Calm during the night.

      13. A ſmall breeze of Northerly wind,
with which they ſteered W. In the
afternoon it fell calm, and continued ſo till the

      16. At noon, when a breeze ſpringing
up at Eaſt, they ſteered W. on
which courſe they continued
during the

      18. with a S. S. E. wind.

From the 19 to the 22. The wind was changeable from the S. W. to N. W.
with which they ſtill made a ſhift
to get to the Weſtward.

      23. The wind E. they ſteered betwixt
N. & W. which courſe they continued the

      24th, 25th, 26th, with a Northerly
wind.

      27. A. M. the wind changed to S. W.

      28, 29, 30. Wind at Weſt.

July   1. The wind changed to E. with
which they ſteered between W.
and

and S. W. with little variations,
till the 3d.

July 4. They reached Kamtchatkoi Nofs,
and on the

5th. Brought the fhip, in good
condition, into Kamtchatka river.

Soloviof's defcription of thefe iflands and
the inhabitants, being more circumftantial
than the accounts given by former navigators,
deferves to be inferted at full length. According to his eftimation, the ifland Unalafhka lies between 1500 and 2000 verfts due
Eaft from the mouth of the Kamtchatka
river: the other iflands to the Eaftward ftretch
towards N. E. He reckons the length of
Akutan at eighty verfts; Umnak at an hundred and fifty; and Unalafhka at two hundred. No large trees were feen upon any of
the iflands which he vifited. They produce
underwood, fmall fhrubs, and plants, for the
moft part fimilar to the common fpecies found
in Kamtchatka. The winter is much milder
than the Eaftern parts of Siberia, and continues only from November to the end of
March. The fnow feldom lies upon the
ground for any time.

Rein-

Rein-deer, bears, wolves, ice-foxes, are
not to be found on these islands; but they
abound in black, grey, brown, and red foxes;
for which reason they have got the name of
Lyssie Ostrova, or Fox Islands. These foxes
are stronger than those of Yakutsk; and their
hair is much coarser. During the day they
lie in caves and clifts of rocks; towards
evening they come to the shore in search of
food : they have long extirpated the brood of
mice, and other small animals. They are
not in the smallest degree afraid of the inhabitants, but distinguish the Russians by the
scent; having experienced the effects of their
fire-arms. The number of sea-animals, such
as sea-lions, sea-bears, and sea-otters, which
resort to these shores, are very considerable.
Upon some of the islands warm springs and
native sulphur are to be found.

The Fox-islands are in general very populous; Unalashka, which is the largest island,
is supposed to contain several thousand inhabitants. These savages live together in
separate communities, composed of fifty, and
sometimes of two or even three hundred persons; they dwell in large caves from forty
to eighty yards long, from six to eight broad,
and

and from four to five high. The roof of thefe caves is a kind of wooden grate, which is firft fpread over with a layer of grafs, and then covered with earth. Several openings are made in the top, through which the inhabitants go up and down by ladders : the fmalleft dwellings have two or three entrances of this fort, and the largeft five or fix. Each cave is divided into a certain number of partitions, which are appropriated to the feveral families; and thefe partitions are marked by means of ftakes driven into the earth. The men and women fit on the ground ; and the children lie down, having their legs bound together under them, in order to make them learn to fit upon their hams.

Although no fire is ever made in thefe caves, they are generally fo warm, that both fexes fit naked. Thefe people obey the calls of nature openly, and without efteeming it indecent. They wafh themfelves firft with their own urine, and afterwards with water. Even in winter they are always bare-footed : and when they want to warm themfelves, efpecially before they lie down to fleep, they fet fire to dry grafs and walk over it. Their habita-

tions

tions being almoft dark, they ufe particularly
in winter a fort of large lamps, made by hol-
lowing out a ftone, into which they put a
rufh-wick and burn train oil. A ftone fo
hollowed is called Tfaaduck. The natives *
are whites with black hair ; they have flat
faces, and are of a good ftature. The men
fhave with a fharp ftone or knife the circumference and top of the head, and let the hair
which remains hang from the crown †. The
women cut their hair in a ftreight line over
the forehead ; behind they let it grow to a
confiderable length, and tie it in a bunch.
Some of the men wear their beards ; others
fhave or pull them out by the roots.

They mark various figures on their faces,
the backs of their hands, and lower parts of
their arms, by pricking them firft with a needle,
and then rubbing the parts with a fort of
black clay. They make three incifions in
the under-lip ; they place in the middle one
a flat bone, or a fmall coloured ftone ; and in

---

* Von geficht find fic platt un dweifs durchgaengig mit
fchwarzen haaren.

† The original in this paffage is fomewhat obfcure. Die
maenner fcheeren mit einem Scharfen Stein oder Meffer den
Umkreifs des Haatkopfs und die Platte, und laffen die Haare
um die Krone des Kopfs rundum ueberdangen.

each

each of the fide-ones they fix a long pointed piece of bone, which bends and reaches almoft to the ears. They likewife make a hole through the griftle of the nofe, into which they put a fmall piece of bone in fuch a manner as to keep the noftrils extended. They alfo pierce holes in their ears, and wear in them what little ornaments they can procure.

Their drefs confifts of a cap and a furcoat, which reaches down to the knee. Some of them wear common caps of a party coloured bird-fkin, upon which they leave part of the wings and tail. On the fore-part of their hunting and fifhing caps they place a fmall board like a fcreen, adorned with the jawbones of fea-bears, and ornamented with glafs beads, which they receive in barter from the Ruffians. At their feftivals and dancing parties they ufe a much more fhowy fort of caps. Their fur-coats are made like fhirts, being clofe behind and before, and are put on over the head. The drefs of the men is made of bird fkins, that of the women of fea-otters and fea-bears. Thefe fkins are died with a fort of red earth, and neatly fewed with finews, and ornamented with various ftripes of fea-otter fkins and leathern fringes.

They

They have alfo upper garments made of the
inteftines of the largeft fea-calves and fea-
lions.

Their veffels confift of two forts : the
larger are leathern boats or baidars, which have
oars on both fides, and are capable of holding
thirty or forty people. The fmaller veffels
are rowed with a double paddle, and refemble
the canoes of the Greenlanders, containing
only one or two perfons : they never weigh
above thirty pounds, being nothing but a
thin fkeleton of a boat covered with leather.
In thefe however they pafs from one ifland
to another ; and even venture out to fea to a
confiderable diftance. In calm weather they
go out in them to catch turbot and cod with
bone-hooks and lines made of finews or fea-
weed. They ftrike fifh in the rivulets with
darts. Whales and other fea-animals thrown
afhore by the waves are carefully looked after,
and no part of them is loft. The quantity
of provifions which they procure by hunting
and fifhing being far too fmall for their wants,
the greateft part of their food confifts of fea-
wrack and fhell-fifh, which they find on the
fhore.

No

No ftranger is allowed to hunt or fifh near a village, or to carry off any thing fit for food. When they are on a journey, and their provifions are exhaufted, they beg from village to village, or call upon their friends and relations for affiftance.

They feed upon the flefh of all forts of fea-animals, and generally eat it raw. But if at any time they choofe to drefs their victuals, they make ufe of an hollow ftone : having placed the fifh or flefh therein, they cover it with another, and clofe the inter-ftices with lime or clay. They then lay it horizontally upon two ftones, and light a fire under it. The provifion intended for keeping is dried without falt in the open air. They gather berries of various forts, and lily roots of the fame fpecies with thofe which grow wild at Kamtchatka. They are unacquainted with the manner of dreffing the cow-parfnip, as practifed in that Peninfula ; and do not underftand the art of diftilling brandy or any other ftrong liquor from it. They are at prefent very fond of fnuff, which the Ruffians have introduced among them.

No traces were found of any worfhip, neither

ther did they feem to have any forcerers *
among them. If a whale happens to be caft
on fhore, the inhabitants affemble with great
marks of joy, and perform a number of extraordinary ceremonies. They dance and beat
drums † of different fizes : they then cut up
the fifh, of which the greateft and beft part
is confumed on the fpot. On fuch occafions
they wear fhowy caps ; and fome of them
dance naked in wooden mafks, which reach
down to their fhoulders, and reprefent various
forts of fea-animals. Their dances confift of
fhort fteps forwards, accompanied with many
ftrange geftures.

Marriage ceremonies are unknown among
them ; and each man takes as many wives as he
can maintain, but the number feldom exceeds

* In the laft chapter it is faid that there are forcerers
among them.

† The expreffion in the original is, " Schlagen auf groffen
" platten Handpauken von verfchiedenen Klang," which,
being literally tranflated, fignifies " They beat upon large
" flat hand-kettle drums of different founds."

By the accounts which I procured at Peterfburg, concerning the form of thefe drums, they feem to refemble in fhape
thofe made ufe of by the forcerers of Kamtchatka, and
are of different fizes. I had an opportunity of feeing one
of the latter in the Cabinet of Curiofities. It is of an
oval form, about two feet long and one broad : it is covered
only at one end like the tambour de bafque, and is worn
upon the arm like a fhield.

four.

four. Thefe women are occafionally allowed to cohabit with other men ; they and their children are alfo not unfrequently bartered in exchange for commodities. When an iflander dies, the body is bound with thongs, and afterwards expofed to the air in a fort of wooden cradle hung upon a crofs-bar, fupported by forks. Upon thefe occafions they cry, and make bitter lamentations.

Their Toigons or Princes are thofe who have numerous families, and are fkilful and fuccefsful in hunting and fifhing.

Their weapons confift of bows, arrows, and darts : they throw the latter very dexteroufly, and to a great diftance, from a handboard. For defence they ufe wooden fhields, called kuyaki. Thefe iflanders are, notwithftanding their favagenefs, very docile ; and the boys, whom the Ruffians keep as hoftages, foon acquire a knowledge of their language.

C H A P.

C H A P. XII.

Voyage of Otcheredin *in the* St. Paul 1765—
He winters upon Umnak—*Arrival of* Leva-
fheff *upon* Unalafhka—*Return of* Otcheredin *to* Ochotfk.

IN the year 1765 three merchants, namely,
Orekhof of Yula, Lapin of Solikamfk,
and Shilof of Uftyug, fitted out a new veffel
called the St. Paul, under the command of
Aphanaffei Otcheredin. She was built in the
harbour of Okotfk : his crew confifted of
fixty-two Ruffians and Kamtchadals ; and fhe
carried on board two inhabitants of the Fox
Iflands, named John and Timothy Surgef,
who had been brought to Kamtchatka and
baptifed.

September 10, they failed from Okotfk,
and arrived the 22d in the bay of Bolcheretfk,
where they wintered. Auguft 1, 1776, they
continued their voyage, and having paffed
the fecond of the Kuri Ifles, fteered on the
6th into the open fea ; on the 24th they
reached the neareft of the Fox Iflands, which

the

the interpreters called * Atchak. A ftorm
arifing, they caft anchor in a bay, but-faw no
inhabitants upon the fhore. On the 26th
they failed again, difcovered on the 27th Sagaugamak, along which they fteered North
Eaft, and on the 31ft cam^e within feven miles
of the ifland Umnak ; where, on account of
the latenefs of the feafon and the want of
provifion and water, they determined to winter. Accordingly on the 1ft of September,
by the advice of the interpreters, they brought
the veffel into a convenient bay near a point
of land lying N. W. where they faftened it
to the fhore with cables.

Upon their landing they difcovered feveral
pieces of a wreck ; and two iflanders, who
dwelled on the banks of a rivulet which empties itfelf into the bay, informed them, that
thefe were the remains of a Ruffian veffel,
whofe commander's name was Denys. From
this intelligence they concluded that this
was Protaffof's veffel, fitted out at Okotfk.
The inhabitants of Umnak, Unalafhka, and
of the Five Mountains, had affembled, and
murdered the crew, when feparated into different hunting parties. The fame iflanders

* Called in a former journal Atchu, p. 70.

alfo

alſo mentioned the fate of Kulkof's and Trapeſnikof's ſhips upon the iſland Unalaſhka·
Although this information occaſioned general
apprehenſions ; yet they had no other re-
ſource than to draw the veſſel aſhore, and to
take every poſſible precaution againſt a ſur-
prize. Accordingly they kept a conſtant
watch ; made preſents to the Toigons and the
principal inhabitants ; and demanded ſome
children as hoſtages. For ſome time the
iſlanders behaved very peaceably, until the
Ruſſians endeavoured to perſuade them to become tributary : upon which they gave ſuch
repeated ſigns of their hoſtile intentions, that
the crew lived under continual alarms. In
the beginning of September information was
brought to them of the arrival of a veſſel,
fitted out by Ivan Popof, merchant of Lalſk,
at Unalaſhka.

About the end of the ſaid month the Toigon
of the Five Mountains came to Otcheredin ;
and was ſo well ſatisfied with his reception,
that he brought hoſtages ; and not only aſ-
ſured them of his own friendſhip, but pro-
miſed to uſe his influence with the other
Toigons, and to perſuade them to the ſame
peaceable behaviour. But the other Toigons
not

not only paid no regard to his perfuafions, but even barbaroufly killed one of his children. From thefe and other circumftances the crew paffed the winter under continual apprehenfions; and durft not venture far from the harbour upon hunting parties. Hence enfued a fcarcity of provifions; and hunger, joined to the violent attacks of the fcurvy, made great havock amongft them; infomuch that fix of them died; and feveral of the furvivors were reduced to fo weak a condition, that they were fcarcely able to move.

The health of the crew being re-eftablifhed in the fpring, twenty-three men were fent on the 25th of June in two boats to the Five Mountains, in order to perfuade the inhabitants to pay tribute. On the 26th they landed no the ifland Ulaga, where they were attacked with great fpirit by a large body of the inhabitants; and though three of the Ruffians were wounded, yet the favages were repulfed with confiderable lofs: they were fo terrified by this defeat, that they fled before the Ruffians during their continuance on that ifland. The latter were detained there by tempeftuous weather until the 9th of July;

during

during which time they found two rufty fire-
locks belonging to Protaffof's crew. On the
10th they returned to the harbour ; and it
was immediately refolved to difpatch fome
companies upon hunting expeditions.

Accordingly on the 1ft of Auguft Matthew
Polofkof, a native of Ilinfk, was fent with
twenty-eight men in two boats to Unalafhka ;
if the weather and other circumftances were
favourable, they were to make to Akutan
and Akun, the two neareft iflands to the Eaft,
but to proceed no further. Polofkof reached
Akutan about the end of the month ; and
being kindly received by the inhabitants, he
left fix of his party to hunt ; with the remainder he went to Akun, which lies about
two verfts from Akutan. From thence he
difpatched five men to the neighbouring
iflands, where he was informed by the interpreters there were great quantities of foxes.

Polofkof and his companions continued the
whole autumn upon Akun without being annoyed; but on the 12th of December the inhabitants of the different iflands affembled in great
numbers, and attacked them by land and fea.
They informed Polofkof, by means of the interpreters,

terpreters, that the Ruffians whom he had fent to the neighbouring iflands were killed; that the two veffels at Umnak and Unalafhka were plundered, and the crew put to death; and that they were now come to make him and his party fhare the fame fate. The Ruffian fire-arms however kept them in due refpect; and towards evening they difperfed. The fame night the interpreter deferted, probably at the inftigation of his countrymen, who neverthelefs killed him, as it was faid, that winter.

January 16, the favages ventured to make a fecond attack. Having furprifed the guard by night, they tore off the roof of the Ruffian dwelling, and fhot down into the hut, making at the fame time great outcries: by this unexpected affault four Ruffians were killed, and three wounded; but the furvivors no fooner had recourfe to their fire-arms, than the enemy was driven to flight. Meanwhile another body of the natives attempted to feize the two veffels, but without fuccefs: they however cut off the party of fix men left by Polofkof at Akutan, together with the five hunters difpatched to the contiguous iflands,

and

and two of Popof's crew who were at the Wefternmoft part of Unalafhka.

Polofkof continued upon Akun in great danger until the 20th of February; when, the wounded being recovered, he failed over with a fair wind to Popof's veffel at Unalafh-ka; and on the 10th of May returned to Otcheredin.

In April, Popof's veffel being ready for the voyage, all the hoftages, whofe number amounted to forty, were delivered to Otche-redin. July the 30th, a veffel belonging to the fame Popof arrived from Beering's Ifland, and caft anchor in the fame bay where Otcheredin's lay; and both crews entered in-to an agreement to fhare in common the pro-fits of hunting. Strengthened by this alli-ance, Otcheredin prevailed upon a number of the inhabitants to pay tribute. Auguft the 22d Otcheredin's mate was fent with fix boats and fifty-eight men to hunt upon Una-lafhka and Akutan; and there remained thirty men with the veffels in the harbour, who kept conftant watch.

Soon afterwards Otcheredin and the other commander received a letter from Levafhef Captain Lieutenant of the Imperial fleet, who

accom-

accompanied Captain Krenitzin in the fecret expedition to thofe iflands. The letter was dated September 11, 1768 ; it informed them he was arrived at Unalafhka in the St. Paul, and lay at anchor in the fame bay in which Kulkof's veffel had been loft. He likewife required a circumftantial account of their voyages. By another order of the 24th he fent for four of the principal hoftages ; and demanded the tribute of fkins which had been exacted from the iflanders. But as the weather was generally tempeftuous at this feafon of the year, they deferred fending them till the fpring. May the 31ft Levafhef fet fail for Kamtchatka ; and in 1771 returned fafely from his expedition at St. Peterfburg.

The two veffels remained at Umnak until the year 1770, during which time the crews met with no oppofition from the iflanders. They continued their hunting parties, in which they had fuch good fortune, that the fhare of Otcheredin's veffel (whofe voyage is here chiefly related) confifted in 530 large fea-otter fkins, 40 young ones and 30 cubs, the fkins of 656 fine black foxes, 100 of an inferior fort, and about 1250 red fox fkins.

With

With this large cargo of furs Otcheredin set
sail, on the 22d of May, 1770, from Umnak,
leaving Popof's crew behind. A short time
before their departure, the other interpreter
Ivan Surgef, at the instigation of his relations,
deserted.

After having touched at the nearest of the
Aleütian Islands, Otcheredin and his crew arrived on the 24th of July at Okotsk. They
brought two islanders with them, whom they
baptized. The one was named Alexèy So-
lovief; the other Boris Otcheredin. These
islanders unfortunately died on their way to
Petersburg; the first between Yakutsk and
Irkutsk; and the latter at Irkutsk, where he
arrived on the 1st of February, 1771.

CHAP.

C H A P. XIII.

Conclufion—General pofition and fituation of the
Aleütian and Fox Iflands—their diftance from
each other—Farther defcription of the drefs,
manners, and cuftoms, of the inhabitants—
their feafts and ceremonies, &c.

ACCORDING to the lateft informa-
tions brought by Otcheredin's and
Popof's veffels, the North Weft point of
Commandorfkoi Oftrof, or Beering's Ifland, lies
due Eaft from the mouth of the Kamtckatka
river, at the diftance of 250 verfts. It is
from 70 to 80 verfts long, and ftretches from
North Weft to South Eaft, in the fame direction as Copper Ifland. The latter is fituated
about 60 or 70 verfts from the South Eaft
point of Beering's Ifland, and is about 50
verfts in length.

About 300 verfts Eaft by South of Copper
Ifland lie the Aleütian Ifles, of which Attak
is the neareft : it is rather larger than Beering's Ifland, of the fame fhape, and ftretches
from Weft to South Eaft. From thence about
20 verfts Eaftwards is fituated Semitfhi, extending

tending from Weſt to Eaſt, and near its Eaſtern
point another ſmall iſland.   To the South of
the ſtrait, which ſeparates the two latter
iſlands, and at the diſtance of 40 verſts from
both of them, lies Shemiya in a ſimilar poſition, and not above 25 verſts in length.   All
theſe iſlands ſtretch between 54 and 55 degrees of North latitude.

The Fox Iſlands are ſituated E. N. E. from
the Aleütians : the neareſt of theſe, Atchak,
is about 800 verſts diſtant ; it lies in about
56 degrees North latitude, and extends from
W. S. W. towards E. N. E.   It greatly re-
ſembles Copper Iſland, and is provided with a
commodious harbour on the North.   From
thence all the other iſlands of this chain ſtretch
in a direction towards N. E. by Eaſt.

The next to Atchak is Amlak, about 15
verſts diſtant ; it is nearly of the ſame ſize ;
and has an harbour on its South ſide.   Next
follows Sagaugamak, at about the ſame diſtance, but ſomewhat ſmaller ; from that it
is 50 verſts to Amukta, a ſmall rocky iſland ;
and the ſame diſtance from the latter to
Yunakſan, another ſmall iſland.   About 20
verſts from Yunakſan there is a cluſter of five
ſmall

fmall iflands, or rather mountains, Kigalgift, Kagamila, Tfigulak, Ulaga, and Tana-Unok, and which are therefore called by the Ruffians *Pät Sopki*, or the Five Mountains. Of thefe Tana-Unok lies moft to the N. E. towards which the Weftern point of Umnak advances within the diftance of 20 verfts.

Umnak ftretches from S. W. to N. E. ; it is 150 verfts in length, and has a very confiderable bay on the Weft end of the Northern coaft, in which there is a fmall ifland or rock, called Adugak ; and on the South fide is Shamelga, another rock. The Weftern point of Aghunalafhka, or Unalafhka, is feparated from the Eaft end of Umnak by a ftrait near 20 verfts in breadth. The pofition of thefe two iflands is fimilar ; but Aghunalafhka is much the largeft, and is above 200 verfts long. It is divided towards the N. E. into three promontories, one of which runs out in a Wefterly direction, forming one fide of a large bay on the North coaft of the ifland : the fecond ftretches out N. E. ends in three points, and is connected with the ifland by a fmall neck of land. The third or moft Southerly one is feparated from the laft mentioned promontory by

by a deep bay. Near Unalafhka towards the
Eaft lies another fmall ifland, called Skirkin.

About 20 verfts from the North Eaft promontory of Aghunalafhka lie four iflands : the
firft, Akutan, is about half as big as Umnak;
a verft further is the fmall ifland Akun ; a
little beyond is Akunok ; and laftly Kigalga,
which is the fmalleft of thefe four, and
ftretches with Akun and Akunok almoft from
N. to S. Kigalga is fituated about the 61ft
degree of latitude. About 100 verfts from
thence lies an ifland called Unimak *, upon
which Captain Krenitzin wintered ; and beyond it the inhabitants faid there was a large
tract of country called Alafhka, of which
they did not know the boundaries.

The Fox Iflands are in general very rocky,
without containing any remarkably high
mountains : they are deftitute of wood, but
abound in rivulets and lakes, which are moftly without fifh. The winter is much milder
than in Siberia : the fnow feldom falls before the beginning of January, and continues
on the ground till the end of March.

* Krenitzin wintered in the ftraits of Alaxa, which feparate Uuimak from Alaxa. See Part II. p. 208.

Their

There is a volcano in Amuchta; in Kagamila fulphur flows from a mountain; in Taga-
Unok there are warm fprings, hot enough to
boil provifions; and flames of fulphur are occafionally feen at night upon the mountains
of Unalafhka and Akutan.

The Fox Iflands are tolerably populous in
propotion to their fize. The inhabitants are
entirely free, and pay tribute to no one : they
are of a middle ftature; and live, both in
fummer and winter, in holes dug in the earth.
No figns of religion were found amongft
them. Several perfons indeed pafs for forcerers, pretending to know things paft and to
come, and are accordingly held in high efteem,
but without receiving any emolument. Filial
duty and refpect towards the aged are not
held in eftimation by thefe iflanders. They
are not however deficient in fidelity to each
other; they are of lively and chearful tem-
pers, though rather impetuous, and naturally
prone to anger. In general, they do not obferve any rules of decency, but follow all the
calls of nature publicly, and without the
leaft referve. They wafh themfelves with
their own urine.

There

Their principal food confifts in fifh and other fea-animals, fmall fhell-fifh, and fea-plants : their greateft delicacies are wild lilies and other roots, together with different kinds of berries. When they have laid in a ftore of provifions, they eat at any time of the day without diftinction ; but in cafe of neceffity they are capable of fafting feveral days together. They feldom heat their dwellings ; but when they are defirous of warming themfelves, they light a bundle of hay, and ftand over it ; or elfe they fet fire to train oil, which they pour into a hollow ftone.

They feed their children when very young with the coarfeft flefh, and for the moft part raw. If an infant cries, the mother immediately carries it to the fea-fide, and be it fummer or winter holds it naked in the water until it is quiet. This cuftom is fo far from doing the children any harm, that it hardens them againft the cold, and they accordingly b are-footed through the winter without the leaft inconvenience. They are alfo trained to bathe frequently in the fea ; and it is an opinion generally received among the iflanders, that by that means they are rendered bold, and become fortunate in fifhing.

The

The men wear fhirts made of the fkins of cormorants, fea-divers, and gulls ; and, in order to keep out the rain, they have upper garments of the bladders and other inteftines of fea-lions, fea-calves, and whales, blown up and dried. They cut their hair in a circular form clofe to their ears ; and fhave alfo a round place upon the top. The women, on the contrary, let the hair defcend over the forehead as low as the eye-brows, and tie the remaining part in a knot upon the top of the head. They pierce the ears, and hang therein bits of coral, which they get from the Ruffians. Both fexes make holes in the griftle of the nofe, and in the under-lip, in which they thruft pieces of bone, and are very fond of fuch kind of ornaments. They mark alfo and colour their faces with different figures. They barter among one another fea-otters, fea-bears, clothes made of bird-fkins and of dried inteftines, fkins of fea-lions and fea-calves for the coverings of baidars, wooden mafks, darts, thread made of finews and reindeer hair, which they get from the country of Alafka.

Their houfhold utenfils are fquare pitchers and large troughs, which they make out of the

the wood driven afhore by the fea. Their weapons are bows and arrows pointed with flints, and javelins of two yards in length, which they throw from a fmall board. In-ftead of hatchets they ufe crooked knives of flint or bone. Some iron knives, hatchets, and lances, were obferved amongft them, which they had probably obtained by plundering the Ruffians.

According to the reports of the oldeft inhabitants of Umnak and Unalafhka, they have never been engaged in any war either amongft themfelves or with their neighbours, except once with the people of Alafhka, the occafion of which was as follows : The Toigon of Umnak's fon had a maimed hand; and fome inhabitants of Alafhka, who came upon a vifit to that ifland, faftened to his arm a drum, out of mockery, and invited him to dance. The parents and relations of the boy being offended at this infult, a quarrel enfued; and from that time the two people have lived in continual enmity, attacking and plundering each other by turns. According to the reports of the iflanders, there are mountains upon Alafhka, and woods of great extent at fome diftance from the coaft. The natives

tives wear clothes made of the fkins of rein-
deer, wolves, and foxes, and are not tributary
to any of their neighbours. The inhabitants
of the Fox-iflands feem to have no knowledge
of any country beyond Alafhka.

Feafts are very common among thefe iflanders ; and more particularly when the inhabitants of one ifland are vifited by thofe of the
others. The men of the village meet their
guefts beating drums, and preceded by the
women, who fing and dance. At the conclufion of the dance the hofts invite them to
partake of the feaft; after which ceremony
the former return firft to their dwellings, place
mats in order, and ferve up their beft provifion. The guefts next enter, take their places,
and after they are fatisfied the diverfions
begin.

Firft, the children dance and caper, at the
fame time making a noife with their fmall
drums, while the owners of the hut of both
fexes fing. Next, the men dance almoft naked, tripping after one another, and beating
drums of a larger fize : when thefe are weary,
they are relieved by the women, who dance
in their clothes, the men continuing in the
mean

mean time to sing and beat their drums. At last
the fire is put out, which had been kindled for
the ceremony. The manner of obtaining fire is
by rubbing two pieces of dry wood, or most
commonly by striking two flints together,
and letting the sparks fall upon some sea-ot-
ter's hair mixed with sulphur. If any for-
cerer is present, it is then his turn to play his
tricks in the dark ; if not, the guests immediately retire to their huts, which are made
on that occasion of their canoes and mats.
The natives, who have several wives, do not
withhold them from their guests ; but where
the owner of the hut has himself but one
wife, he then makes the offer of a female
servant.

Their hunting season is principally from
the end of October to the beginning of December, during which time they kill large
quantities of young sea-bears for their clothing.
They pass all December in feastings and di-
versions similar to that above mentioned :
with this difference, however, that the men
dance in wooden masks, representing various
sea-animals, and painted red, green, or black,
with coarse coloured earths found upon these
islands.

During

During thefe feftivals they vifit each other from village to village, and from ifland to ifland. The feafts concluded, mafks and drums are broken to pieces, or depofited in caverns among the rocks, and never afterwards made ufe of. In fpring they employ themfelves in killing old fea-bears, fea-lions, and whales. During fummer, and even in winter when it is calm, they row out to fea, and catch cod and other fifh. Their hooks are of bone ; and for lines they make ufe of a ftring made of a long tenacious fea-weed, which is fometimes found in thofe feas near one hundred and fixty yards in length.

Whenever they are wounded in any encounter, or bruifed by any accident, they apply a fort of yellow root to the wound, and faft for fome time. When their head achs, they open a vein in that part with a ftone lancet. When they want to glue the points of their arrows to the fhaft, they ftrike their nofe till it bleeds, and ufe the blood as glue.

Murder is not punifhed amongft them, for they have no judge. Their ceremonies of burying the dead are as follow : The bodies of poor people are wrapped up in their own clothes,

clothes, or in mats ; then laid in a grave, and covered over with earth. The bodies of the rich are put, together with their clothes and arms, in a fmall boat made of the wood driven afhore by the fea : this boat is hung upon poles placed crofs-ways ; and the body is thus left to rot in the open air.

The cuftoms and manners of the inhabitants of the Aleütian Ifles are nearly fimilar to thofe of the inhabitants of the Fox Iflands. The former indeed are rendered tributary, and entirely fubject to Ruffia ; and moft of them have a flight acquaintance with the Ruffian language, which they have learned from the crews of the different veffels who have landed there.

PART

PART II.

CONTAINING

SUPPLEMENTARY ACCOUNTS

OF THE

RUSSIAN DISCOVERIES.

CHAP. I.

Extract from the journal of a voyage made by Captain Krenitzin *and Lieutenant* Levashef *to the* Fox Islands, *in* 1768, 1769, *by order of the Emprefs of* Ruffia—*they fail from* Kamtchatka—*arrive at* Beering's *and* Copper Iflands—*reach the* Fox Iflands—Krenitzin *winters at* Alaxa—Levashef *upon* Unalashka—*productions of* Unalashka—*defcription of the inhabitants of the* Fox Iflands—*their manners and cuftoms, &c.*

ON the 23d of July Captain Krenitzin failed in the Galliot St. Catherine from the mouth of the Kamtchatka river towards America : he was accompanied by Lieutenant Levashef, in the Hooker St. Paul. Their inftructions were regulated by information derived from Beering's expedition in 1741. Shaping their courfe accordingly, they found themfelves more to the North than they expected ; and were told by the Ruffian traders and hunters, that a fimilar * miftake was committed

* This paffage is obfcurely expreffed. Its meaning may be afcertained by comparing Krenitzin's chart with that of Beering's voyage prefixed to Muller's account of the Ruffian Difcoveries. The route of Krenitzin's veffel was confiderably

mitted in the chart of that expedition. Thefe
traders, who for fome years paft were accuftomed to ramble to the diftant iflands in
queft of furs, faid that they were fituated
much more to the South, and farther Eaft,
than was imagined. On the 27th they faw
Commodore's or Beering's Ifland, which is
low and rocky, efpecially to the S. W. On
this fide they obferved a fmall harbour, diftinguifhed by two hillocks like boats, and
not far from it they found a frefh-water lake.

To the S. E. lies another ifland, called by
the Ruffians Mednoi Oftrof, or Copper Ifland,
from a great quantity of copper found upon
its N. E. coaft, the only fide which is known
to the Ruffians. It is wafhed up by the fea,
and covers the fhore in fuch abundance, that
many fhips may load with it. Perhaps an
India trader might make a profitable voyage
from thence to China, where this metal is
in high demand. This copper is moftly in a
metallic or malleable ftate, and many pieces
feem as if they had formerly been in fufion.

ably to the North of the courfe held by Beering and Tfchi-
tikof, and confequently he failed through the middle of
what they had fuppofed to be a continent, and which he
found to be an open fea. See Robertfon's Hiftory of America,
p. 461 ; and p. 27, 28. of this work.

The

The iſland is not high, but has many hillocks, each of which has the appearance of
having formerly been the crater of a volcano.
We may here, once for all, obſerve, that all
the iſlands repreſented in this chart * abound
with ſuch craters, called in Ruſſian *Sopka*, in
ſo much that no iſland, however ſmall, was
found without one ; and many of them conſiſted of nothing elſe. In ſhort, the chain of
Iſlands here laid down may, without any
violent ſtretch of imagination, be conſidered
as thrown up by ſome late volcanos. The
apparent novelty of every thing ſeems to
juſtify this conjecture : nor can any objection
be derived from the vegetable productions with
which theſe iſlands abound ; for the ſummer
after the lower diſtrict of Zutphen in Holland
was gained from the ſea, it was covered over
with wild muſtard. All theſe lands are ſubject to violent and frequent earthquakes, and
abound in ſulphur. The writer of the journal
was not able to inform us whether any lava
was found upon them ; but he ſpeaks of a
party-coloured ſtone as heavy as iron. From
this account it is by no means improbable,

* Namely, the chart prefixed to this journal.

that

that the copper above-mentioned has been melted in fome eruption.

After leaving Copper Ifland, no land was feen from either of the fhips (which had parted company in a fog) till, on the S. E. quarter of their track, was difcovered the chain o. iflands or head-lands laid down in the chartf Thefe in general appeared low, the fhore bad, without creeks, and the water between them very fhallow. During their courfe out-wards, as well as during their return, they had frequent fogs. It appears from the journal, as well as from the relation of the hunters, that it is very uncommon to have clear wea-ther for five days together, even during fum-mer.

The St. Catherine wintered in the ftraits of Alaxa, where they hauled her into fhoal wa-ter. The inftructions given to the captain fet forth, that a private fhip had in 1762 found there a commodious haven ; but he looked for it in vain. The entrance of this ftrait from the N. E. was extremely difficult on account of flats, and ftrong currents both flood and ebb : the entrance however from the S. E. was afterwards found to be much eafier with not

lefs

lefs than 5½ fathoms water. Upon furveying this ftrait, and the coaft of Alaxa, many
craters were obferved in the low grounds clofe
to the fhore ; and the foil produced few plants.
May not this allow us to fuppofe that the
coaft had fuffered confiderable changes fince
the year 1762 ? Few of the iflands produce
wood, and that only in the vallies by the
rivulets. Unalga and Alaxa contain the moft :
they abound with frefh-water ftreams, and
even rivers ; from which we may infer that
they are extenfive. The foil is in general
boggy, and covered with mofs ; but Alaxa
has more foil, and produces much grafs.

The St. Paul wintered in Unalafhka. This
wintering place was obferved to lie in 53°
29′ North latitude ; and its longitude from the
mouth of Kamtchatka river, computed by
the fhip's journal, was 27° 05′ Eaft *. Unalafhka is about fifty miles long from N. E.
to S. W. and has on the N. E. fide three bays.
One of them, called Udagha, ftretches thirty
miles E. N. E. and W. S. W. nearly through
the middle of the ifland. Another, called

* According to the general map of Ruffia, the mouth
of the Kamtchatka river is in 178° 25′ from Fero. Unalafhka therefore, according to this eftimation, is 205° 30′ from
Fero, or 187° 55′ 15″ from Greenwich.

Igunok,

Igunok, lying N. N. E. and S. S. W. is a
tolerably good harbour, with three and a half
fathom water at high tide, and fandy ground.
It is well fheltered from the North fwell at its
entrance by rocks, fome of which are under
water. The tide flows here five feet at full
and change ; and the fhore is in general bold
and rocky, except in the bay, at the mouth
of a fmall river. There are two burning
mountains on this Ifland, one called Ayaghifh,
and the other (by the Ruffians) the Roaring
Mountain. Near the former is a very copious
hot fpring. The land is in general rocky,
with loamy and clayey grounds; but the
grafs is extremely coarfe, and unfit for pafture.
Scarcely any wood is to be found on it. Its
plants are dwarf cherry (* Xylofteum of
Tournefort), wortle berry (Vaccinium Uliginofum of Linnæus), rafberry, farana and fhik-
fhu of Kamtchatka, and kutage, larch, white
poplar, pine, and birch †. The land animals are foxes of different colours, mice,

* The Lonicera Pyrenaica of Linnæus. It is not a dwarf
cherry, but a fpecies of honeyfuckle.

† All the other journalifts uniformly defcribe Unalafhka
as containing nothing but underwood ; we muft therefore
fuppofe that the trees here mentioned were very low and
fmall ; and this agrees with what goes before, " fcarcely
" any wood is to be found on it."

and

and weafels ; there are alfo beavers *, fea cats, and fea lions, as at Kamtchatka. Among their fifh we may reckon cod, perch, pilchards, fmelts, roach, needle fifh, terpugh, and tchavitcha. The birds are eagles, partridges, ducks, teals, urili, ari, and gadi. The animals, for whofe Ruffian names I can find no tranflations, are (excepting the Ari) defcribed in Krafhininikoff's Hiftory of Kamtchatka, or in Steller's relation contained in the fecond volume of the Memoirs of the Academy of St. Peterfburg.

The inhabitants of Alaxa, Umnak, Unalafhka, and the neighbouring iflands, are of a middle ftature, tawny brown colour, and black hair. In fummer they wear coats *(parki†)* made of bird fkins, over which, in bad weather, and in their boats, they throw cloaks, called *kamli*, made of thin whale guts. On their heads they wear wooden caps, ornamented with ducks feathers, and the ears of the fea-animal, called *Scivutcha* or fealion ; they alfo adorn thefe caps with beads of different colours, and with little figures of

* By beavers the journalifts certainly mean fea-otters, called by the Ruffians fea-beavers. See p. 13.

† Parki in Ruffian fignifies a fhirt, the coats of thefe iflanders being made like fhirts.

bone

bone or ftone. In the partition of the noftrils they place a pin, about four inches long,
made of bone, or of the ftalk of a certain
black plant ; from the ends of this pin or
bodkin they hang, in fine weather and on
feftivals, rows of beads, one below the other.
They thruft beads, and bits of pebble cut
like teeth, into holes made in the under-lips.
They alfo wear ftrings of beads in their ears,
with bits of amber, which the inhabitants
of the other iflands procure from Alaxa, in
exchange for arrows and *kamli.* They cut
their Hair before juft abo/e the eyes, and fome
fhave the top of their heads like monks. Behind, the hair is loofe.   The drefs of the women fcarcely differs from that of the men, excepting that it is made of fifh-fkins.   They
few with bone needles, and thread made of
fifh guts, faftening their work to the ground
before them with bodkins.   They go with
the head uncovered, and the hair cut like
that of the men before, but tied up behind in
a high knot.   They paint their cheeks with
ftrokes of blue and red, and wear nofe-pins,
beads, and ear-rings like the men : they hang
beads round their neck, and checkered ftrings
round their arms and legs.

In

In their perfons we fhould reckon them extremely nafty. They eat the vermin with which their bodies are covered, and fwallow the mucus from the nofe. Having wafhed themfelves, according to cuftom, firft with urine, and then with water, they fuck their hands dry. When they are fick, they lie three or four days without food ; and if bleeding is neceffary, they open a vein with lancets made of flint, and fuck the blood.

Their principal nourifhment is fifh and whale fat, which they commonly eat raw. They alfo feed upon fea-wrack and roots, particularly the *faran*, a fpecies of lily ; they eat an herb, called *kutage*, on account of its bitternefs, only with fifh or fat. They fometimes kindle fire by catching a fpark among dry leaves and powder of fulphur : but the moft common method is by rubbing two pieces of wood together, in the manner practifed at Kamtchatka *, and which Vakfel, Beering's lieutenant, found to be in ufe in

* The inftrument made ufe of by the Kamtchadals, t°
procure fire, is a board with feveral holes in it, and a ftick ;
the latter is put into the holes, and turned about fwiftly'
until the wood within the holes begins to burn, and the
fparks fall upon the tinder placed in fuch a manner as to
receive them.

that

that part of North America which he faw in
1741. They are very fond of Ruffian oil
and butter, but not of bread. They could
not be prevailed upon to tafte any fugar until
the commander fhewed the example; finding
it fweet, they put it up to carry it home to
their wives.

The houfes of thefe iflanders are huts
built precifely in the manner of thofe in
Kamtchatka, with the entry through a hole
in the middle of the roof. In one of thefe
huts live feveral families, to the amount of
thirty or forty perfons. They keep themfelves warm by means of whale fat burnt in
fhells, which they place between their legs.
The women fit apart from the men.

Six or feven of thefe huts or yourts make
a village, of which there are fixteen in Unalafhka. The iflands feem in general to be
well inhabited, as may be conjectured from
the great number of boats which are feen
continually plying along the fhore. There
are upwards of a thoufand inhabitants on
Unalafhka, and they fay that it was formerly
much more populous. They have fuffered
greatly by their difputes with the Ruffians,
and by a famine in the year 1762; but moft
of

of all from a change in their way of life.
No longer contented with their original fim-
plicity, they long for Ruffian luxuries : in
order therefore to obtain a few delicacies,
which are prefently confumed, they dedicate
the greateft part of their time to hunting,
for the purpofe of procuring furs for the
Ruffians; by which means, they neglect to
lay up a provifion of fifh and roots, and
fuffer their children frequently to die of
hunger.

Their principal food is fifh, which they
catch with bone hooks. Their boats, in
which they row to a great diftance from
land, are made, like thofe of the Innuet or
Efquimaux, of thin flips of wood and fkins :
thefe fkins cover the tops as well as the fides
of the boat, and are drawn tight round the
waift of the rower. The oar is a paddle,
broad at both ends. Some of their boats hold
two perfons; one of whom rows, and the
other fifhes : but this kind of boats feem
appropriated to their chiefs. They have alfo
large boats capable of holding forty men.
They kill birds and beafts with darts made
of bone, or of wood tipped with fharpened
ftone : they ufe thefe kind of darts in war,

which

which break with the blow given by them, and leave the point in the wound.

The manners and character of thefe people are what we fhould expect from their neceffi-tous fituation, extremely rude and favage. The inhabitants however of Unalafhka are fomewhat lefs barbarous in their manners and behaviour to each other, and alfo more civil to ftrangers than the natives of the other iflands; but even the former are engaged in frequent and bloody quarrels, and commit murder without the leaft compunction. Their difpofition engages them in continual wars, in which they always endeavour to gain their point by ftratagem. The inhabitants of Unimak are formidable to all the reft; they frequently invade the other iflands, and carry off women, the chief object of their wars. Alaxa is moft fubject to thefe incurfions, probably becaufe it is more populous and ex-tenfive. They all agree in hating the Ruf-fians, whom they confider as general inva-ders, and therefore kill them wherever they can. The people of Unalafhka however are more friendly; for Lieutenant Levafhef, being informed that there was a Ruffian veffel in the ftraits of Alaxa, prevailed on fome

Una-

Unalafhkans to carry a letter, which they
undertook, notwithftanding the danger they
were expofed to from the inhabitants of the
intervening iflands,

The journalift fays, that thefe people have
no kind of religion, nor any notion of a
God. We obferve however among them fufficient marks of fuch a religion, as might
be expected from people in their fituation.
For the journalift informs us, that they have
fortune-tellers employed by them at their
feftivals. Thefe perfons pretend to foretel
events by the information of the Kugans or
Dæmons. In their divinations they put on
wooden mafks, made in the form in which
they fay the Kugan appeared to them; they
then dance with violent motions, beating at
the fame time drums covered with fifh fkins.
The inhabitants alfo wear little figures on
their caps, and place others round their
huts, to keep off the devils. Thefe are fufficient marks of a favage religion.

It is common for them to have two, three,
or four wives; who do not all live together,
but, like the Kamtchadals, in different
yourts. It is not unufual for the men to
exchange their wives, and even fell them,

in

in time of dearth, for a bladder of fat. The hufband afterwards endeavours to get back his wife, if fhe is a favourite, and in cafe he is unfuccefsful he fometimes kills himfelf. When ftrangers arrive at a village, it is always cuftomary for the women to meet them, while the men remain at home: this is confidered as a pledge of friendfhip and fecurity. When a man dies in the hut belonging to his wife, fhe retires into a dark hole, where fhe remains forty days. The hufband pays the fame compliment to his favourite wife upon her death. When both parents die, the children are left to fhift for themfelves. The Ruffians found many in this fituation, and fome were brought for fale.

In each village there is a fort of chief called Tookoo*: he decides differences by arbitration, and the neighbours enforce the fentence. When he embarks at fea he is exempt from working, and has a fervant called *Kalè*, for the purpofe of rowing the canoe: this is the only mark of his dignity; at other times he labours like the reft. The office is not hereditary; but is generally con-

* This is probably a miftake for Toigon.

ferred

ferred on him who is moſt remarkable for his perſonal qualities; or who poſſeſſes a great influence by the number of his friends. Hence it frequently happens, that the perſon who has the largeſt family is choſen.

During their feſtivals, which are held at the concluſion of the fiſhing ſeaſon in April, the men and women ſing ſongs : the women dance ſometimes ſingly, and ſometimes in pairs, waving in their hands blown bladders; they begin with gentle movements, which become at laſt extremely violent.

The inhabitants of Unalaſhka are called Kogholaghi; thoſe of Akutan, and further Eaſt to Unimak, Kighiguſi; and thoſe of Unimak and Alaxa, Kataghayekiki. They cannot tell from whence theſe appellations are derived; and now begin to call themſelves by the general name of Aleyut, given to them by the Ruſſians, and borrowed from ſome of the * Kuril iſlands. Upon being aſked concerning their origin, they ſaid that they had always inhabited theſe iſlands, and knew nothing of any other

* I cannot find, that any of the Kuril Iſles are called Aleyut in the catalogue of thoſe iſlands given by Mr. Muller, S. R. G. III. p. 86—92. Neither are any of them laid down under that name in the Ruſſian charts.

country

country beyond them. All that could be gathered from them was, that the greateft numbers came from Alaxa, and that they did not know whether that land had any bounds. The Ruffians furveyed this ifland very far to the N.E. in boats, being out about a fortnight, and fet up a crofs at the end of their furvey. The boats of the iflanders are like thofe of the Americans. It appears however from their cuftoms and way of life, fo far as thefe are not neceffarily prefcribed to them by their fituation, that they are of Kamtchadal original. Their huts, their manner of kindling fire, and other circum-ftances, lead to this conjecture. Add to this, the almoft continued Wefterly winds, which muft render the paffage Weftward extremely difficult. Beering and Tchirikoff could never obtain Eafterly winds but by going to the outhward.

The Ruffians have for fome years paft been accuftomed to repair to thefe iflands in queft of furs, of which they have impofed a tax on the inhabitants. The manner of carrying on this trade is as follows. The Ruffians go in autumn to Beering's and Copper Ifland, and there winter; they then employ themfelves

felves in catching the fea-cat, and afterwards the Scivutcha, or fea-lion. The flesh
of the latter is prepared for food, and is
efteemed very delicate. They carry the fkins
of thefe fea-animals to the Eaftern iflands.
Next fummer they fail Eaftward, to the Fox-
iflands; and again lay their fhips up for the
winter. They then endeavour to procure,
either by perfuafion or force, the children of
the inhabitants, particularly of the Tookoos,
as hoftages. This being accomplifhed, they
deliver to the inhabitants fox-traps, and alfo
fkins for their boats, for which they expect
in return furs and provifions during the winter. After obtaining from them a certain
quantity of furs, by way of tax, for which
they give quittances; the Ruffians pay for
the reft in beads, falfe pearls, goats wool,
copper kettles, hatchets, &c. In the fpring
they get back their traps, and deliver up
their hoftages. They dare not hunt alone,
nor in fmall numbers, on account of the
hatred of the natives. Thefe people could
not, for fome time, comprehend for what
purpofe the Ruffians impofed a tribute of
fkins, which were not to be their own property, but belonged to an abfent perfon; for
their

their Tookoos have no revenue. Nor could
they be made to believe, that there were any
more Ruffians than thofe who came among
them; for in their own country all the men
of an ifland go out together. At prefent
they comprehend fomething of Kamtchatka,
by means of the Kamtchadals and Koriacs
who come with the Ruffians; and on their
arrival love to affociate with people whofe
manner of life refembles their own.

Krenitzin and Levafhef returned from this
expedition into the mouth of Kamtchatka
river in autumn 1769.

The chart which accompanies this journal
was compofed by the pilot Jacob Yakof,
under the infpection of the commanders
* Krenitzin and Levafhef. The track of the
St. Paul is marked both in going out and
returning. The harbour of the St. Paul in
the ifland Unalafhka, and the ftraits of Alaxa,
are laid down from obfervations made during the winter 1768; and the iflands connected by bearings and diftances taken during a cruife of the St. Paul twice repeated.

* Krenitzin was drowned foon after his return to Kamtchatka, in a canoe belonging to the natives.

In

In this chart the variation is said to be

In Lat.	Long.	Points
54° 40′.	204.	2 Eaſt.
52 20	201	1½
52 50	198	1½
53 20	192 30	1
53 40	188	1
54 50	182 30	0¾
55 00	180 30	0¾

But the arrows in the compaſs imply that the variation is *Weſt*; probably the miſtake is in the arrows.

CHAP. II.

Voyage of Lieutenant Synd *to the North Eaſt of* Siberia—*He diſcovers a cluſter of iſlands, and a promontory, which he ſuppoſes to belong to the continent of* America, *lying near the coaſt of the* Tſchutſki.

IN 1764 lieutenant Synd ſailed from Okotſk, upon a voyage of diſcovery towards the continent of America. He was ordered to take a different courſe from that held by the late Ruſſian veſſels, which lay due Eaſt from the coaſt of Kamtchatka. As
he

he steered therefore his course more to the North East than any of the preceding navigators; and as it appears from all the voyages related in the first part of this work *, that the vicinity of America is to be sought for in that quarter alone, any accurate account of this expedition would not fail of being highly interesting. It is therefore a great mortification to me, that, while I raise the reader's curiosity, I am not able fully to satisfy it. The following intelligence concerning this voyage is all which I was able to procure. It is accompanied with an authentic chart.

In 1764 Synd put to sea from the port of Okotsk, but did not pass (we know not by what accident) between the Southern Cape of Kamtchatka and Shushu, the first Kuril Isle, before 1766. He then steered his course North at no great distance from the coast of the peninsula, but made very little progress that year ; for he wintered South of the river Uka.

The following year he sailed from Ukinski Point due East and North East, until he fell in with a cluster of islands † stretching

* See p. 28.

† These are certainly some of the islands which the Tschutski resort to in their way to what they call the continent of America,

between

between 61 and 62 degrees of latitude, and 195°
and 202° longitude. Thefe iflands lie South
Eaft and Eaft of the coaft of the Tfchutfki ;
and feveral of them are fituated very near the
fhore. Befide thefe fmall iflands, he difcovered alfo a mountainous coaft lying within
one degree of the coaft of the Tfchutfki,
between 64 and 66° North latitude ; its moft
Weftern extremity was fituated in longitude
38° 15′ from Okotfk, or 199° 1′ from Fero.
This land is laid down in his chart as part of
the continent of America ; but we cannot determine upon what proofs he grounds this
reprefentation, until a more circumftantial
account of his voyage is communicated to the
public. Synd feems to have made but a fhort
ftay afhore. Inftead of endeavouring to furvey
its coafts, or of fteering more to the Eaft, he
almoft inftantly fhaped his courfe due Weft
towards the courfe of the Tfchutfki, then
turned directly South and South Weft, until
he came oppofite to Katyrfkoi Nofs. From
that point he continued to coaft the peninfula
of Kamtchatka ; doubled the cape ; and
reached Okotfk in 1768.

CHAP

C H A P. III.

Summary of the proofs tending to shew, that
Beering *and* Tschirikof *reached* America
in 1741, *or came very near it.*

THE coast which Beering reached, and
called Cape St. Elias, lay, according
to his estimation, in 58° 28′ N. latitude, and
in longitude 236° from Fero : the coast
touched at by Tschirikof was situated in lat.
56° long. 241°*.

Steller, who accompanied Beering in his
expedition towards America, endeavours to
prove, that they discovered that continent by
the following arguments † : The coasts were
bold, presenting continual chains of high
mountains, some of which were so elevated,
that their tops were covered with snow :
their sides were cloathed from the bottom

* The reader will find the narrative of this voyage made
by Beering and Tschirikoff in Muller's account of the Russian Discoveries, S. R. G. III. p. 193, &c.
† See Krashininikoff's account of Kamtchatka, Chap. X.
French Translation ; Chap. IV. English translation.

to the top with large tracts of thick and fine wood *.

Steller went afhore, and although he re-mained only a few hours, yet he obferved feveral fpecies of birds which are not known in Siberia : amongft thefe was the bird de-fcribed by † Catefby, under the name of Blue Jay ; and which has never yet been found in any country but North America. The foil was very different from that of the neigh-bouring iflands, and at Kamtchatka ; and he collected feveral plants, which are deemed by botanifts peculiar to America.

The following lift of thefe plants was com-municated to me by Mr. Pallas : I infert them however without prefuming to decide,

* The recent navigations in thofe feas ftrongly confirm this argument. For in general all the New-difcovered Iflands are quite deftitute of trees ; even the largeft produce nothing but underwood, one of the moft Eafterly Kadyak alone ex-cepted, upon which fmall willows and alders were obferved growing in vallies at fome diftance from the coaft. See p. 137.

† See Catefby's Natural Hiftory of Florida, Carolina, &c. This bird is called, by Linnæus, Corvus Chriftatus. I have feen in Mr. Pennant's MS account of the hiftory of the animals, birds, &c. of N. America, and the Northern hemifphere, as high as lat. 60, an exact defcription of this bird. Whenever that ingenious author, to whom we are indebted for many elegant and interefting publications, gives this part of his labours to the world, the zoology of thefe countries will be fully and accurately confidered

whether

whether they are the exclufive growth of
North America : the determination of this
point is the province of botany.

Trillium Erectum. Fumaria Cucullaria.
A fpecies of Dracontium, with leaves like the
Canna Indica. Uvularia Perfoliata. Heu-
chera Americana. Mimulus Luteus, a Peru-
vian plant. A fpecies of Rubus, probably
a variety of the Rubus Idæus, but with larger
berries, and a large lacinated red calyx. None
of thefe plants are found in Kamtchatka, or
in any of the neighbouring iflands *.

Though thefe circumftances fhould not be
confidered as affording decifive proofs, that
Beering reached America ; yet they will

* According to Mr. Pallas, the plants of the New-difcovered Iflands are moftly alpine, like thofe of Siberia ;
this he attributes to the fhortnefs and coldnefs of the fummer, occafioned by the frequency of the North winds.
His words are : " Quoique les hivers de ces ifles foient
affez temperés par l'air de la mer, de façon que les neiges
ne couvrent jamais la terre que par intervalles, la plupart
des plantes y font alpines, comme en Siberie, par la raifon
que l'eté y eft auffi courte et froide, à caufe des vents de
nord qui y regnent." This paffage is taken from a MS
treatife in the French language, relative to the New-difcovered Iflands, communicated to me by my very learned
and ingenious friend Mr. Pallas, profeffor of natural hiftory at St. Peterfburg ; from which I have been enabled
to collect a confiderable degree of information. This treatife was fent to Monf. Buffon ; and that celebrated naturalift has made great ufe of it in the fifth volume of his
Supplement à l'Hiftoire Naturelle.

furely

furely be admitted as ſtrong preſumptions, that he very nearly approached that continent *.

C H A P. IV.

Poſition of the Andreanoffsky Iſles *aſcertained —Number of the* Aleütian Iſles.

WHEN the anonymous author publiſhed his account of the Ruſſian Diſcoveries in 1766, the poſition of the Andreanoffsky Iſles was not aſcertained. It was generally ſuppoſed, that they formed part of that cluſter of iſlands, which Synd † fell in with in his voyage towards Tſchukotſkoi Noſs ; and Buffon ‡ repreſents them to be the ſame with thoſe laid down in Stæhlin's chart, under the name of Anadirſky Iſles. The anonymous author, in the paſſage here

* The reader will recollect in this place, that the natives of the contiguous iſlands touched at by Beering and Tſchirikof " preſented to the Ruſſians the calumet, or " pipe of peace, which is a ſymbol of friendſhip univerſal " among the people of North America, and an uſage of " arbitrary inſtitution peculiar to them." See Robertſon's Hiſt. Am. vol. I. p. 276. S. R. G. III. p. 214.

† See p. 223, 224, 225.

‡ Iſles Anadyr ou Andrien. Supp. vol. V. p. 591.

referred

referred to, fuppofes them to be N. E. of the
Aleütian Ifles; "at the diftance of 600 or
" 800 verfts; that their direction is probably
" Eaft and Weft, and that fome of them
" may unite with that part of the Fox Iflands
" which are moft contiguous to the oppofite
" continent." This conjecture was advanced
upon a fuppofition that the Andreanoffsky
Ifles lay near the coaft of the Tfchutfki; and
that fome of the Fox Iflands were fituated in
latitude 61, as they are laid down upon the
general map of Ruffia. But according to
fubfequent information the Andreanoffsky
Ifles lie between the Aleütian and the Fox
Iflands, and complete the connection between
Kamtchatka and America *. Their chain is
fuppofed to begin in about latitude 53, near
the moft Eafterly of the Aleütian Ifles, and
to extend in a fcattered feries towards the Fox
Iflands. The moft North Eafterly of thefe
iflands are faid to be fo near the moft Southerly of the Fox Iflands, that they feem occafionally to have been taken for them. An
inftance of this occurs in p. 61 and 62 of

* P. 64. Some of the remoter iflands are faid to be
E. S. E. of the Aleütian Ifles; thefe muft be either part
of the Andreanoffsky Ifles, or the moft Southerly of the Fox
Iflands.

this

this work ; where Atchu and Amlak are
reckoned among the Fox Iflands. It is however more probable, that they are part of the
group called by the Aleütian chief Negho *,
and known to the Ruffians under the name
of Andreanoffsky Iflands, becaufe they were
fuppofed to have been firft difcovered by
Andrean Tolftyk, whofe voyage is related
in the feventh chapter of the Firft Part.

I take this opportunity of adding, that the
anonymous author, in defcribing the Aleütian Ifles, both in the firft and laft chapter
of the account of the Ruffian difcoveries,
mentions only three ; namely, Attak, Semitfhi, Shemiya. But the Aleütian Ifles
confift of a much larger number ; and their
chain includes all the iflands comprehended
by the iflander in the two groups of Khao
and Safignan +. Many of them are laid down
upon the general map of Ruffia ; and fome
of them are occafionally alluded to in the
journals of the Ruffian voyages ‡.

* See p. 239.
† See p. 238, 239.
‡ See p. 31, and particularly p. 50, where fome of thefe
iflands are mentioned under the names of Ibiya, Kifka,
and Olas.

CHAP.

C H A P. V.

Conjectures concerning the proximity of the Fox Iflands *to the continent of* America.

THE anonymous author, in the courfe of his account of the Ruffian difco-veries, endeavoured to prove, by many cir-cumftances drawn from natural hiftory, that the Fox Iflands muft lie near the continent of America : hence he grounds his conjec-ture, that " the time is not far diftant when " fome of the Ruffian navigators will fall-in " with that coaft."

The fmall willows and alders which, ac-cording to Glottof, were found growing up-on Kadyak, do not appear to have been fuffi-cient either in fize or quantity to afcertain, with any degree of certainty, the clofe vici-nity of that ifland to America. River-otters, wolves, bears, and wild boars, which were obferved upon the fame ifland, will perhaps be thought to afford a ftronger prefumption in favour of a neighbouring continent : mar-tens

tens were alfo caught there, an animal which
is not known in the Eaftern parts of Siberia,
nor found upon any of the other iflands. All
the abovementioned animals, martens alone
excepted, were feen upon Alakfu, which is
fituated more to the North Eaft than Kadyak,
and alfo rein-deers and wild dogs. To thefe
proofs drawn from natural hiftory, we muft add
the reports of a mountainous country covered
with forefts, and of a great promontory called
Ataktak, lying ftill more to the N. E. which
were prevalent among the inhabitants of
Alakfu and Kadyak.

Although thefe circumftances have been
already mentioned *, yet I have thought proper to recapitulate them here, in order to lay
before the reader in one point of view the
feveral proofs advanced by the anonymous
author, which feem to fhew, that the Fox
Iflands are fituated near America. Many of
them afford, beyond a doubt, evident figns of a
lefs open fea; and give certain marks of a
nearer approach towards the oppofite continent.
But how far that diftance may be fuppofed,
muft be left to the judgment of the reader;
and remains to be afcertained by fubfequent

* See p. 76 and 77; 134—137; 198.

navi-

navigators. All that we know for certain is, that, as far as any Ruffian veffels have hither-to failed, a chain of iflands has been difco-vered lying E. or N. E. by E. from Kamt-chatka, and ftretching towards America. Part of this chain has only been touched at ; the reft is unknown ; and all beyond is un-certainty and conjecture.

CHAP. VI.

Of the Tfchutfki—*Reports of the vicinity of* America *to their coaft, firft propagated by them, feem to be confirmed by late accounts from thofe parts.*

THE Tfchutfki, it is well known, in-habit the North Eaftern part of Siberia : their country is a fmall tract of land, bounded on the North by the Frozen Sea, on the Eaft by the Eaftern Occean ; on the South it borders upon the river Anadyr, and on that of Kovyma to the Weft. The N. E. cape of this country is called Tfchukotfkoi-Nofs, or the promontory of the Tfchutfki. Its inhabitants are the only people of Siberia who

who have not yet been fubdued by the Ruffians.

The anonymous author agrees with Mr.
Muller in fuppofing, that America advances
to within a fmall diftance of the coaft of the
Tfchutfki ; which, he fays, "is confirmed by
" the lateft accounts procured from thefe
" parts."

The firft intelligence concerning the fuppofed vicinity between Afia and America was
derived from the reports of the Tfchutfki in
their intercourfe with the Ruffians. Vague
and uncertain accounts, drawn from a barbarous people, cannot deferve implicit credit;
but as they have been uniformly and invariably propagated by the inhabitants of thofe
regions from the middle of the laft century
to the prefent time, they muft merit at leaft
the attention of every curious enquirer.

Thefe reports were firft related in Muller's
account of the Ruffian difcoveries, and have
been lately thought worthy of notice by Dr.
Robertfon *, in his Hiftory of America.
Their probability feems ftill further increafed
by the following circumftances. One Plenifner, a native of Courland, was appointed

* Hift. of America, vol. I. p. 274.—277.

commander of Okotſk, in the year 1760, with an exprefs order from the court to proceed as far as * Anadirſk, and to procure all poſſible intelligence concerning the North Eaſtern part of Siberia, and the oppoſite continent. In confequence of this order, Plenifner repaired to Anadirſk, and proceeded likewife to Kovimſkoi Oſtrog : the former of thefe Ruſſian fettlements is fituated near the Southern, the latter near the Weſtern limits of the Tſchutſki. Not content however with collecting all the information in his power from the neighbouring Koriacs, who have frequent intercourfe with the Tſchutſki ; he alfo fent into their country one Daurkin, a native Tſchutſki, who had been taken prifoner, and bred up by the Ruſſians. Daurkin continued two years with his countrymen ; and made feveral expeditions with them to the neighbouring iflands, which lie off the Eaſtern coaſt of Siberia. The fum of the intelligence brought by this man was as follows : that Tſchukotſkoi-Nofs is a very narrow peninfula ; that the Tſchutſki carry on a trade of barter with the inhabitants of America ;

* Anadirſk has been lately deſtroyed by the Ruſſians themfelves.

that

that they employ fix days in paffing the ftrait which feparates the two continents ; that they direct their courfe from ifland to ifland ; and that the diftance from the one to the other is fo fmall, that they are able to pafs every night afhore. More to the North, he defcribes the two continents as approaching ftill nearer to each other, with only two iflands lying between them.

This intelligence remarkably coincided with the accounts collected by Plenifner him-felf among the Koriacs. Plenifner returned to Peterfburg in 1776, and brought with him feveral* maps and charts of the North Eaftern parts of Siberia, which were afterwards ufed in the compilation of the general map of Ruffia, publifhed by the academy in 1776†.

By

* The moft important of thefe maps comprehends the country of the Tfchutíki, together with the nations which border immediately upon them. This map was chiefly taken during a fecond expedition made by major Paulofsky againft the Tfchutfki ; and his march into that country is traced upon it. The firft expedition of that Ruffian officer, in which he penetrated as far as Tfchukotskoi-Nofs, is re-lated by Mr. Muller, S. R. G. III. p. 134—138. We have no account of this fecond expedition, during which he had feveral fkirmifhes with the Tfchutski, and came off victori-ous ; but upon his return was furprifed and killed by them. This expediton was made about the year 1750.

† The circumftances mentioned in the text were com-municated to me during my continuance at Peterfburg by

feveral

By thefe means the country of the Tfchutfki has been laid down with a greater degree
of accuracy than heretofore. Thefe are probably the late accounts from thofe parts
which the anonymous author alludes to.

C H A P. VII.

*Lift of the New-difcovered Iflands, procured
from an* Aleütian *chief—Catalogue of Iflands
called by different names in the Account of the*
Ruffian *Difcoveries.*

T H E fubfequent lift of the New-difcovered Iflands was procured from an
Aleütian chief brought to Peterfburg in 1771,
and examined at the defire of the Emprefs by
Mr. Muller, who divides them into four
principal groups. He regulates this divifion
partly by a fimilarity of the language fpoken
by the inhabitants, and partly by vicinity of
fituation.

The firft group *, called by the iflander
Safignan, comprehends, 1. Beering's Ifland·

---

feveral perfons of credit, who had frequently converfed with
Plenifner fince his return to the capital, where he died in
the latter end of the year 1778.

* Thefe two firft groups probably belong to the Aleütian
Ifles.

2. Copper

2. Copper Ifland. 3. Otma. 4. Samya, or Shemiya. 5. Anakta.

The fecond group is called Khao, and comprifes eight iflands: 1. Immak. 2. Kifka. 3. Tchetchina. 4. Ava. 5. Kavia. 6. Tfchagulak. 7. Ulagama. 8. Amtfchidga.

The third general name is Negho, and comprehends the iflands known by the Ruffians under the name of Andreanofsky Oftrova : fixteen were mentioned by the iflander, under the following names :

1. Amatkinak. 2. Ulak. 3. Unalga. 4. Navotfha. 5. Uliga. 6. Anagin. 7. Kagulak. 8. Illafk, or Illak. 9. Takavanga, upon which is a volcano. 10. Kanaga, which has alfo a volcano. 11. Leg. 12. Shetfhuna. 13. Tagaloon : near the coaft of the three laft mentioned iflands feveral fmall rocky ifles are fituated. 14. An ifland without a name, called by the Ruffians Goreloi *. 15. Atchu. 16. Amla.

The fourth group is denominated Kavalang, and comprehends fixteen iflands : thefe

---

* Goreloi is fuppofed by the Ruffian navigators to be the fame ifland as Atchu, and is reckoned by them among the Fox Iflands. See p. 68, and p. 229.

are called by the Ruffians Lyffie Oftrova, or
the Fox Iflands.

1. Amukta.　2. Tfchigama.　3. Tfche-
gula.　4. Uniftra.　5. Ulaga.　6. Tana-
gulana.　7. Kagamin.　8. Kigalga.　9.
Schelmaga.　10. Umnak.　11. Aghun-Alafh-
ka.　12. Unimga.　At a fmall diftance from
Unimga, towards the North, ftretches a promontory called by the iflanders the Land of
Black Foxes, with a fmall river called Alafhka, which empties itfelf oppofite to the laft-
mentioned ifland into a gulf proper for a
haven. The extent of this land is not known·
To the South Eaft of this promontory lie four
little iflands.　13. Uligan.　14. Antun-
duffume.　15. Semidit.　16. Senagak.

Many of thefe names are not found either
in journals or charts : while others are wanting in this lift which are mentioned in both
journals and charts. Nor is this to be won-
dered at ; for the names of the Iflands have
been confiderably altered and corrupted by the
Ruffian navigators. Sometimes the fame
name has been applied to different iflands by
the different journalifts ; at other times the
fame ifland has been called by different names.
Several inftances of thefe changes feem to
occur

occur in the account of the Ruffian Difcoveries : namely,

Att, Attak, and Ataku.

Shemiya and Sabiya.

Atchu, Atchak, Goreloi or Burned Ifland.

Amlak, Amleg.

Ayagh, Kayaku.

Alakfu, Alagfhak, Alachfhak.

Aghunalafhka, Unalafhka.

C H A P. VIII.

Attempts of the Ruffians *to difcover a North
Eaft paffage—Voyages from* Archangel *towards the* Lena—*From the* Lena *towards*
Kamtchatka—*Extract from* Muller's *account of* Defchneff's *voyage round* Tfchukotfkoi Nofs—*Narrative of a voyage made
by* Shalauroff *from the* Lena *to* Shelatfkoi
Nofs.

THE only communication hitherto
known between the Atlantic and Pacific Ocean, or between Europe and the Eaft
Indies, is made either by failing round the
Cape of Good Hope, or by doubling Cape
Horn. But as both thefe navigations are extremely tedious, the great object of feveral
late European voyages has been turned towards

wards the difcovery of a North Eaft or a North Weft paffage.   As this work is entirely confined to the Ruffian navigations, any dif-quifition concerning the North Weft paffage is totally foreign to the purpofe ; and for the fame reafon in what relates to the North'Eaft, thefe refearches extend only to the attempts of the Ruffians for the difcovery of that paffage.

The advocates for the North Eaft paffage have divided that navigation into three prin-cipal parts ; and by endeavouring to fhew that the three parts have been feparately paffed at different times, they conclude, that the whole navigation is not impracticable.

The three parts are, 1. from Archangel to the Lena; 2. from the Lena to Kamt-chatka ; 3. from Kamtchatka to Japan. With refpect to the latter, the connection between the feas of Kamtchatka and Japan firft appeared from fome Japanefe veffels wrecked upon the coaft of Kamtchatka in the beginning of this century ; and this com-munication has been unqueftionably proved from feveral voyages made by the Ruffians from Kamtchatka to Japan *.

No one ever afferted that the firft part from Archangel to the Lena was ever performed in one voyage ; but feveral perfons having ad-

* S. R. G. III. p. 78, and p. 166, &c.

vanced

vanced that this navigation has been performed by the Ruffians at different times, it be-
comes neceffary to examine the accounts of
the Ruffian voyages in thofe feas.

In 1734 lieutenant Morovief failed from
Archangel toward the river Oby ; and got no
farther the firft year than the mouth of the
Petchora. The next fummer he paffed through
the ftraits of Weygatz into the fea of Kara ;
and coafted along the Eaftern fide of that fea,
as high as latitude 72° 30′, but did not double
the promontory which feparates the fea of
Kara from the bay of Oby. In 1738, the
lieutenants Malgyn and Skurakof doubled
that promontory with great difficulty, and
entered the bay of Oby. During thefe expeditions the navigators met with great dangers and impediments from the ice. Several
unfuccefsful attempts were made to pafs
from the bay of Oby to the Yenifèi, which
was at laft effected in 1738 by two veffels
commanded by lieutenants Offzin and Kof-
kelef. The fame year the pilot Feodor Me-
nin failed from the Yenifèi towards the Lena :
he fteered North as high as lat. 72°. 15′. but
when he came to the mouth of the Pifida
he

he was ſtopped by the ice ; and finding it impoſſible to force a paſſage, he returned to the Yeniſèi *.

July, 1735, lieutenant Prontſhiſtſhef ſailed from Yakutſk up the Lena to its mouth, in order to paſs by ſea to the Yeniſèi. The Weſtern mouths of the Lena were ſo choaked with ice, that he was obliged to paſs through the moſt Eaſterly one ; and was prevented by contrary winds from getting out until the 13th of Auguſt. Having ſteered North Weſt along the iſlands which lie ſcattered before the mouths of the Lena, he found himſelf in lat. 70° 4'. He ſaw much ice to the North and North Eaſt ; and obſerved ice-mountains from twenty-four to ſixty feet in height. He ſteered betwixt the ice, which in no place left a free channel of greater breadth than an hundred or two hundred yards. The veſſel being much damaged, on the 1ſt of September he ran up the mouth of the Olenek, which, according to his eſtimation, lies in 72° 30', near which place he paſſed the winter †.

He got out of the Olenek the beginning of Auguſt in the following year ; and arrived

* S. R. G. III. p. 145 to 149.
† Gmelin Reiſe, II. 425 to 427.

on the third at the mouth of the Anabara, which he found to lie in lat. 73° 1′. There he continued until the 10th, while fome of the crew reconnoitred the country in fearch of fome mines. On the 10th he proceeded on his voyage : before he reached the mouth of the Katanga, he was fo entirely furrounded and hemmed in with ice, that it was not without great difficulty and danger he was able to get loofe. He then obferved a large field of ice ftretching into the fea, on which account he was obliged to continue near the fhore, and to run up the Khatanga. The mouth of this river was in lat. 74° 9′. From thence he bent his courfe moftly Northward along the fhore, until he reached the mouth of the Taimura on the 18th. He then proceeded further, and followed the coaft towards the Piafida. Near the fhore were feveral fmall iflands, between which and the land the ice was immovably fixed. He then directed his courfe toward the fea, in order to pafs round the chain of iflands. At firft he found the fea more free to the North of the iflands, while he obferved much ice lying between them. He came at length to the laft ifland, fituated in lat. 77° 25′, between which and

the

the fhore, as well as on its northern fide, the
ice was firm and immovable. He attempted
however to fteer ftill more to the North ; and
having advanced about fix miles, he was prevented by a thick fog from proceeding. This
fog being difperfed, he faw on each fide, and
before him, nothing but ice ; that towards
the fea was not fixed ; but the accumulated
maffes were all fo clofe, that the fmalleft veffel could not have worked its way through.
Still attempting however to pafs to the
North, he was forced by the ice N. E. Apprehenfive of being hemmed in, he returned
to the Taimura ; and from thence got, with
much difficulty and danger, to the Olenek,
on the 29th of Auguft.

   This narrative of the expedition is extracted
from the account of profeffor * Gmelin : according to Mr. Muller †, who has given a
curfory relation of the fame voyage, Pront-
fhiftfhef did not quite reach the mouth of the
Taimura ; for he there found the chain of
iflands ftretching from the continent far into
the fea. The channels between them were
fo choaked with ice, that it was impoffible to
force a paffage : after fteering as high as lat.
77° 25', he found fuch a plain of fixed ice

* Gmelin Reife, vol. II. p. 427 to p. 434.
† S. R. G. III. p. 14), 150.

                                    before

before him, that he had no profpect of getting any farther. Accordingly he returned
to the Olenek.

Another voyage, to pafs from the Lena to
the Yenisèi in 1739, was attempted by Khari-
ton Laptief, with the fame bad fuccefs; and
he relates, that between the rivers Piafida
and Taimura there is a promontory which he
could not double, the fea being entirely
frozen before he could pafs round *.

From all thefe circumftances we muft collect, that the whole fpace between Archangel and the Lena has never yet been navigated; for in going Eaft from the Yenisèi
the Ruffians could get no farther than the
mouth of the Piafida; and, in coming
Weft from the Lena, they were ftopped, according to Gmelin, North of the Piafida; and,
according to Muller, Eaft of the Taimura.

The Ruffians, who fail almoft annually
from Archangel, and other towns, to Nova
Zemla, for the purpofe of catching fea-horfes,
feals, and white bears, make to the Weftern
Coaft; and no Ruffian veffel has ever paffed
round its North Eaftern extremity †.

* Gmelin Reife, p. 440. Mr. Muller fays only, that
Laptief met with the fame obftacles which forced Pront-
fhiftfhef to return. S. R. G. III, p. 150.

† Although this work is confined to the Ruffian Difcoveries, yet as the N. E. paffage is a fubject of fuch interesting

The navigation from the Lena to Kamtchatka now remains to be confidered. If we

may

ing curiofity, it might feem an omiffion in not mentioning,
that feveral Englifh and Dutch veffels have paffed through
the Straits of Weygatz into the fea of Kara : they all met
with great obftructions from the ice, and had much difficulty in getting through. See Hiftoire Gen. des Voyages,
tome XV. paffim.

In 1696 Heemfkirk and Barentz, after having failed
along the Weftern coaft of Nova Zemla, doubled the North
Eaftern cape lying in latitude 77° 20', and got no lower
along the Eaftern coaft than 76°, where they wintered.

See an account of this remarkable voyage in Girard Le
Ver's Vraye Defcription des Trois Voyages de Mer, p. 13
to 45 ; and Hift. Gen. des Voy. tom. XV. p. 111 to 139.

No veffel of any nation has ever paffed round that Cape,
which extends to the North of the Piafida, and is laid down
in the Ruffian charts in about 78° latitude. We have already feen that no Ruffian veffel has ever got from the Piafida to the Katanga, or from the Katanga to the Piafida ;
and yet fome authors have pofitively afferted, that this
promontory has been doubled. In order therefore to elude
the Ruffian accounts, which clearly affert the contrary; it
is pretended, that Gmelin and Muller have purpofely concealed fome parts of the Ruffian journals, and have impofed upon the world by a mifreprefentation of facts. But
without entering into any difpute on this head, I can venture to affirm, that no fufficient proof has been as yet advanced in fupport of this affertion ; and therefore, until
fome pofitive information fhall be produced, we cannot deny
plain facts, or prefer hearfay evidence to circumftantial and
well-attefted accounts.

Mr. Engel has a remarkable paffage in his Effai fur une
route par la Nord Eft, which it may be proper to confider
in this place, becaufe he afferts, in the moft pofitive manner, that two Dutch veffels formerly paffed three hundred
leagues to the North Eaft of Nova Zemla ; from whence

he

may believe fome authors, this navigation has
been open for above a century and an half ;
and

he infers, that they muft have doubled the abovementioned Cape, which extends to the North of the Piafida,
and have got at leaft as far Eaft as the mouth of the Olenek. His words are, L'illuftre Societé Royale, fous l'an
1675, rapporte ce voyage, et dit, que peu d'années aupara-
vant une Societé de merchands d'Amfterdam avoit fait une
tentative pour chercher le paffage du Nord Eft, et équippa
deux vaiffeaux les quels etant paffé au feptante neuf ou hui-
tantieme degré de latitude, avoient poufsé felon Wood,
jufqu' à trois cent lieues à l'Eft de la Novelle Zemble, &c.
&c. Upon this fact he founds his proof that the navigation
from Archangel to the Lena has been performed. Par con-
fequent cette partie de la route a été faite. He refts the
truth of this account on the authority of the Philofophical
Tranfactions, and of Captain Wood, who failed upon a
voyage for the difcovery of the North Eaft paffage in 1676.
The latter, in the relation of his voyage, enumerates feveral arguments which induced him to believe the practicability of the North-Eaft paffage.—"The feventh argument,"
he fays, " was another narration, printed in the Tranf-
" actions, of two fhips of late that had attempted the paf-
" fage, failed 300 leagues to the Eaftward of Nova Zemla,
" and had after profecuted the voyage, had there not a
" difference arofe betwixt the undertakers and the Eaft-
" India company." We here find that Captain Wood refers to the Philofophical Tranfactions for his authority.
The narration printed in the Tranfactions, and which is alluded to by both Captain Wood and Mr. Engel, is to be
found in Vol. IX. of the Philofophical Tranfactions, p. 209,
for December 1674. It confifts of a very curious " Nar-
" rative of fome obfervations made upon feveral voyages,
" undertaken to find a way for failing about the North to
" the Eaft-Indies ; together with inftructions given by
" the Dutch Eaft-India Company for the difcovery of the
" famous land of Jeffo near Japan." Thefe inftructions
were, in 1643, given to Martin Geritfes Vries, captain of
the

and feveral veffels have at different times
paffed round the North Eaftern extremity of
Afia.

the fhip Caftricum, " who fet out to difcover the unknown
" Eaftern coaft of Tartary, the kingdom of Kata, and the
" Weft coaft of America, together with the ifles fituate
" to the Eaft of Japan, cried up for their riches of gold
" and filver." Thefe inftructions contain no relation of
two Dutch veffels, which paffed 300 leagues Eaft of Nova
Zemla.   Mention is indeed made of two Dutch veffels,
" who were fent out in the year 1639, under the command
" of Captain Kwaft, to difcover the Eaft coaft of the Great
" Tartary, efpecially the famous gold and filver iflands ;
" though, by reafon of feveral unfortunate accidents,
" they both returned re infectâ." Short mention is afterwards made of Captain Kwaft's journal, together with the
writings of the merchants who were with him, as follows :
" That in the South Sea, at the 37½ degrees Northern
" latitude, and about 400 Spanifh, or 343 Dutch miles,
" that is, 28 degrees longitude Eaft of Japan, there lay a
" very great and high ifland, inhabited by a white, hand-
" fome, kind, and civilized people, exceedingly opulent in
" gold and filver, &c. &c."
    From thefe extracts it appears, that, in the fhort ac-
count of the journals of the two Dutch veffels, no longitude is mentioned to the Eaft of Nova Zemla ; but the difcoveries of Kwaft were made in the South fea, to which
place he, as well as Captain Vries afterwards, muft have
failed round the Cape of Good Hope. The author of the
narrative concludes indeed, that the N. E. paffage is practicable, in the following words : " To promote this paffage
" out of the Eaft-Indies to the North into Europe, it were
" neceffary to fail from the Eaft-Indies to the Weftward of
" Japan, all along Corea, to fee how the fea-coafts tend to
" the North of the faid Corea, and with what conveniency
" fhips might fail as far as Nova Zemla, and to the North
" of the fame.   Where our author faith, that undoubtedly
" it would be found, that having paffed the North corner
" of Nova Zemla, or, through Weygatz, the North end
" of Yelmer land, one might go on South-Eaftward, and
                                            " make

Afia. But if we confult the Ruffian accounts, we fhall find, that frequent expeditions have been unqueftionably made from the Lena to the Kovyma ; but that the voyage from the Kovyma round Tfchukotfkoi Nofs, into the Eaftern ocean, has been performed but once. According to Mr. Muller, this formidable cape was doubled in the year 1648. The material incidents of this remarkable voyage are as follow * :

" In 1648 feven kotches or veffels failed from the mouth of the river Kovyma +, in order to penetrate into the Eaftern Ocean. Of thefe, four were never more heard of ;

" make a fuccefsful voyage." But mere conjectures cannot be admitted as evidence. As we can find no other information relative to the fact mentioned by Captain Wood and Mr. Engel, (namely,, that two Dutch veffels have paffed 300 leagues to the Faft of Nova Zemla), we have no reafon to credit mere affertions without proof : we may therefore advance as a fact, that hitherto we have no authentic account, that any veffel has ever paffed the cape to the Eaft of Nova Zemla, which lies North of the river Piafida. See Relation of Wood's Voyage, &c. in the Account of feveral late Voyages and Difcoveries to the South and North, &c. London, 1694, p. 148. See alfo Engel, Mem. et Obf. Geo. p. 231—234.

* I fhould not have fwelled my book with this extract, if the Englifh tranflation of Mr. Muller's work was not extremely erroneous in fome material paffages. S. R. G. III. p. 8—20.

† Mr. Muller calls it Kolyma.

the

the remaining three were commanded by
Simon Defhnef, Gerafim Ankudinof, two
chiefs of the Coffacs, and Fedot Alexeef, the
head of the Promyfhlenics. Defhnef and
Ankudinof quarrelled before their departure:
this difpute was owing to the jealoufy of
Defhnef, who was unwilling that Ankudinof fhould fhare with him the honour, as
well as the profits, which might refult from
the expected difcoveries. Each veffel was
probably manned with about thirty perfons;
Ankudinof's, we certainly know, carried that
number. Defhnef promifed before-hand a
tribute of feven fables, to be exacted from
the inhabitants on the banks of Anadyr; fo
fanguine were his hopes of reaching that
river. This indeed he finally effected; but
not fo foon, nor with fo little difficulty, as
he had prefumed.

On the 20th of June, 1648, the three veffels failed upon this remarkable expedition
from the river Kovyma. Confidering the
little knowledge we have of the extreme
regions of Afia, it is much to be regretted,
that all the incidents of this voyage are not
circum-

circumftantially related. Defhnef *, in an
account of his expedition fent to Yakutfk,
feems

* In order thoroughly to underftand this narrative, it is
neceffary to inform the reader, that the voyage made by
Defhnef was entirely forgotten until the year 1736, when
Mr. Muller found, in the archives of Yakutfk, the ori-
ginal accounts of the Ruffian navigations in the Frozen
Ocean.

Thefe papers were extracted, under his infpection, at
Yakutfk, and fent to Petersburg ; where they are now preferved in the library belonging to the Imperial Academy
of Sciences: they confift of feveral folio volumes. The
circumftances relating to Defhnef are contained in the fecond
volume. Soliverftof and Stadukin, having laid claim to the
difcovery of the country on the mouth of the Anadyr, had
afferted, in confequence of this claim, that they had arrived there by fea, after having doubled Tfchukotskoi
Nofs. Defhnef, in anfwer, fent feveral memorials, peti-
tions, and complaints, againft Stadukin and Soliverftof,
to the commander of Yakutsk, in which he fets forth, that
he had the fole right to that difcovery, and refutes the arguments advanced by the others. From thefe memorials
Mr. Muller has extracted his account of Defhnef's voyage.
When I was at Peterfburg, I had an opportunity of feeing
thefe papers : and as they are written in the Ruffian language, I prevailed upon my ingenious friend Mr. Pallas to
infpect the part which relates to Defhnef. Accordingly
Mr. Pallas, with his ufual readinefs to oblige, not only
compared the memorials with Mr. Muller's account, but
even took the trouble to make fome extracts from the moft
material parts : thefe extracts are here fubjoined ; becaufe
they will not only ferve to confirm the exactnefs of Mr.
Muller, but alfo becaufe they tend to throw fome light on
feveral obfcure paffages. In one of Defhnef's memorials he
fays, " To go from the river Kovyma to the Anadyr, a
" great promontory muft be doubled, which ftretches
" very far into the fea : it is not that promontory which
" lies next to the river Tfchukotskia. Stadukin never
" arrived at this great promontory : near it are two
                                                " iflands,

feems only as it were accidentally to hint at
his adventures by fea : he takes no notice of
any

" iflands, whofe inhabitants make holes in their under-
" lips, and infert therein pieces of the fea-horfe tufh,
" worked into the form of teeth. This promontory
" ftretches between North and North Eaft : it is known
" on the Ruffian fide by the little river Stanovie, which
" flows into the fea, near the fpot where the Tfchutski
" have erected a heap of whale-bones like a tower. The
" coaft from the promontory turns round towards the
" Anadyr, and it is poffible with a good wind to fail from
" the point to that river in three days and nights : and
" it will take up no more time to go by land to the fame
" river, becaufe it difcharges itfelf into a bay." In another memorial Defhnef fays, " that he was ordered to
" go by fea from the Indigirka to the Kovyma ; and
" from thence with his crew to the Anadyr, which was
" then newly difcovered. That the firft time he failed
" from the Kovyma, he was forced by the ice to return
" to that river ; but that next year he again failed from
" thence by fea, and after great danger, misfortunes,
" and with the lofs of part of his fhipping, arrived at
" laft at the mouth of the Anadyr. Stadukin, having in
" vain attempted to go by fea, afterwards ventured to
" pafs over the chain of mountains then unknown ; and
" reached by that means the Anadyr. Soliverftof and
" his party, who quarrelled with Defhnef, went to the
" fame place from the Kovyma by land ; and the tribute
" was afterwards fent to the laft mentioned river acrofs
" the mountains, which were very dangerous to pafs
" amidft the tribes of Koriacs and Yukagirs, who had
" been lately reduced by the Ruffians."
    In another memorial Defhnef complains bitterly of So-
liverftof ; and afferts, " that one Severka Martemyanof,
" who had been gained over by Soliverftof, was fent to
" Yakutsk, with an account that he (Soliverftof) had dif-
" covered the coafts to the North of the Anadyr, where
" large numbers of fea-horfes are found." Defhnef here-
upon

any occurrence untill he reached the great promontory of the Tſchutſki; he mentions no obſtructions from the ice, and probably there were none; for he obſerves, upon another occaſion, that the ſea is not every year ſo free from ice as it was at this time. He commences his narrative with a deſcription of the great promontory : " It is," ſays he, " very different from that which " is ſituated Weſt of the Kovyma, near the " river Tſchukotſkia. It lies between North " and North Eaſt, and bends, in a circular " direction, towards the Anadyr. It is diſtin- " guiſhed on the Ruſſian (namely, the Weſ- " tern) ſide by a rivulet which falls into " the ſea, cloſe to which the Tſchutſki " have raiſed a pile, like a tower, with the " bones of whales. Oppoſite the promon- " tory (it is not ſaid on which ſide) are two

upon ſays, " that Soliverſtof and Stadukin never reached " the rocky promontory, which is inhabited by numerous " bodies of the Tſchutſki ; over-againſt which are iſlands " whoſe inhabitants wear artificial teeth thruſt through " their under lips. This is not the firſt promontory from " the river Kovyma, called Svatoi Noſs ; but another far " more conſiderable, and verywell known to him (Deſhnef), " becauſe the veſſel of Ankudinof was wrecked there, and " becauſe he had there taken priſoners ſome of the pſople " who were rowing in their boats ; and ſeen the iſlanders " with teeth in their lips. He alſo well knew, that it was " ſtill far from that promontory to the river Anadyr."

" iſlands,

" iflands, on which he obferved people of
" the nation of the Tfchutfki, who had
" pieces of the fea horfe tooth thruft into
" holes made in their lips. With a good wind
" it is poffible to fail from this promontory to
" the Anadyr in three days ; and the jour-
" ney by land may be performed in the fame
" fpace of time, becaufe the Anadyr falls
" into a bay." Ankudinof's kotche was
wrecked on this promontory, and the crew
was diftributed on board the two remaining
veffels. On the 20th of September, Defhnef and Fedot Alexeef went on fhore, and
had a fkirmifh with the Tfchutfki, in which
Alexeef was wounded. The two veffels foon
afterwards loft fight of each other, and never
again rejoined. Defhnef was driven by tempeftuous winds until October, when he was
fhipwrecked (as it appears from circumftances)
confiderably to the South of the Anadyr,
not far from the river Olutora. What became of Fedot Alexeef and his crew will
be mentioned hereafter. Defhnef and his
companions, who amounted to twenty-five
perfons, now fought for the Anadyr ; but
being entirely unacquainted with the country,
ten weeks elapfed before they reached its
banks

banks at a small distance from its mouth: here he found neither wood nor inhabitants, &c.

The following year he went further up the river, and built Anadirskoi Ostrog: here he was joined by some Russians on the 25th of April, 1650, who came by land from the river Kovyma. In 1652, Deshnef having constructed a vessel, sailed down the Anadyr as far as its mouth, and observed on the North side a sand bank, which stretched a considerable way into the sea. A sand bank of this kind is called, in Siberia, Korga. Great numbers of sea-horses were found to resort to the mouth of the Anadyr. Deshnef collected several of their teeth, and thought himself amply compensated by this acquisition for the trouble of his expedition. In the following year, Deshnef ordered wood to be felled for the purpose of constructing a vessel, in which he proposed sending the tribute which he had collected .by sea to Yakutsk *. But this design was laid aside from the want of other materials. It was also reported,

* That is, by sea, from the mouth of the Anadyr, round Tschukotskoi Nofs to the river Lena, and then up that river to Yakutsk.

that

that the fea about Tfchukotfkoi Nofs was not
every year free from ice.

Another expedition was made in 1654 to
the Korga, for the purpofe of collecting fea-
horfe teeth.   A Coffac, named Yufko Soliverftof, was one of the party, the fame who
not long before had accompanied the Coffac
Michael Stadukin, upon a voyage of difcovery in the Frozen Sea.   This perfon was
fent from Yakutfk to collect fea-horfe teeth,
for the benefit of the crown.   In his inftructions mention is made of the river Yentfhen-
don, which falls into the bay of Penfhinfk,
and of the Anadyr ; and he was ordered to
exact a tribute from the inhabitants dwelling
near thefe rivers ; for the adventures of Defhnef were not as yet known at Yakutsk.
This was the occafion of new difcontents.
Soliverftof claimed to himfelf the difcovery
of the Korga, as if he had failed to that
place in his voyage with Stadukin in 1649.
Defhnef, however, proved that Soliverftof
had not even reached Tfchukotskoi Nofs,
which he defcribes as nothing but bare rock,
and it was but too well known to him, becaufe the veffel of Ankudinof was fhipwrecked
there.   "Tfchukotski Nofs," adds Defhnef,

nef, " is not the firft promontory * which
" prefents itfelf under the name of Svatoi
" Nofs. It is known by the two iflands
" fituated oppofite to it, whofe inhabitants
" (as is before-mentioned) place pieces of
" the fea-horfe tufh into holes made in their
" lips. Defhnef alone had feen thefe peo-
" ple, which neither Stadukin nor Soliver-
" ftof had pretended to have done : and the
" Korga, or fand-bank, at the mouth of the
" river Anadyr, was at fome diftance from
" thefe iflands'."

While Defhnef was furveying the fea-
coaft, he faw in an habitation belonging to
fome Koriacs a woman of Yakutfk, who,

* We may collect from Defhnef's reafoning, that Soliverftof, in endeavouring to prove that he had failed round
the Eaftern extremity of Afia, had miftaken a promontory
called Svatoi Nofs for Tfchukotskoi Nofs : for otherwife,
why fhould Defhnef, in his refutation of Soliverftof, begin
by afferting, that Svatoi Nofs was not Tfchukotskoi Nofs ?
The only cape laid down in the Ruffian maps, under the
name of Svatoi Nofs, is fituated 25 degrees to the Weft
of the Kovyma ; but we cannot poffibly fuppofe this to
be the promontory here alluded to ; becaufe, in failing
from the Kovyma towards the Anadyr, " the firft promon-
" tory which prefents itfelf" muft neceffarily be Eaft of the
Kovyma. Svatoi Nofs, in the Ruffian language, fignifies
Sacred Promontory ; and the Ruffians occafionally apply
it to any cape, which it is difficult to double. It therefore moft probably here relates to the firft cape, which
Soliverftof reached after he had failed from Kovyma.

as

as he recollected, belonged to Fedot Alexeef. Upon his enquiry concerning the fate of her master, she replied, " that Fedot and Gera- " sim (Ankudinof) had died of the scurvy ; " that part of the crew had been slain ; that " a few had escaped in small vessels, and " have never since been heard of." Traces of the latter were afterwards found in the peninsula of Kamtchatka ; to which place they probably arrived with a favourite wind, by following the coast, and running up the Kamtchatka river.

When Vladimir Atlassof, in 1697, first attempted the reduction of Kamtchatka, he found that the inhabitants had previous knowledge of the Russians. A common tradition still prevails amongst them, that, long before the expedition of Atlassof, one * Fedotof (who was probably the son of Fedot Alexeef) and his companions had resided amongst them, and had intermarried with the natives. They still shew the spot where the Russian habitations stood ; namely, at the mouth of the small river Nikul, which falls into the Kamtchatka river, and is called by the Russians Fedotika. Upon Atlassof's

* Fedotof, in the Russian language, signifies the son of Fedot.

arrival

arrival none of the firſt Ruſſians remained. They are ſaid to have been held in great veneration, and almoſt deified by the inhabitants, who at firſt imagined that no human power could hurt them ; until they quarreled amongſt themſelves, and the blood was ſeen to flow from the wounds which they gave each other : and upon a ſeparation taking place between the Ruſſians, part of them had been killed by the Koriacs, as they were going to the ſea of Penſhinſk, and the remainder by the Kamtchadals. The river Fedotika falls into the Southern ſide of the Kamtchatka river about an hundred and eighty verſts below Upper Kamtchatkoi Oſtrog. At the time of the firſt expedition to Kamtchatka, in 1697, the remains of two villages ſtill ſubſiſted, which had probably been inhabited by Fedotof and his companions : and no one knew which way they came into the peninſula, until it was diſcovered from the archives of Yakutſk in 1636."

* No other navigator, ſubſequent to Deſhnef, has ever pretended to have paſſed the

* Mr. Engel indeed pretends that lieutenant Laptieff, in 1739, doubled Tſchukotskoi-Noſs, becauſe Gmelin ſays,
that

North Eaftern extremity of Afia, notwithftanding all the attempts to accomplifh this
paffage, as well from * Kamtchatka, as from
the Frozen Ocean.

The

that " he paffed from the Kovyma to Anadirfk partly by
" water and partly by land." For Mr. Engel afferts the
impoffibility of getting from the Kovyma to Anadirfk, partly
by land and partly by water, without going from the Kovyma
to the mouth of the Anadyr by fea, and from thence to Anadirsk by land. But Mr. Muller (who has given a more particular account of the conclufion of this expedition) informs us, that Laptief and his crew, after having wintered near the Indigirka, paffed from its mouth in fmall
boats to the Kovyma ; and as it was dangerous, on account of the Tfchutski, to follow the coaft any farther,
either by land or water, he went through the interior part
of the country to Anadirsk, and from thence to the mouth
of the Anadyr. Gmelin Reife, vol. II. p. 440. S. R. G.
III. p. 157.

Mention is alfo made by Gmelin of a man who paffed
in a fmall boat from the Kovyma round Tfcukotskoi-Nofs
into the fea of Kamtchatka ; and Mr. Engel has not
omitted to bring this paffage in fupport of his fyftem, with
this difference, that he refers to the authority of Muller,
inftead of Gmelin, for the truth of the fact. But as we
have no account of this expedition, and as the manner in
which it is mentioned by Gmelin implies that he had it
merely from tradition, we cannot lay any ftrefs upon fuch
vague and uncertain reports. The paffage is as follows :
" Es find fo gar Spuren vorhanden, dafs ein Kerl mit einem
" Schifflein, das nicht viel groeffer als ein Schifferkahn
" gevefen, von Kolyma bis Tfchukotski-Nofs vorbey, und
" bis nach Kamtfchatka gekommen fey." Gmelin Reife
II. p. 437. Mem. et Obf. Geog. &c. p. 10.

    * Beering, in his voyage from Kamtchatka, in 1628,
towards Tfchukotskoi-Nofs, failed along the coaft of the
Tfchutski as high as lat. 67°. 18'. and obferving the coaft
take a Wefterly direction, he too haftily concluded, that
he

The following narrative of a late voyage, performed by one Shalaurof, from the Lena towards Tfchukotfki-Nofs, will fhew the great impediments which obftruct a coafting navigation in the Frozen Sea, even at the moft favourable feafon of the year.

Shalaurof, a Ruffian merchant of Yakutfk, having conftructed a fhitik at his own expence, went down the Lena in 1761 *. He was accompanied by an exiled midfhipman, whom he found at Yakutfk, and to whom we are indebted for the chart of this expedition. Shalaurof got out of the Southern mouth of the Lena in July, but was fo much embarraffed by the ice, that he ran the veffel into the mouth of the Yana, where he was

he had paffed the North Eaftern extremity. Apprehenfive, if he had attempted to proceed, of being locked in by the ice, he returned to Kamtchatka. If he had followed the fhore, he would have found that what he took for the Northern ocean was nothing more than a deep bay ; and that the coaft of the Tfchutski, which he confidered as turning uniformly to the Weft, took again a Northerly direction. S. R. G. III. p. 117.

* According to another MS. account of Shalaurof's voyage, which I have in my poffeffion, he is faid to have fet out upon this expedition in 1760 ; and was prevented by the continued drifts of floating ice, which the Northerly winds drove towards the fhore, from penetrating that year any further than the mouth of the Yana, where he wintered. In 1761, he put to fea on the 29th of July, paffed Svatoi-Nofs, &c &c.

detained

detained by the ice until the 29th of Auguft,
when he again fet fail. Being prevented by
the ice from keeping the open fea, he coafted
the fhore ; and, having doubled Svatoi-Nofs
on the 6th of September, difcovered at a fmall
diftance at Sea, to the North, a mountainous
land, which is probably fome unknown ifland,
in the Frozen Ocean. He was employed
from the 7th to the 15th in getting through
the ftrait between Diomed's ifland and the
coaft of Siberia ; which he effected, not without great difficulty. From the 16th he had
a free fea and a fair S. W. wind, which carried him in 24 hours beyond the mouth of
the Indigirka. The favourable breeze continuing, he paffed on the 18th the Alafca.
Soon afterwards, the veffel approaching too
near the fhore was entangled amongft vaft
floating maffes of ice, between fome iflands *
and the main land. And now the late feafon

* Thefe iflands are Medviedkie Oftrova, or the Bear
Iflands ; they are alfo called Krefftofskie Oftrova, becaufe
they lie oppofite the mouth of the fmall river Kreftova.
For a long time vague reports were propagated that the
continent of America ftretched along the Frozen Ocean,
very near the coafts of Siberia ; and fome perfons pretended
to have difcovered its fhore not far from the rivers Kovyma
and Kreftova. But the falfity of thefe reports was proved
by

fon of the year obliging Shalaurof to look out
for a wintering place, he ran the veffel into
one of the mouths of the river Kovyma,
where fhe was laid up. The crew immediately conftructed an hut, which they fecured with a rampart of frozen fnow, and a
battery of fmall guns. Wild rein-deer reforted to this place in large herds, and were
fhot in great plenty from the enclofure. Before the fetting-in of winter, various fpecies
of falmon and trout afcended the river in
fhoals; affording to the crew a plentiful fubfiftence, and preferving them from the
fcurvy *.

The mouth of the Kovyma was not freed
from ice before the 21ft of July, 1762, when

by an expedition made in 1764, by fome Ruffian officers
fent by Denys Ivanovitch Tfchitcherin, governor of Tobolsk. Thefe officers went in winter, when the fea was
frozen, in fledges drawn by dogs, from the mouth of the
Kreftova. They found nothing but five fmall rocky iflands,
fince called the Bear Iflands, which were quite uninhabited;
but fome traces were found of former inhabitants, namely,
the ruins of huts. They obferved alfo on one of the iflands
a kind of wooden ftage built of drift wood, which feemed
as if it had been intended for defence. As far as they
durft venture out over the Frozen Sea, no land could be
feen; but high mountains of ice obftructed their paffage,
and forced them to return. See the map of this expedition upon the chart of Shalaurof's voyage.

* Raw fifh are confidered in thofe Northern countries
as a prefervative againft the fcurvy.

Shalaurof

Shalaurof again put to fea, and fteered until the
28th N. E. by N. E. ¼ E.   Here he obferved
the variation of the compafs afhore, and
found it to be 11° 15″ Eaft.   The 28th
a contrary wind, which was followed by
calm, obliged him to come to an anchor, and
kept him ftationary until the 10th of Auguft,
when a favourable breeze fpringing up, he
fet fail.   He then endeavoured to fteer at
fome diftance from fhore, holding a more
Eafterly courfe, and   N. E. by E ;   but the
veffel was impeded by large bodies of floating ice, and a ftrong current, which feemed
to bear Weftward at the rate of a verft an
hour.   Thefe circumftances very much retarded his courfe.   On the 18th, the weather being thick and foggy, he found himfelf unexpectedly near the coaft with a number of ice iflands before him, which on the
19th entirely furrounded and hemmed in the
veffel.   He continued in that fituation, and
in a continual fog, until the 23d, when he
got clear, and endeavoured by fteering N. E.
to regain the open fea, which was much lefs
clogged with ice than near the fhore.   He
was forced, however, by contrary winds,
S. E. and E. among large maffes of floating
ice.

ice. This drift of ice being paffed, he again ftood to the N. E. in order to double She-latſkoi-Nofs *; but before he could reach the iflands lying near it, he was ſo retarded by contrary winds, that he was obliged, on account of the advanced feafon, to fearch for a wintering place. He accordingly failed South towards an open bay, which lies on the Weſt fide of Shelatſkoi-Nofs, and which no navigator had explored before him. He fteered into it on the 25th, and got upon a fhoal between a ſmall ifland, and a point of land which juts from the Eaftern coaft of this bay. Having got clear with much difficulty, he continued for a fhort time a S. E. courfe, then turned S. W. He then landed in order to difcover a fpot proper for their winter refidence; and found two ſmall rivulets, but neither trees nor drift-wood. The veffel was towed along the Southerly fide of the bay as far as the ifland Sabedèi. On the 5th of September, he faw fome huts of the Tfchut-

---

* He does not feem to have been deterred from proceeding by any ſuppofed difficulty in paffing Shelatſkoi-Nofs, but to have veered about merely on account of the late feafon of the year. Shelatſkoi-Nofs is fo called from the Shelagen, a tribe of the Tfchutski, and has been ſuppofed to be the fame as Tfchukotski-Nofs. S. R. G. III. p. 52.

fki

fki clofe to the narrow channel between Sabadèi and the main land ; but the inhabitants
fled on his approach.

Not having met with a proper fituation,
he ftood out to fea, and got round the ifland
Sabadèi on the 8th, when he faftened the
veffel to a large body of ice, and was carried along by a current towards W. S. W. at
the rate of five verfts an hour.   On the 1cth,
he faw far to the N. E. by N. a mountain,
and fteered the 11th and 12th towards his
former wintering place in the river Kovyma.
Shalaurof propofed to have made the following year another attempt to double Shelat-
fkoi-Nofs ; but want of provifion, and the
mutiny of the crew, forced him to return to
the Lena in 1763.   It is worth remarking,
that during his whole voyage he found the
currents fetting in almoft uniformly from
the Eaft.   Two remarkable rocks were obferved by Shalaurof near the point where the
coaft turns to the N. E. towards the channel
which feparates the ifland Sabadèi from the
continent ; thefe rocks may ferve to direct
future navigators : one is called Saetfhie
Kamen, or Hare's Rock, and rifes like a
crooked horn ; the other Baranèi Kamen, or
                                       Sheep's

Sheep's Rock ; it is in the fhape of a pear, narrower at the bottom than at top, and rifes twenty-nine yards above high-water mark.

Shalaurof, concluding from his own experience, that the attempt to double Tfchukotfkoi-Nofs, though difficult, was by no means impracticable, and not difcouraged by his former want of fuccefs from engaging a fecond time in the fame enterprize, fitted out the fame fhitik, and in 1764 departed as before from the river Lena. We have no pofitive accounts of this fecond voyage : for neither Shalaurof nor any of his crew have ever returned. The following circumftances lead us to conclude, that both he and his crew were killed near the Anadyr by the Tfchutfki, about the third year after their departure from the Lena. About that time the Koriacs of the Anadyr refufed to take from the Ruffians the provifion of flour, which they are accuftomed to purchafe every year. Inquiry being made by the governor of Anadirfk, he found that they had been amply fupplied with that commodity by the Tfchutfki. The latter had probably procured it from the plunder of Shalaurof's veffel, the crew of
whicn

which appeared to have perished near the
Anadyr. From these facts, which have been
since confirmed by repeated intelligence
from the Koriacs and Tschutski, it has been
afferted, that Shalaurof had doubled the N.
E. cape of Afia. But this affertion amounts
only to conjecture; for the arrival of the
crew at the mouth of the Anadyr affords
no decifive proof that they had paffed round
the Eaftern extremity of Afia; for they
might have penetrated to that river by land,
from the Weftern fide of Tfchukotfkoi-
Nofs.

In reviewing thefe feveral accounts of the
Ruffian voyages in the Frozen Sea, as far
as they relate to a North Eaft paffage, we
may obferve, that the cape which ftretches
to the North of the Piafida has never been
doubled; and that the exiftence of a paffage
round Tfchukotfkoi-Nofs refts upon the fingle
authority of Defhnef. Admitting however
a practicable navigation round thefe two promontories; yet, when we confider the difficulties and dangers which the Ruffians encountered in thofe parts of the Frozen Sea
which they have unqueftionably failed
through,

through, how much time they employed in making an inconfiderable progrefs, and how often their attempts were unfuccefsful ; when we reflect, at the fame time, that thefe voyages can only be performed in the midft of a fhort fummer, and even then only when particular winds drive the ice into the fea, and leave the fhores lefs obftructed ; we fhall reafonably conclude, that a navigation, purfued along the coafts in the Frozen Ocean, would probably be ufelefs for commercial purpofes.

A navigation therefore in the Frozen Ocean, calculated to anfwer any end of general utility, muft (if poffible) be made in an higher latitude, at fome diftance from the fhores of Nova Zemla and Siberia. And fhould we even grant the poffibility of failing N. E. and Eaft of Nova Zemla, without meeting with any infurmountable obftacles from land or ice ; yet the final completion of a N. E. voyage muft depend upon the exiftence of a free paffage * between the coaft

* I have faid a *free paffage*, becaufe if we conclude from the narrative of Defhnef's voyage, that there really does exift fuch a paffage ; yet, if that paffage is only occafionlly navigable (and the Ruffians do not pretend to have paffed it more than once), it can never be of any general and commercial utility.

of

of the Tſchutſki and the continent of America.
But ſuch diſquiſitions as theſe do not fall
under the intention of this work, which is
meant to ſtate and examine facts, not to lay
down an hypotheſis, or to make theoretical
enquiries *.

* I beg leave to aſſure the reader, that throughout this
whole work I have entirely confined myſelf to the Ruſſian
accounts ; and have carefully avoided making uſe of any
vague reports concerning the diſcoveries lately made by
captains Cooke and Clerke in the ſame ſeas. Many of
the geographical queſtions, which have been occaſionally
treated in the courſe of this performance, will probably
be cleared up, and the true poſition of the Weſtern coaſts
of America aſcertained, from the journals of thoſe experienced navigators.

PART

PART III.

CONTAINING

THE CONQUEST OF SIBERIA;

AND

THE HISTORY

OF THE

TRANSACTIONS AND COMMERCE

BETWEEN RUSSIA AND CHINA.

CHAP

CHAP. I.

First irruption of the Ruffians *into* Siberia—
fecond inroad—Yermac, *driven by the Tzar
of* Mufcovy *from the* Volga, *retires to* Orel,
a Ruffian *fettlement*—*Enters* Siberia, *with
an army of* Coffacs—*his progrefs and exploits
—Defeats* Kutchum Chan—*conquers his dominions—cedes them to the Tzar—receives a
reinforcement of* Ruffian *troops—is furprized
by* Kutchum Chan—*his defeat and death—
veneration paid to his memory—*Ruffian *troops
evacuate* Siberia—*re-enter and conquer the
whole country—their progrefs ftopped by the*
Chinefe.

SIBERIA was fcarcely known to the
Ruffians before the middle of the fixteenth century *: for although an expedition was made, under the reign of Ivan Vaffilievitch I. into the North-Weftern Parts of
that country, as far as the river Oby, by
which feveral Tartar tribes were rendered
tributary, and fome of their chiefs brought

* S. R. G. VI. p. 119—211. Fif. Sib. Gef. Tom. I.

prifoners

prifoners to Mofcow ; yet this incurfion bore
a greater refemblance to the defultory inroads of barbarians, than to any permanent
eftablifhment of empire by a civilized nation.
Indeed, the effects of that expedition foon va-
nifhed ; nor does any trace of the leaft fubfequent communication with Siberia appear
in the Ruffian hiftory before the reign of
Ivan Vaffilievitch II. At that period Siberia
again became an object of attention, by
means of one Anika Strogonof, a Ruffian
merchant, who had eftablifhed fome falt-
works at Solvytfhegodfkaia, a town in the
government of Archangel.

Strogonof carried on a trade of barter with
the inhabitants of the North-Weftern parts
of Siberia, who brought every year to the
abovementioned town large quantities of the
choiceft furs. Upon their return to their
country, he was accuftomed to fend with
them fome Ruffian merchants, who croffed
the mountains, and traded with the natives.
By thefe means a confiderable number of
very valuable furs were procured at an eafy
rate, in exchange for toys and other commodities of trifling value. This traffick was continued for feveral years, without any interruption;
during

during which Strogonof rapidly amaſſed a very conſiderable fortune *. At length the Tzar Ivan Vaſſilievitch II. foreſeeing the advantages which would accrue to his ſubjects, from eſtabliſhing a more general and regular commerce with theſe people, determined to enlarge the communication already opened with Siberia. Accordingly he ſent a body of troops into that country. They followed the ſame route which had been diſcovered by the Ruſſians in the former expedition; and which was lately frequented by the merchants of Solvytſhegodſkaia. It lay along the banks of the Petſchora, and from thence croſſed the Yugorian mountains, which form the North-Eaſtern boundary of Europe. Theſe troops, however, do not ſeem to have paſſed the Irtiſh, or to have penetrated further than the Weſtern branch of the river Oby. Some Tartar tribes were indeed laid under contribution; and a chief, whoſe name was Yediger, conſented to pay an annual tribute of a thouſand ſables. But this expedition was not productive of any laſting effects; for ſoon afterwards Yediger was defeated,

* S. R. G. VI. p. 220—223. Fiſ. Sib. Gef. p. 182.

and

and taken prifoner by Kutchum Chan, a
lineal defcendant of the celebrated Zinghis
Chan, who had newly eftablifhed his empire
in thofe parts.

This fecond inroad was probably made
about the middle of the fixteenth century ;
for the Tzar Ivan Vaffilievitch affumed the
title of Lord of all the Siberian lands fo early
as 1558, before the conquefts of Yermac in
thofe regions *. But probably the name of
Siberia was at that time only confined to the
diftrict then rendered tributary ; and, as the
Ruffians extended their conquefts, this appellation was afterwards applied to the whole
tract of country which now bears that
name.

For fome time after the above-mentioned
expedition, the Tzar does not appear to have
made any attempts towards recovering his
loft authority in fo remote a country. But
his attention was again turned to that quarter
by a concurrence of incidents ; which, though
begun without his immediate interpofition,
terminated in a vaft acceffion of territory.

Strogonof, in recompence for having firft
opened a trade with the inhabitants of Si-

* S. R. G. VI. p. 217.

beria,

beria, obtained from the Tzar large grants of land. Accordingly he founded colonies upon the banks of the rivers Kama and Tchuffovaia ; and thefe fettlements gave rife to the entire fubjection of Siberia by the re- fuge which they not long afterwards afforded to Yermac Timofeef, a fugitive Coffac of the Don, and chief of a troop of banditti who infefted the fhores of the Cafpian fea. And as Yermac was the inftrument by which fuch a vaft extent of dominion was added to the Ruffian Empire, it will not be uninterefting to follow him from the fhores of the Cafpian to the banks of the Kama ; and to trace his fubfequent progrefs in the diftant regions of Siberia.

By the victories which the Tzar Ivan Vaffilievitch had gained over the Tartars of Cafan and Aftracan, that monarch extended his dominions as far as the Cafpian Sea ; and thereby eftablifhed a commerce with the Per- fians and Bucharians. But as the mer- chants trading to thofe parts were continually pillaged by the Coffacs of the Don ; and as the roads which lay by the fide of that river, and of the Volga, were infefted with thofe

thofe banditti ; the Tzar fent a confiderable force againft them. Accordingly, they were attacked and routed ; part were flain, part made prifoners ; and the reft efcaped by flight : among the latter was a corps of fix thoufand Coffacs, under the command of Yermac Timofeef *.

This celebrated adventurer, being driven from his ufual haunts, retired with his followers into the interior part of the province of Cafan ; and directed his courfe along the banks of the Kama, until he reached Orel †, one of the Ruffian fettlements recently planted, and governed by Maxim grandfon of Anika Strogonof. Yermac, inftead of ftorming the place, and pillaging the inhabitants, acted with a degree of moderation unufual in a chief of banditti. Being hofpitably received by Strogonof, and fupplied with all things neceffary for the fubfiftence of his troops, he fixed his winter quarters at that fettlement. His reftlefs genius however did not fuffer him to continue for any length of time in a ftate of inactivity ; and, from the intelligence he procured concerning the fitua-

* S. R. G. VI. p. 232. Fif. Sib. Gef. I. p. 185.
† S. R. G. VI. p. 233.

tion

tion of the neighbouring Tartars of Siberia,.
he turned his arms toward that quarter.

Siberia was at that time partly divided
among a number of feparate princes ; and
partly inhabited by the various tribes of independent Tartars.   Of the former Kutchum
Chan was the moft powerful Sovereign.   His
dominions comprifed that tract of country
which now forms the South-Weftern part of
the province of Tobolfk ; and ftretched from
the banks of the Irtifh and Oby to thofe of
the Tobol and Tura.   His principal refidence was at Sibir *, a fmall fortrefs upon
the river Irtifh,   not far from the prefent
town of Tobolfk ; and of which fome ruins
ftill remain.   Although his power was very
confiderable ; yet there were fome circumftances which feemed to enfure fuccefs to an

* Several authors have fuppofed the name of Siberia to
derive its origin from this fortrefs, foon after it was firft
taken by the Ruffians under Yermac. But this opinion is advanced without fufficient foundation ; for the name of
Sibir was unknown to the Tartars, that fort being by them
called Isker.   Befides, the Southern part of the province
of Tobolsk, to which the name of Siberia was originally
applied, was thus denominated by the Ruffians before the
invafion of Yermac.   This denomination probably firft
came from the Permians and Sirjanians, who brought the
firft accounts of Siberia to the Ruffians.

S. R. G. VI. p. 180.

enter-

enterprizing invader. He had newly acquired a large part of his territories by conqueſt ; and had, in a great meaſure, alienated
the affections of his idolatrous ſubjects by the
intolerant zeal with which he introduced and
diſſeminated the Mahometan religion *.

Strogonof did not fail of diſplaying to
Yermac this inviting poſture of affairs, as well
with a view of removing him from his preſent
ſtation, as becauſe he himſelf was perſonally
exaſperated againſt Kutchum Chan : for the
latter had ſecretly inſtigated a large body of
Tartars to invade the Ruſſian ſettlements
upon the river Tchuſſovaia ; and had afterwards commenced open hoſtilities with a body
of forces under the command of his couſin
Mehemet Kul. And although both theſe attempts had failed of ſucceſs ; yet the troops
engaged in them had left traces of havoc and
devaſtation too laſting to be eaſily effaced †.

All theſe various conſiderations were not
loſt upon Yermac : having therefore employed
the winter in preparations for his intended
expedition, he began his march in the ſummer of the following year, 1578, along the

* S. R. G. VI. p. 180.
† Fiſ. Sib. Geſ. I. p. 187.

banks

banks of the Tchuffovaia. The want of
proper guides, and a neglect of other neceffary precautions, greatly retarded his march ;
and he was overtaken by the winter before he
had made any confiderable progrefs. And
at the appearance of fpring he found his
ftock of provifions fo nearly exhaufted, that he
was reduced to the neceffity of returning to
Orel. But this failure of fuccefs, inftead of ex-
tinguifhing his ardour for the profecution of
the enterprize, only ferved to render him
ftill more folicitous in guarding againft the
poffibility of a future mifcarriage. By threats
he extorted from Strogonof every affiftance
which the nature of the expedition feemed
to require. Befide a fufficient quantity of
provifions, the greateft part of his followers,
who were before unprovided with fire-arms,
were fupplied with mufkets and ammunition ;
and, in order to give the appearance of a
regular army to his troops, colours were
diftributed to each company, which were
ornamented with the images of faints, after
the manner of the Ruffians.

Having thus made all previous arrange-
ments, he found himfelf in a condition to
force his way into Siberia ; and in the month
of

of June, 1579, he commenced this second
expedition. His followers amounted to five
thoufand men ; adventurers inured to hard-
fhips, and regardlefs of danger : they placed
implicit confidence in their leader, and feemed
to be all animated with the fame fpirit. He
continued his route partly by land, and partly
by water : the navigation however of the
rivers was fo tedious, and the roads fo rugged
and difficult, that eighteen months elapfed
before he reached Tchingi, a fmall town upon
the banks of the Tura *. Here he muftered
his troops, and found his army confiderably
reduced : part had been exhaufted by fatigue ;
part carried off by ficknefs ; and part deftroyed in fkirmifhing with the Tartars.
The whole remaining number amounted to
about fifteen hundred effective men ; and
yet with this handful of troops Yermac did
not hefitate for a moment in advancing a-
gainft Kutchum Chan. That prince was
already upon his guard ; and refolved to defend his crown to the laft extremity. Having
collected his forces, he difpatched feveral fly-
ing parties againft Yermac, himfelf remaining behind with the flower of his troops :

* S. R. G. VI. p. 243 – 248—262.

but

but all thefe detachments were repulfed with confiderable lofs; and worfted in many fucceffive fkirmifhes. Yermac continued his march without intermiffion, bearing down all refiftance until he reached the center of his adverfary's dominions.

Thefe fucceffes however were dearly bought; for his army was now reduced to five hundred men. Kutchum Chan was encamped * at no great diftance upon the banks of the Irtifh, with a very fuperior force, and determined to give battle. Yermac, not daunted by the inequality of numbers, prepared for the engagement, with a confidence which never forfook him: his troops were equally impatient for action, and knew no medium between conqueft and death. The event of the combat correfponded with this magnanimity. After an obftinate and well-fought battle, victory declared in favour of Yermac: the Tartars were entirely routed, and the carnage was fo general, that Kutchum Chan himfelf efcaped with difficulty.

* The place where the Tartar army lay encamped was called Tfchuvatch: it is a neck of land wafhed by the Irtifh, near the fpot where the Tobol falls into that river. Fif. Sib. Gef. I. p. 203.

This

This defeat proved decifive : Kutchum Chan was deferted by his fubjects ; and Yermac, who knew how to improve as well as gain a victory, marched without delay to Sibir, the refidence of the Tartar princes. Being well aware, that the only method to fecure his conqueft was to obtain poffeffion of that important fortrefs, he expected to have been oppofed by a confiderable garrifon, determined to facrifice their lives in its defence. But the news of the late defeat had diffufed univerfal confternation ; and a body of troops, whom he had difpatched in order to reduce the fortrefs, finding it quite deferted, he himfelf made his triumphant entry, and feated himfelf upon the throne without the leaft oppofition. Here he fixed his refidence, and received the allegiance of the neighbouring people, who flocked from all quarters upon the news of fo unexpected a revolution. The Tartars, ftruck with his gallant intrepidity and brilliant exploits, fubmitted to his authority without hefitation, and acquiefced in the payment of the ufual tribute.

Thus this enterprifing Coffac was fuddenly exalted, from the ftation of a chief of banditti,

to

to the rank of a fovereign prince. It does not appear from hiftory whether his firft defign was to conquer Siberia, or folely to amafs a confiderable booty. The latter indeed feems the more probable conjecture. The rapid tide of fuccefs with which he was carried on, and the entire defeat of Kutchum Chan, after-wards expanded his views, and opened a larger fcene to his ambition. But, whatever were his original projects, he feems worthy, fo far as intrepidity and prudence form a bafis of merit, of the final fuccefs which flowed in upon him. For he was neither elated with unexpected profperity, nor dazzled with the fudden glare of royalty : on the contrary, the dignity of his deportment was as confiftent and unaf-fected, as if he had been born a fovereign.

And now Yermac and his followers feemed to enjoy thofe rewards which they had dearly purchafed by a courfe of unremitted fatigue, and by victories which almoft exceeded belief. Not only the tribes in the neighbourhood of Sibir wore the appearance of the moft unre-ferved fubmiffion ; but even princes from the moft diftant parts acknowledged themfelves tributary, and claimed his protection. This calm, however, was of fhort duration. In-

furrections

furrections were concerted by Kutchum Chan ; who, though driven from his dominions, yet ftill retained no fmall degree of influence over his former fubjects.

Yermac faw and felt the precarioufnefs of his prefent grandeur : the inconfiderable number of his followers, who had furvived the conqueft of Sibir, had been ftill further diminished by an ambufcade of the enemy ; and, as he could not depend on the affection of his new fubjects, he found himfelf under the neceffity either of calling in foreign affiftance, or of relinquifhing his dominion. Under thefe circumftances he had recourfe to the Tzar of Mufcovy ; and made a tender of his new acquifitions to that monarch, upon condition of receiving immediate and effectual fupport. The judicious manner in which he conducted this meafure fhews him no lefs able in the arts of negotiation than of war.

One of his moft confidential followers was difpatched to Mofcow at the head of fifty Coffacs. He had orders to reprefent the progrefs which the Ruffian troops, under the command of Yermac, had made in Siberia : he was artfully to add, that an extenfive empire was conquered in the name of the Tzar ;
that

that the natives were reduced to fwear allegiance to that monarch ; and confented to pay
an annual tribute. This reprefentation was
accompanied with a prefent of the choiceft and
moft valuable furs *. The embaffador was
received at Mofcow with the ftrongeft marks
of fatisfaction : a public thankfgiving was celebrated in the cathedral ; the Tzar acknowledged and extolled the good fervices of Yermac ; he granted a pardon for all former of-
fences ; and, as a teftimony of royal favour,
diftributed prefents for him and his followers.
Among thofe that were fent to Yermac was a
fur robe, which the Tzar himfelf had worn,
and which was the greateft mark of diftinction
that could be conferred upon a fubject. To
thefe was added a fum of money, and a promife of fpeedy and effectual affiftance.

Meanwhile Yermac, notwithftanding the
inferior number of his troops, did not remain
inactive within the fortrefs of Sibir. He defeated all attempts of Kutchum Chan to recover his crown ; and took his principal general prifoner : he made occafional inroads
into the adjacent provinces, and extended his

* S. R. G. VI. p. 304.

con-

conquests to the source of the Taffda on one side, and on the other as far as the district which lies upon the Oby above its junction with the Irtish.

At length the promised succours arrived at Sibir. They consisted of five hundred Russians, under the command of prince Bolkosky, who was appointed wayvode or governor of Siberia. Strengthened by this reinforcement, Yermac continued his excursions on all sides with his usual activity; and gained several bloody victories over different princes, who imprudently asserted their independence.

In one of these expeditions he laid siege to Kullara, a small fortress upon the banks of the Irtish, which still belonged to Kutchum Chan: but he found it so bravely defended by that monarch, that all his efforts to carry it by storm proved ineffectual. Upon his return to Sibir he was followed at some distance by that prince, who hung unperceived upon his rear; and was prepared to seize any fortunate moment of attack which might occur: nor was it long before a favourable opportunity presented itself. The Russians to the number of about three hundred lay negligently posted

in

in a fmall ifland, formed by two branches of
the Irtifh. The night was obfcure and rainy;
and the troops, fatigued with a long march,
repofed themfelves without fufpicion of danger. Kutchum Chan, apprifed of their fituation, filently advanced at midnight with a
felect body of men; and, having forded the
river, came with fuch rapidity upon the Ruffians, as to preclude the ufe of their arms. In
the darknefs and confufion of the night, the
latter were cut to pieces almoft without oppofition; and fell a refiftlefs prey to thofe ad-
verfaries, whom they had been accuftomed to
conquer and defpife. The maffacre was fo
univerfal, that only one man is recorded to
have efcaped, and to have brought the news
of this cataftrophe to his countrymen at Sibir.

Yermac himfelf perifhed in the rout, though
he did not fall by the fword of the enemy. In
all the hurry of furprife, he was not fo much
infected with the general panic, as to forget
his ufual intrepidity, which feemed to be encreafed rather than abated by the danger of
his prefent fituation. After many defperate
acts of heroifm, he forced his way through
the furrounding troops, and made to the banks
of

of the Irtifh *. Being clofely purfued by a de-
tachment of the enemy, he endeavoured to
throw himfelf into a boat which lay near the
fhore ; but ftepping fhort, he fell into the
water ; and, being incumbered with the
weight of his armour, funk inftantly to the
bottom †.

His body was expofed, by order of Kutchum
Chan, to all the infults, which revenge ever
fuggefted to barbarians in the frenzy of fuccefs. But thefe firft tranfports of refentment

---

* Many difficulties have arifen concerning the branch of
the Irtifh in which Yermac was drowned ; but it is now
fufficiently afcertained that it was a canal, which fome time
before this cataftrophe had been cut by order of that Coffac. Not far from the fpot where the Vagai falls into the
Irtifh, the latter river forms a bend of fix verfts ; by cutting
a canal in a ftraight line from the two extreme points of this
fweep, he fhortened the length of the navigation. S. R. G.
p. 365, 366.

† Cyprian was appointed the firft archbifhop of Siberia
in 1621. Upon his arrival at Tobolfk, he enquired for feveral of the antient followers of Yermac who were ftill alive ;
and from them he made himfelf acquainted with the principal circumftances attending the expedition of that Coffac,
and the conqueft of Siberia. Thofe circumftances he committed to writing ; and thefe papers may be confidered as
the archives of the Siberian hiftory ; from which the feveral hiftorians of that country have drawn their relations.
Sava Yefimof, who was himfelf one of Yermac's followers,
is one of the moft accurate hiftorians of thofe times. He
carries down his hiftory to the year 1636. Fif. Sib. Gef. I.
p. 430.

had

had no fooner fubfided, than the Tartars tef-
tified the moft pointed indignation at the un-
generous ferocity of their leader. The prowefs
of Yermac, his confummate valour and magnanimity, virtues which barbarians know how
to prize, rofe upon their recollection. They
made a fudden tranfition from one extreme to
the other : they reproached their leader for
ordering, and themfelves for being the inftruments of indignity to fuch venerable remains.
At length their heated imaginations proceeded
even to confecrate his memory : they interred
his body with all the rites of Pagan fuperftition ; and offered up facrifices to his manes.

Many miraculous ftories were foon fpread
abroad, and met with implicit belief. The
touch of his body was fuppofed to have proved
an inftantaneous cure for all diforders ; and
even his clothes and arms were faid to be en-
dowed with the fame efficacy. A flame of fire
was reprefented as fometimes hovering about
his tomb, and fometimes as ftretching in one
luminous body from the fame fpot towards the
heavens. A prefiding influence over the affairs
of the chace and of war was attributed to his
departed fpirit ; and numbers reforted to his
tomb to invoke his tutelary aid in concerns fo

in-

interesting to uncivilized nations. These idle fables, though they prove the superstitious credulity of the Tartars, convey at the same time the strongest testimony of their veneration for the memory of Yermac; and this veneration greatly contributed to the subsequent progress of the Russians in those regions *.

With Yermac expired for a time the Russian empire in Siberia. The news of his defeat and death no sooner reached the garrison of Sibir, than a hundred and fifty troops, the sad remains of that formidable army, which had gained such a series of almost incredible victories, retired from the fortress, and evacuated Siberia. Notwithstanding this disaster, the court of Moscow did not abandon its design upon that country; which a variety of favourable circumstances still concurred to render a flattering object of Russian ambition.

* Even so late as the middle of the next century, this veneration for the memory of Yermac had not subsided. Al-lai, a powerful prince of the Calmucs, is said to have been cured of a dangerous disorder, by mixing some earth taken from Yermac's tomb in water, and drinking the infusion. The same is also reported to have carried with him a small portion of the same earth, whenever he engaged in any important enterprize. This earth he superstitiously considered as a kind of charm; and was persuaded that he always secured a prosperous issue to his affairs by such a precaution. S. R. G. VI. p. 391.

Yer-

Yermac's fagacity had difcovered new and commodious routes for the march of troops acrofs thofe inhofpitable regions : the rapidity with which he overran the territories of Kutchum Chan, taught the Ruffians to confider the Tartars as an eafy prey. Many of the tribes, who had been rendered tributary by Yermac, had teflified a chearful acquiefcence under the fovereignty of the Tzar ; and were inclined to renew their allegiance upon the firft opportunity : others looked upon all refiftance as unavailing ; and had learned, from dear-bought experience, to tremble at the very name of a Ruffian. The natural ftrength of the country, which proved not to be irrefiftible even when united, was confiderably weakened by its inteftine commotions. Upon the retreat of the Ruffian garrifon from Sibir, that fortrefs, together with the adjacent diftrict, was feized by Seyidyak, fon of the former fovereign, whom Kutchum Chan had dethroned and put to death : other princes availed themfelves of the general confufion to affert independency ; and Kutchum Chan was able to regain only a fmall portion of thofe dominions, of which he had been ftripped by Yermac.

In-

Influenced by thefe motives, the court o[f] Mofcow difpatched a body of three hundred troops into Siberia, who penetrated to the banks of the Tura as far as Tfchingi almoft without oppofition; and, having built the fort of Tumen, re-eftablifhed their authority over the neighbouring diftrict. Being foon afterwards reinforced by an additional number of men, they were enabled to extend their operations, and to erect the fortreffes of Tobolfk, Sirgut, and Tara. The conftruction of thefe and other fortreffes was foon attended with a fpeedy recovery of the whole territory, which Yermac had reduced under the Ruffian yoke.

This fuccefs was only the fore-runner of ftill greater acquifitions. The Ruffians pufhed their conqueft far and wide: wherever they appeared, the Tartars were either reduced or exterminated; new towns were built; and colonies were planted on all fides. Before a century had well elapfed, all that vaft tract of country now called Siberia, which ftretches from the confines of Europe to the Eaftern Ocean, and from the Frozen Sea to the prefent frontiers of China, was annexed to the Ruffian dominions. A ftill larger extent of

ter-

territory had probably been won ; and all the
various tribes of independent Tartary, which
lie between the South-Eaftern extremity of
the Ruffian empire and the Chinefe Wall,
would have followed the fate of the Siberian
hordes ; if the power of China had not fuddenly interpofed.

C H A P. II.

Commencement of hoftilities between the Ruffians
and Chinefe—*Difputes concerning the limits*
of the two empires—Treaty of Nerfhinfk—
Embaffies from the court of Ruffia *to* Pekin—
Treaty of Kiakta—*Eftablifhment of the com-*
merce between the two nations.

TOWARDS the middle of the feventeenth century the Ruffians were rapidly extending themfelves Eaftward through
that important territory which lies on each
fide of the river * Amoor. They foon reduced feveral independent Tungufian hordes ;
and built a chain of fmall fortreffes along the
banks of the above mentioned river, of which

---

* Amoor is the name given by the Ruffians to this river ;
it is called Sakalin-Ula by the Manfhurs, and was formerly
denominated Karamuran, or the Black River, by the Mongols. S. R. G. II. p. 293.

the

the principal were Albafin, and Kamarſkoi
Oſtrog. Not long afterwards, the Chinefe
under * Camhi conceived a fimilar defign of
fubduing the fame hordes. Accordingly the
two great powers of Ruffia and China, thus
pointing their views to the fame object, unavoidably claſhed ; and, after feveral jealoufies
and intrigues, broke into open hoftilities about
the year 1680. The Chinefe laid fiege to
Kamarſkoi Oſtrog; and, though repulfed in
this attempt, found means to cut off feveral
ſtraggling parties of Ruffians. Thefe animo-
fities induced the Tzar Alexèy Michaelovitch
to fend an embaffy to Pekin ; a meafure,

* Camhi was the fecond emperor of the Manſhur race,
who made themfelves maſters of China in 1624.
The Manſhurs were originally an obfcure tribe of the
Tungufian Tartars, whofe territories lay South of the
Amoor, and bordered upon the kingdom of Corea, and the
province of Leaotong. They began to emerge from ob-
fcurity at the beginning of the feventeenth century. About
that time, their chief Aifchin-Giord reduced feveral neighbouring hordes ; and, having incorporated them with his
own tribe, under the general name of Manſhur, he became
formidable even to the Chinefe. Shuntſchi, grandfon of
this chief, by an extraordinary concurrence of circumftances,
was raifed while an infant to the throne of China, of which
his fucceffors ftill continue in poffeffion. Shuntſchi died in
1662, and was fucceeded by Camhi, who is well known from
the accounts of the Jefuit miffionaries.
For an account of the revolution of China, fee Duhalde
Defcr. de la Chine, Bell's Journey to Pekin, and Fif. Sib.
Gef. tom. I. p. 463.

which

which did not produce the defired effect. The Chinefe attacked Albafin with a confiderable force : having compelled the Ruffian garrifon to capitulate, they demolifhed that and all the Ruffian forts upon the Amoor; and returned, with a large number of prifoners, to their own country.

Not long after their departure, a body of fixteen hundred Ruffians advanced along the Amoor; and conftructed a new fort, under the old name of Albafin. The Chinefe, ap-prifed of their return, marched inftantly to-wards that river; and laid fiege to Albafin with an army of feven thoufand men, and a large train of artillery. They battered the new fortrefs for feveral weeks, without being able to make a breach, and without attempt-ing to take it by ftorm. The befieged, though not much annoyed by the unfkilful operations of the enemy, were exhaufted with the com-plicated miferies of ficknefs and famine ; and, notwithftanding they continued to make a gallant refiftance, muft foon have funk under their diftreffes, if the Chinefe had not volun-tarily retired, in confequence of a treaty in agitation between the two courts of Mofcow and Pekin. For this purpofe the Ruffian embaffador

baſſador Golovin had quitted Moſcow in 1685, accompanied by a large body of troops, in order to ſecure his perſon, and enforce reſpect to his embaſſy. The difficulty of procuring ſubſiſtence for any conſiderable number of men in ſuch deſolate regions, joined to the ruggedneſs of the roads, and the length of the march, prevented his arrival at Selenginſk until the year 1687. From thence meſſengers were immediately diſpatched to Pekin, with overtures of peace.

After ſeveral delays, occaſioned partly by policy, and partly by the poſture of affairs in the Tartar country through which the Chineſe were to paſs, embaſſadors left Pekin in the beginning of June 1689. Golovin had propoſed to receive them at Albaſin; but, while he was proceeding to that fortreſs, the Chineſe embaſſadors preſented themſelves at the gates of Nerſhinſk, eſcorted by ſuch a numerous army, and ſuch a formidable train of artillery, that Golovin was conſtrained, from motives of fear, to conclude the negotiation almoſt upon their own terms. The conferences were held under tents, in an open plain, near the town of Nerſhinſk; and a treaty concluded, which firſt checked the pro-

greſs

grefs of the Ruffian arms in thofe parts ; and laid the foundations of an important and regular commerce between the two nations. By the firft and fecond articles, the South-Eaftern boundaries of the Ruffian empire were formed by a ridge of mountains, ftretching North of the Amoor from the fea of Okotfk to the fource of the fmall river Gorbitza *, then by that river to its influx into the Amoor, and laftly by the Argoon, from its junction with the Shilka up to its fource. By the fifth article reciprocal liberty of trade was granted to all the fubjects of the two empires, who fhould be provided with paffports from their refpective courts †.

This treaty was figned on the 27th of Auguft, in the year 1689, under the reign of

* There are two Gorbitzas ; the firft falls into the Amoor, near the conflux of the Argoon and Shilka ; the fecond falls into the Shilka. The former was meant by the Ruffians ; but the Chinefe fixed upon the latter, for the boundary, and have carried their point. Accordingly the prefent limits are fomewhet different from thofe mentioned in the text. They are carried from the point where the Shilka and Argoon unite to form the Amoor, Weftward along the Shilka, until they reach the mouth of the Weftern Gorbitza ; from thence they are continued to the fource of the laft-mentioned river, and along the chain of mountains as before. By this alteration the Ruffian limits are fomewhat abridged.

† S. R. G. II. p. 435.

Ivan

Ivan and Peter Alexiewitch, by which the Ruffians loft, exclufively of a large territory, the navigation of the river Amoor. The importance of this lofs was not at that time underftood ; and has only been felt fince the difcovery of Kamtchatka, and of the iflands between Afia and America. The products of thefe new-difcovered countries might, by means of the Amoor, have been conveyed by water into the diftrict of Nerfhinfk, from whence there is an eafy tranfport by land to Kiakta: whereas the fame merchandife, after being landed at Okotfk, is now carried over a large tract of country, partly upon rivers of difficult navigation, and partly along rugged and almoft impaffable roads.

In return, the Ruffians obtained, what they had long and repeatedly defired, a regular and permanent trade with the Chinefe. The firft intercourfe between Ruffia and China commenced in the beginning of the feventeenth century * ; at which period a fmall quantity of Chinefe merchandife was procured, by the merchants of Tomfk and other adjacent towns, from the Calmucs. The rapid and profitable

---

* S. R. G. VIII. p. 504, & feq.

fale

fale of thefe commodities encouraged certain wayvodes of Siberia to attempt a direct and open communication with China. For this purpofe feveral perfons were deputed at different times to Pekin from Tobolfk, Tomfk, and other Ruffian fettlements; and although thefe deputations failed of obtaining the grant of a regular commerce, they were neverthelefs attended with fome important confequences. The general good reception, which the agents met with, tempted the Ruffian merchants to fend occafional traders to Pekin. By thefe means a faint connection with that metropolis was kept alive: the Chinefe learned the advantages of the Ruffian trade; and were gradually prepared for its fubfequent eftablifhment. This commerce, carried on by intervals, was entirely fufpended by the hoftilities upon the river Amoor: but no fooner was the treaty of Nerfhinfk concluded, than the Ruffians engaged with extraordinary alacrity in their favourite branch of traffic. And its advantages were foon found to be fo confiderable, that Peter I. conceived an idea of ftill farther enlarging it. Accordingly, in 1692, he difpatched Ifbrand Ives, a Dutchman in his fervice, to Pekin; who requefted

and

and obtained, that the liberty of trading to China, which by the late treaty was granted to individuals, fhould be extended to caravans.

In confequence of this arrangement, fuccef-five caravans went from Ruffia to Pekin; where a caravanfary was allotted for their reception; and all their expences during their continuance in that metropolis were defrayed by the Emperor of China. The right of fending thefe caravans, and the profits refulting from them, belonged to the crown of Ruffia. In the mean time, private merchants continued as before to carry on a feparate trade with the Chinefe, not only at Pekin, but alfo at the head quarters of the Mongols. The camp of thefe roving Tartars was generally ftationed near the conflux of the Orkon and Tola, between the Southern frontiers of Siberia and the Mongol defert. A kind of annual fair was held at this fpot by the Ruffian and Chinefe merchants, who brought their refpe&ive goods for fale. This rendezvous foon became a fcene of riot and confufion; and repeated complaints of the drunkennefs and mifcondu& of the Ruffians were tranf-mitted to the Chinefe Emperor. Thefe com-

plaints

plaints made a ftill greater impreffion from a
coincidence of fimilar exceffes, for which the
Ruffians at Pekin had become notorious. Ex-
afperated by the frequent reprefentations of
his fubjects, Camhi threatened to expel the
Ruffians from his dominions, and to prohibit
them from carrying on any commerce, as
well in China as in the country of the Mongols.

Thefe untoward circumftances occafioned
another embaffy to Pekin in the year 1719.
Leff Vaffilievitch Ifmailof, the embaffador
upon this occafion, fucceeded in the negotiation ; and adjufted every difficulty to the
fatisfaction of both parties. At his departure
Laurence Lange, who had accompanied him
in the character of agent for the caravans,
was permitted to remain at Pekin for the purpofe of fuperintending the conduct of the Ruffians. His refidence however in that metropolis was but fhort ; for he was foon afterwards compelled, by the Chinefe, to return.
His difmiffion was owing partly to a fudden
caprice of that fufpicious people ; and partly
to a frefh mifunderftanding between the two
courts, in relation to fome Mongol tribes who
bordered upon Siberia. A fmall number of
thefe

thefe Mongols had placed themfelves under the protection of Ruffia, and were immediately demanded by the Chinefe; but the Ruffians refufed compliance, under pretence that no article in the treaty of Nerfhinfk could, with any appearance of probability, be conftrued as extending to the Mongols. The Chinefe were incenfed at this refufal; and their refentment was ftill farther inflamed by the diforderly conduct of the Ruffian traders, who, freed from all controul by the departure of their agent, had indulged, without reftraint, their ufual propenfity to excefs. This concurrence of unlucky incidents extorted in 1722, an order from Camhi for the total expulfion of the Ruffians from the Chinefe and Mongol territories; and all intercourfe between the two nations immediately ceafed.

Affairs continued in this ftate until the year 1727; when the count Sava Vladiflavitch Ragufinfki, a Dalmatian in the fervice of Ruffia, was difpatched to Pekin. He was inftructed at all events to compofe the differences between the two courts relating to the Mongol tribes; to fettle the Southern frontiers of the Ruffian empire in that quarter; and to obtain the permiffion of renewing the trade with China.

China. He accordingly prefented a new plan for a treaty of limits and commerce to Yund-fchin, fon and fucceffor of Camhi; by which the frontiers of the two empires were finally traced as they exift at prefent ; and the commerce eftablifhed upon a permanent bafis, calculated to prevent as far as poffible all future fources of mifunderftanding. This plan being approved by the emperor, Chinefe commiffioners were immediately appointed to negotiate with the Ruffian embaffador upon the banks of the Bura, a fmall river which flows, South of the confines of Siberia, into the Orkon near its junction with the Selenga.

At this conference, the old limits, fettled by the treaty of Nerfhinfk, were continued from the fource of the Argoon Weftwards as far as the mountain Sabyntaban, which is fituated at a fmall diftance from the fpot where the conflux of the two rivers Uleken and Kemtzak form the Yenisèi : this boundary feparates the Ruffian dominions from the territory of the Mongols, who are under the protection of China. It was likewife ftipulated, that for the future all negotiations fhould be tranfacted between the tribunal of foreign affairs at Pekin, and the board of foreign

reign affairs at St. Peterſburg ; or in matters of
inferior moment between the two commanders of the frontiers *.

The moſt important articles relating to
commerce were as follow :

A caravan was allowed to go to Pekin every
three years, on condition of its not conſiſting
of more than two hundred perſons ; and that
during their reſidence in that metropolis, their
expences ſhould be no longer defrayed by the
emperor of China. Notice was likewiſe to be
ſent to the Chineſe court immediately upon
their arrival at the frontiers ; where an officer was to meet and accompany them to
Pekin. The privilege before enjoyed by individuals of carrying on a promiſcuous traffic
in the Chineſe and Mongol territories was
aboliſhed ; and no merchandize belonging to
private perſons was permitted to be brought
for ſale beyond the frontiers. For the purpoſe of preſerving, conſiſtently with this re-
gulation, the privilege of commerce to individuals, two places of reſort were appointed
on the confines of Siberia : one called Kiakta,

* This article was inſerted, becauſe the Chineſe emperor, from a ridiculous idea of ſuperiority, had contemp-
tuouſly refuſed to hold any correſpondence with the court of
Ruſſia.

from

from a rivulet of that name near which it
ſtands ; and the other Zurukaitu ; at which
places a free trade was reciprocally indulged to
the ſubjeċts of the two nations. A permiſſion was at the ſame time obtained for building a Ruſſian church within the precinċts of
their caravanſary ; and, for the celebration of
divine ſervice, four prieſts were allowed to re-
ſide at Pekin *. The ſame favour was alſo
extended to ſome Ruſſian ſcholars † for the
purpoſe of learning the Chineſe tongue : in

* The firſt Ruſſian church at Pekin was built for the ac-
commodation of the Ruſſians taken priſoners at Albaſin.
Theſe perſons were carried to Pekin, and the place appointed for their habitation in that city was called the Ruſſian
Street, a name it ſtill retains. They were ſo well received
by the Chineſe, that, upon the concluſion of the treaty of
Nerſhinſk, they refuſed to return to their native country.
And, as they intermarried with the Chineſe women, their
deſcendants are quite naturalized ; and have for the moſt
part adopted not only the language, but even the religion
of China. Hence, the above-mentioned church, though
it ſtill exiſts, is no longer applied to the purpoſe of divine
worſhip : its prieſt was transferred to the church, which
was built within the walls of the caravanſary.

† The good effeċts of this inſtitution have already been
perceived. A Ruſſian, whoſe name is Leontief, after having reſided ten years at Pekin, is returned to Petersburg.
He has given ſeveral tranſlations and extraċts of ſome in-
tereſting Chineſe publications, viz. Part of the Hiſtory of
China ; the Code of the Chineſe Laws ; Account of the
Towns and Revenues, &c. of the Chineſe empire, extraċted
from a Treatiſe of Geography, lately printed at Pekin. A
ſhort account of this Extraċt is given in the Journal of St.
Petersburg for April, 1779.

or-

order to qualify themfelves for interpreters between the two nations.

This treaty, called the treaty of Kiakta, was, on the fourteenth of June, 1728, concluded and ratified by count Ragufinſki and three Chinefe plenipotentaries upon the ſpot where Kiakta was afterwards built; it is the baſis upon which all the ſubſequent tranſactions between Ruſſia and China have been founded *.

One innovation in the mode of carrying on the trade to China, which has been introduced ſince the acceſſion of the preſent empreſs Catherine II. deſerves to be mentioned in this place. Since the year 1755 no caravans have been ſent to Pekin. Their firſt diſcontinuance was occaſioned by a miſunderſtanding between the two courts of Peterſburg and Pekin; and their diſuſe, after a reconciliation had taken place, aroſe from the following circumſtances. The exportation and importation of many principal commodities, particularly the moſt valuable furs, were formerly prohibited to individuals, and ſolely appropriated to caravans belonging to the crown. By theſe reſtrictions the Ruſſian trade to China was greatly ſhackled

* S. R. G. VIII. p. 513.

and

and circumſcribed. The preſent empreſs
(who, amidſt many excellent regulations
which charaċteriſe her reign, has ſhewn her-
ſelf invariably attentive to the improvement
of the Ruſſian commerce) aboliſhed, in 1762,
the monopoly of the fur trade; and renounced
in favour of her ſubjeċts the excluſive privilege which the crown enjoyed of ſending caravans to Pekin *. By theſe conceſſions the
profits of the trade have been conſiderably encreaſed; the great expence, hazard, and delay, of tranſporting the merchandiſe occaſionally from the frontiers of Siberia to Pekin,
has been retrenched; and Kiakta is now rendered the center of the Ruſſian and Chineſe
commerce.

C H A P. III.

Account of the Ruſſian *and* Chineſe *ſettlements
upon the confines of* Siberia—*deſcription of
the* Ruſſian *frontier town* Kiakta—*of the* Chineſe *frontier town* Maimatſchin—*its buildings, pagodas, &c.*

BY the laſt-mentioned treaty it was ſtipu-
lated, that the commerce between Ruſſia and China ſhould be tranſaċted at the fron-

* S. R. G. VIII. p. 520.

tiers.

tiers. Accordingly two ſpots were marked out for that purpoſe upon the confines of Si-beria, where they border upon the Mongol deſert ; one near the brook Kiakta, and the other at Zurukaitu. The deſcription of the former of theſe places ſhall be the ſubject of the preſent chapter.

This ſettlement conſiſts of a Ruſſian and Chineſe town, both ſituated in a romantic valley, ſurrounded by high, rocky, and for the moſt part well-wooded, mountains. The valley is interſected by the brook Kiakta, which riſes in Siberia, and, after waſhing both the Ruſſian and Chineſe town, falls into the Bura, at a ſmall diſtance from the frontiers.

The Ruſſian ſettlement is called Kiakta from the abovementioned brook : it lies in 124 degrees 18 minutes longitude from the iſle of Fero, and 35 degrees N. latitude, at the diſtance of 3676 miles from Moſcow, and 1025 from Pekin.

It conſiſts of a fortreſs and a ſmall ſuburb. The fortreſs, which is built upon a gentle riſe, is a ſquare encloſed with paliſadoes, and ſtrengthened with wooden baſtions at the ſe-veral angles. There are three gates, at which
guards

guards are conftantly ftationed : one of the
gates faces the North, a fecond the South towards the Chinefe frontiers, and a third the
Eaft clofe to the brook Kiakta. The principal
public buildings in the fortrefs are a wooden
church, the governor's houfe, the cuftom-
houfe, the magazine for provifions, and the
guard-houfe. It contains alfo a range of fhops
and warehoufes, barracks for the garrifon, and
feveral houfes belonging to the crown ; the
latter are generally inhabited by the principal
merchants. Thefe buildings are moftly of
wood.

The fuburb, which is furrounded with a
wooden wall covered at the top with chevaux
de frize, contains no more than an hundred
and twenty houfes very irregularly built ; it
has the fame number of gates as the fortrefs,
which are alfo guarded. Without this fuburb, upon the high road leading to Selenginfk,
ftand a few houfes, and the magazine for
rhubarb.

This fettlement is but indifferently provided with water ; for although the brook
Kiakta is dammed up as it flows by the fortrefs ; yet it is fo fhallow in fummer, that,
unlefs after heavy rains, it is fcarcely fufficient

cient to fupply the inhabitants. Its ftream is
alfo turbid and unwholefome ; and the fprings
which rife in the neighbourhood are either
foul or brackifh : from thefe circumftances,
the principal inhabitants are obliged to fend
for water from a fpring in the Chinefe diftrict. The foil of the adjacent country is
moftly fand or rock, and extremely barren.
If the frontiers of Ruffia were extended about
fix miles more South to the rivulet of Bura ;
the inhabitants of Kiakta would enjoy good
water, a fruitful foil, and plenty of fifh, all
which advantages are at prefent confined to
the Chinefe.

The garrifon of Kiakta confifts of a company of regular foldiers, and a certain number of Coffacs ; the former are occafionally
changed, but the latter are fixed inhabitants
of the place. It is the province of the commander to infpect the frontiers, and, in con-
junction with the prefident of the Chinefe
merchants, to fettle all affairs of an inferior
nature ; but in matters of importance recourfe
muft be had to the chancery of Selenginfk,
and to the governor of Irkutfk. The Ruffian
merchants, and the agents of the Ruffian
trading

trading company, are the principal inhabitants of Kiakta.

The limits Weftwards from this fettlement
to the river Selenga, and Eaftwards as far as
Tchikoi, are bounded with chevaux de frize,
in order to prevent a contraband trade in cattle,
for the exportation of which a confiderable
duty is paid to the crown. All the outpofts
along the frontiers Weftwards as far as the
government of Tobolfk, and Eaftwards to the
mountains of fnow, are under the command
of the governor of Kiakta.

The moft elevated of the mountains that
furround the valley of Kiakta, and which is
called by the Mongols Burgultei, commands
the Ruffian as well as the Chinefe town: for
this reafon, the Chinefe, at the conclufion of
the laft frontier treaty, demanded the ceffion
of this mountain, under the pretext that fome
of their deified anceftors were buried upon its
fummit. The Ruffians gave way to their re-
queft; and fuffered the boundary to be brought
back to the North fide of the mountain.

The Chinefe town is called, by the Chinefe
and Mongols, Maimatfchin, which fignifies
fortrefs of commerce. The Ruffians term it
the Chinefe Village (Kitaifkaia Sloboda), and
alfo

alfo Naimatfchin, which is a corruption of
Maimatfchin. It is fituated about an hundred
and forty yards South of the fortrefs of Kiakta,
and nearly parallel to it. Midway between
this place and the Ruffian fortrefs, two pofts
about ten feet high are planted in order to
mark the frontiers of the two empires : one is
infcribed with Ruffian, the other with Man-
fhur characters *.

Maimatfchin has no other fortification than
a wooden wall, and a fmall ditch of about
three feet broad ; the latter was dug in the
year 1756, during the war between the Chinefe and the Calmucs. The town is of an
oblong form : its length is about feven hundred yards, and its breadth four hundred. On
each of the four fides a large gate faces the
principal ftreets ; over each of thefe gates
there is a wooden guard-houfe for the Chinefe
garrifon, which confifts of Mongols in tat-
tered clothes, and armed with clubs. Without the gate, which looks to the Ruffian
frontiers, and about the diftance of eight yards

* Upon the mountain to the Weft of Kiakta, the limit
is again marked; on the Ruffian fide by an heap of ftones
and earth, ornamented on the top with a crofs ; and on the
Chinefe by a pile of ftones in the fhape of a pyramid. Pallas
Reife, P. III. p. 110.

from

from the entrance, the Chinefe have raifed a wooden fcreen, fo conftructed as to intercept all view of the ftreets from without.

This town contains two hundred houfes and about twelve hundred inhabitants. It has two principal ftreets of about eight yards broad, croffing each other in the middle at right angles, with two by-ftreets running from North to South. They are not paved, but are laid with gravel, and kept remarkably clean.

The houfes are fpacious, uniformly built of wood, of only one ftory, not more than fourteen feet high, plaiftered and white-wafhed; they are conftructed round a court-yard of about feventy feet fquare, which is ftrewed with gravel, and has an appearance of neatnefs. Each houfe confifts of a fitting-room, fome warehoufes, and a kitchen. In the houfes of the wealthier fort the roof is made of plank; but in meaner habitations of lath covered over with turf. Towards the ftreets moft of the houfes have arcades of wood projecting forwards from the roof, like a penthoufe, and fupported by ftrong pillars. The windows are large after the European manner, but, on account of the dearnefs of glafs and

Ruf-

Ruffian talc, are generally of paper, excepting a few panes of glafs in the fitting-room.

The fitting-room is feldom turned towards the ftreets; it is a kind of fhop, where the feveral patterns of merchandize are placed in receffes, fitted up with fhelves, and fecured with paper-doors for the purpofe of keeping out the duft. The windows are generally ornamented with little paintings; and the walls are hung with Chinefe paper. Half the floor is of hard-beaten clay; the other half is covered with boards, and rifes about two feet. Here the family fit in the day-time, and fleep at night. By the fide of this raifed part, and nearly upon the fame level, there is a fquare brick ftove, with a ftreight perpendicular cylindrical excavation, which is heated with fmall-pieces of wood. From the bottom of this ftove a tube defcends, and is carried zigzag under the boarded floor above-mentioned, and from thence to a chimney which opens into the ftreet. By this contrivance, although the ftove is always open and the flame vifible; yet the room is never troubled in the leaft degree with fmoke. There is fcarcely any furniture in the room, excepting one large dining-table in the lower part, and

two

two fmall lackered ones upon the raifed floor: one of thefe tables is always provided with a chaffing-difh, which ferves to light their pipes when the ftove is not heated.

In this room there are feveral fmall niches covered with filken curtains, before which are placed lamps that are lighted upon feftivals: thefe niches contain painted paper idols; a ftone or metal veffel, wherein the afhes of incenfe are collected; feveral fmall ornaments and artificial flowers: the Chinefe readily allow ftrangers to draw afide the curtains, and look at the idols.

The Bucharian * merchants inhabit the South Weft quarter of Maimatfchin. Their houfes are not fo large nor commodious as thofe of the Chinefe, although the greateft part of them carry on a very confiderable commerce.

The Surgutfchèi, or governor of Maimatfchin, has the care of the police, as well as the direction of all affairs relating to com

* " The chief merchandizes, which the Bucharians " bring to Ruffia, are cotton, ftuffs, and half-filks, fpun " and raw cotton, lamb-skins, precious ftones, gold-duft, " unprepared nitre, fal-ammoniac, &c." See Ruffia, or a complete Hiftorical Account of all the nations that compofe that Empire, V. II. p. 141, a very curious and interefting work lately publifhed by Mr. Tooke.

merce:

merce : he is generally a perfon of rank, of-
tentimes a Mandarin, who has mifbehaved
himfelf in another ftation, and is fent here as
a kind of punifhment. He is diftinguifhed
from the reft by the cryftal button of his cap,
and by a peacock's * feather hanging behind.
The Chinefe give him the title of Amban,
which fignifies commander in chief ; and no
one appears before him without bending the
knee, in which pofture the perfon who brings
a petition muft remain until he receives the
governor's anfwer. His falary is not large ;
but the prefents which he receives from the
merchants amount annually to a confiderable
fum.

The moft remarkable public buildings in
Maimatfchin, are the governor's houfe, the
theatre, and two pagodas. The governor's
houfe is larger than the others, and better
furnifhed ; it is diftinguifhed by a chamber
where the court of juftice is held, and by two
high poles before the entrance ornamented

* In China the princes of the blood wear three peacocks
feathers ; nobles of the higheft diftinction, two ; and the
lower clafs of the nobility, one. It is alfo a mark of high
rank to keep a carriage with four wheels. The governor of
Maimatfchin rode in one with only two wheels. All the
Chinefe wear buttons of different colours in their caps,
which alfo denote the rank.   Pallas Reife, P. III. p. 126.

with

with flags. The theatre is fituated clofe to the wall of the town near the great Pagoda : it is a kind of fmall fhed, neatly painted, open in front, and merely fpacious enough to contain the ftage; the audience ftand in the ftreet. Near it are two high poles, upon which large flags with Chinefe infcriptions are hoifted on feftivals. On fuch occafions the fervants belonging to the merchants act fhort burlefque farces, in honour of their idols. The fmalleft of the two Pagodas is a wooden building, ftanding upon pillars, in the center of the town, at the place where the two principal ftreets crofs. It is a Chinefe tower of two ftories, adorned on the outfide with fmall columns, paintings, and little iron bells, &c. The firft ftory is fquare, the fecond octangular. In the lower ftory is a picture reprefenting the God Tien, which fignifies, according to the explanation of the moft intelligent Chinefe, the Moft High God, who rules over the thirty-two heavens. The Manfhurs, it is faid, call this idol Abcho ; and the Mongols, Tingheru, heaven, or the God of heaven. He is reprefented fitting with his head uncovered, and encircled with a

ray

ray * of glory fimilar to that which furrounds
the head of our Saviour in the Roman ca-
tholic paintings : his hair is long and flowing ;
he holds in his right hand a drawn fword,
and his left is extended as in the act of giving
a benediction.   On one fide of this figure two
youths, on the other a maiden and a grey-
headed old man, are delineated.

The upper ftory contains the picture of
another idol in a black and white checquered
cap, with the fame figures of three young
perfons and a little old man.   There are no
altars in this temple, and no other ornaments
excepting thefe pictures and their frames.   It
is opened only on feftivals, and ftrangers cannot fee it without permiffion.

The great Pagoda +, fituated before the
governor's houfe, and near the principal gate
look-

* When Mr. Pallas obtained permiffion of the governor to
fee this temple, the latter affured him that the Jefuits of
Pekin, and their converts, adored this idol.   From whence
he ingenioufly conjectures, either that the refemblance between this idol, and the reprefentation of our Saviour by
the Roman Catholicks, was the occafion of this affertion ;
or that the Jefuits, in order to excite the devotion of the
converts, have, out of policy, given to the picture of our
Saviour a refemblance to the Tien of the Chinefe.   Pallas
Reife, P. III. p. 119.

+ The great Pagoda is omitted in the engraving of Maimatfchin prefixed to this chapter ; an omiffion owing to the
ar-

looking to the South, is larger and more mag-
nificent than the former. Strangers are allowed to fee it at all times, without the leaft
difficulty, provided they are accompanied by
one of the priefts, who are always to be found
in the area of the temple. This area is furrounded with chevaux de frize : the entrance is from the South through two gates
with a fmall building between them. In
the infide of this building are two receffes
with rails before them, behind which the
images of two horfes as big as life are
coarfely moulded out of clay : they are
faddled and bridled, and attended by two human figures dreffed like grooms. The horfe
to the right is of a chefnut colour, the other
is dun with a black mane and tail ; the former is in the attitude of fpringing, the latter
of walking. Near each horfe a banner of
yellow filk, painted with filver dragons, is
difplayed.

In the middle of this area are two wooden
turrets furrounded with galleries : a large bell

artift's being obliged to leave Kiakta before he had time to
finifh the drawing. In every other refpect, the view, as I
was informed by a gentleman who has been on the fpot,
is complete, and reprefented with the greateft exactnefs.

of

of caſt iron, which is ſtruck occaſionally with a large wooden mallet, hangs in the Eaſtern turret ; the other contains two kettle-drums of an enormous ſize, ſimilar to thoſe uſed in the religious ceremonies of the Calmucs. On each ſide of this area are ranges of buildings inhabited by the prieſts of the temple.

The area communicates by means of a handſome gateway with the inner court, which is bordered on each ſide by ſmall compartments open in front, with rails before them ; in the inſide of theſe compartments the legendary ſtories of the idols are exhibited in a ſeries of hiſtorical paintings. At the farther extremity of this court ſtands a large building, conſtructed in the ſame ſtyle of architecture as the temple. The inſide is ſixty feet long and thirty broad : it is ſtored with antient weapons, and inſtruments of war of a prodigious ſize ; ſuch as ſpears, ſcythes, and long pikes with broad blades, ſhields, coats of arms, and military enſigns repreſenting hands *, dragons heads, and other carved figures. All theſe warlike inſtruments are richly gilded, and ranged in order upon ſcaf-

* Theſe hands reſemble the manipulary ſtandards of the Romans.

folds

folds along the wall. Oppofite the entrance
a large yellow ftandard, embroidered with foliage and filver dragons, is erected; under it,
upon a kind of altar, there is a feries of
little oblong tables, bearing Chinefe infcriptions.

An open gallery, adorned on both fides
with flower-pots, leads from the back-door of
the armoury to the colonade of the temple.
In this colonade two flate tablets are placed,
in wooden frames, about fix feet high and
two broad, with long infcriptions relating to
the building of the temple. Before one of
thefe plates a fmall idol of an hideous form
ftands upon the ground, enclofed in a wooden
cafe.

The temple itfelf is an elegant building,
richly decorated on the outfide with columns,
lackered and gilded carved-work, fmall bells,
and other ornaments peculiar to the Chinefe
architecture. Within there is a rich profufion of gilding, which correfponds with
the gaudinefs of the exterior. The walls
are covered thick with paintings, exhibiting
the moft celebrated exploits of the principal
idol.

This

This temple contains five idols of a coloffal ftature, fitting crofs-legged upon pedeftals in three receffes, which fill the whole Northern fide.

The principal idol is feated alone, in the middle recefs, between two columns ornamented with gilded dragons. Large ftreamers of filk, hanging from the roof of the temple, veil in fome meafure the upper part of the image. His name is Ghedfur, or Gheffur Chan * ; the Chinefe call him Loo-ye, or the firft and moft antient; and the Manfhurs, Guanlöe, or the fuperior god. He is of a gigantic fize, furpaffing more than fourfold the human ftature, with a face gliftening like burnifhed gold, black hair and beard. He

* The Mongols and Calmucs call him by this name of Gheffur Chan; and although they do not reckon him among their divinities, yet they confider him as a great hero, the Bacchus and Hercules of Eaftern Tartary, who was born at the fource of the Koango, and who vanquifhed many monfters. They have in their language a very long hiftory of his heroical deeds. His title, in the Mongul tongue, is as follows : Arban Zeeghi Effin Gheffur Bogdo Chan : the king of the ten points of the compafs, or the monarch Gheffur Chan.

I have in my poffeffion a copy of this manufcript, containing the Hiftory of Gheffur Chan ; it is in the original Mongol language, and was a prefent to me from Mr. Pallas : I fhould be very happy to communicate it to any perfon verfed in the Eaftern langurges.

wears

wears a crown upon his head, and is richly drefsed in the Chinefe fafhion : his garments are not moulded out of clay, as thofe of the other idols; but are made of the fineft filk. He holds in his hands a kind of tablet, which he feems to read with deep attention. Two fmall female figures, refembling girls of about fourteen years of age, ftand on each fide of the idol, upon the fame pedeftal ; one of which grafps a roll of paper. At the right-hand of the idol lie feven golden arrows, and at his left a bow.

Before the idol is a fpacious enclofure, furrounded with rails, within which ftands an altar with four coloffal figures, intended probably to reprefent the principal mandarins of the deified Gheffur. Two of thefe figures are drefsed like judges, and hold before them fmall tablets, fimilar to that in the hands of the principal idol. The two other figures are accoutred in complete armour : one wears a turban ; and carries, upon the left fhoulder, a large fword fheathed, with the hilt upwards. The other has an hideous copper-coloured face, a large belly ; and grafps in his right-hand a lance with a broad blade. Although all the remaining idols in the temple
ple

ple are of an enormous fize, yet they are greatly furpaffed in magnitude by Gheffur Chan.

The firft idol in the recefs to the right is called Maooang, or the Otfchibanni of the Mongols. He has three ghaftly copper-coloured faces, and fix arms: two of his arms brandifh two fabres crofs-ways over the head; a third bears a looking glafs; and a fourth a kind of fquare, which refembles a piece of ivory. The two remaining arms are employed in drawing a bow, with an arrow laid upon it, ready to be difcharged. This idol has a mirror upon his breaft, and an eye in his navel: near it are placed two fmall figures; one holds an arrow, and the other a little animal.

The next idol in the fame recefs is called by the Chinefe Tfaudfing, or the gold and filver god; and by the Mongols Tfagan-Dfambala. He wears a black cap, and is dreffed, after the Chinefe fafhion, in fumptuous robes of ftate; he bears in his hand a fmall jewel cafket. Near him alfo ftand two little figures, one of which holds a truncated branch.

In

In the recefs to the left is the god Kufho,
called by the Manfhurs Kua-fchan, and by
the Mongols Galdi, or the Fire God. He is
reprefented with a frightful firey reddifh face:
clad in complete armour, he wields a fword
half-drawn out of the fcabbard; and feems as
in the act of ftarting up from his feat. He is
attended by two little halberdeers, one of
whom is crying; and the other bears a fowl
upon his hand, which refembles a fea-phea-
fant.

The other idol in the fame recefs is the god
of oxen, Niu-o. He appears to be fitting in
a compofed pofture, is habited like a Mandarin, and diftinguifhed by a crown upon his
head. He has, in common with the other
idols, a mirror upon his breaft. The Chinefe imagine him to be the fame with the Ya-
mandaga of the Mongols; and it is faid his
Manfhurifh name is Kain Killova; his Mongol name, which relates to the hiftory of
Gheffur, is Bars-Batir, the Hero of Tygers.

Before thefe feveral idols there are tables,
or altars, on which cakes, paftry, dried fruit,
and flefh, are placed on feftivals and prayer-
days: on particular occafions even whole car-
caffes of fheep are offered up. Tapers and
lamps

lamps burn day and night before the idols.
Among the utenfils of the temple, the moft
remarkable is a veffel fhaped like a quiver,
and filled with flat pieces of cleft reed, on
which fhort devices are infcribed. Thefe devices are taken out by the Chinefe on New-
year's day ; and are confidered as oracles,
which foretell the good or ill luck of the perfon, by whom they are drawn, during the
following year. There lies alfo upon a table
an hollow wooden black lackered helmet,
which all perfons of devotion ftrike with a
wooden hammer, whenever they enter the
temple. This helmet is regarded with fuch
peculiar awe, that no ftrangers are permitted
to handle it, although they are allowed to
touch even the idols themfelves.

The firft day of the new and full moon is
appointed for the celebration of worfhip.
Upon each of thofe days no Chinefe ever fails
to make his appearance once in the temple :
he enters without taking off his cap *, joins
his hands before his face ; bows five times to
each idol ; touches with his forehead the pedeftal on which the idol fits; and then re-

* Among the Chinefe, as well as other Eaftern nations,
it is reckoned a mark of difrefpect to uncover the head before a fuperior.

tires.

tires. Their principal feftivals are held in the firft month of their year, which anfwers to February. It is called by them, as well as by the Mongols, the white month; and is confidered as a lucky time for the tranfaction of bufinefs: at that time they difplay flags before the temples; and place meat upon the tables of the idols, which the priefts take away in the evening, and eat in the fmall apartments of the interior court. On thefe folemnities plays are performed in the theatre, in honour of the idols: the pieces are generally of the fatyrical kind, and pointed againft unjuft magiftrates and judges.

But although the Chinefe have fuch few ceremonies in their fyftem of religious worfhip; yet they are remarkably infected with fuperftition. Mr. Pallas gives the following defcription of their behaviour at Maimatfchin during an eclipfe of the moon. At the clofe of the evening in which the eclipfe appeared, all the inhabitants feemed to vie with each other indefatigably in raifing an inceffant uproar, fome by hideous fhrieks, others by knocking wood, and beating cauldrons: the din was heightened by ftriking the bell and beating the kettle-drums of the great Pagoda.

The

The Chinese suppose, that during an eclipse
the wicked spirit of the air, called by the
Mongols Arakulla, is attacking the moon;
and that he is frightened away by these hideous shrieks and noises. Another instance
of superstition fell under the observation of
Mr. Pallas, while he was at Maimatschin. A
fire breaking out with such violence that several houses were in flames, none of the inhabitants attempted to extinguish it; they
stood indeed in idle consternation round the
fire; and some of them sprinkled occasionally
water among the flames, in order to sooth the
fire god, who, as they imagined, had chosen
their houses for a sacrifice. Indeed, if the
Russians had not exerted themselves in quench-
ing the fire, the whole place would probably
have been reduced to ashes *.

CHAP.

* This account of Kiakta and Maimatschin is taken from
Mr. Pallas's description of Kiakta, in the journal of his travels through Siberia, P. III. p. 109—126. Every circum-
stance relating to the religious worship of the Eastern nations
is in itself so interesting, that I thought it would not be unacceptable to my readers to give a translation of the above
passages respecting the Chinese Pagodas and Idols; although
in a work treating of the new discoveries, and the commerce
which is connected with them. In the abovementioned
journal the ingenious author continues to describe from his
own observations the manners, customs, dress, diet, and several other particulars relative to the Chinese; which, although exceedingly curious and interesting, are too foreign

to

RUSSIA AND CHINA.433

CHAP. IV.

Commerce between the Chinefe *and* Ruffians—
*lift of the principal exports and imports—
duties—average amount of the* Ruffian *trade.*

THE merchants of Maimatfchin come
from the Northern provinces of China,
chiefly from Pekin, Nankin, Sandchue, and
other principal towns. They are not fettled
at this place with their wives and families:
for it is a remarkable circumftance, that there
is not one woman in Maimatfchin. This re-

to the immediate purpofe of thefe fheets to have been inferted
in the prefent work.

No writer has placed the religion and hiftory of the Mongol nations in a more explicit point of view than Mr. Pallas; eyery page in his interefting journal affords ftriking
proofs of this affertion. He has lately thrown new lights
upon this obfcure fubject, in a recent publication concerning
the Mongols, who inhabit parts of Siberia, and the territory
which lies between that country and the Chinefe-wall. Of
this excellent work the firft volume appeared in 1776, and
contains the genealogy, hiftory, laws, manners, and cuftoms, of this extraordinary people, as they are divided into
Calmucs, Mongols, and Burats. The fecond volume is expected with impatience, and will afcertain, with minutenefs
and accuracy, the tenets and religious ceremonies which
diftinguifh the votaries of Shamanifm from the followers of
Dalai-Lama, the two great fects into which thefe tribes are
diftinguifhed. Pallas Samlung hiftorifcher Nachrichten ueber
die Mongolifchen Volkerfchafter,

ftriction

striction arises from the policy of the Chinese government, which totally prohibits the women from having the slightest intercourse with foreigners. No Chinese merchant engages in the trade to Siberia who has not a partner. These persons mutually relieve each other. One remains for a stated time, usually a year, at Kiakta; and, when his partner arrives with a fresh cargo of Chinese merchandize, he returns home with the Russian commodities *.

Most of the Chinese merchants understand the Mongol tongue, in which language commercial affairs are generally transacted. Some few indeed speak broken Russian; but their pronunciation is so soft and delicate, that it is difficult to comprehend them. They are not able to pronounce the R, but instead of it use an L; and when two consonants come together, which frequently occurs in the Russian tongue, they divide them by the interposition of a vowel †. This failure in articulating

* Pallas Reise, P. III. p. 125.

† Bayer, in his Museum Sinicum, gives several curious instances of the Chinese mode of articulating those sounds, which they have not in their own language. For instance they change BDRXZ into PTLSS.

Thus

culating the Ruffian language feems peculiar to the Chinefe; and is not obfervable in the Calmucs, Mongols, and other neighbouring nations *.

The commerce between the Ruffians and Chinefe is entirely a trade of barter, or an exchange of one merchandize for another. The Ruffians are prohibited to export their own coin : nor indeed could the Chinefe receive it, even fhould that prohibition be taken off; for no fpecie is current amongft them except bullion †. And the Ruffians find it

more

Thus for Maria they fay Ma-li-ya ;
  for crux,   cu-lu-fu ;
  for baptizo,   pa-pe-ti-fo ;
  for cardinalis,   kia-ul-fi-na-li-fu ;
  for fpiritus,   fu-pi-li-tu-fu ;
  for Adam,   va-tam ;
  for Eva,   nge-va ;
  for Chriftus,   ki-li-fu-tu-fu ;
Hoc, eft, corpus, meum——ho-ke, nge-fu-tu, co-ul-pu-fu-me-vum.
              Bayer, Muf. Sin. Tom. I. p. 15.

* Pallas Reife, P. III. p. 134.
† The Chinefe have no gold or filver coin. Thefe metals are always paid in bullion ; and for the purpofe of afcertaining the weight, every Chinefe merchant is conftantly provided with a pair of fcales. As gold is very fcarce in China, filver is the great medium of commerce. When feveral authors affirm that the Ruffians draw large quantities of filver from China, they miftake an accidental occurrence for a general and ftanding fact. During the war between the Chinefe and Calmucs, the former had occafion to purchafe at Kiakta provifion, horfes, and camels, for which

they

more advantageous to take merchandize in exchange, than to receive bullion at the Chinefe ftandard. The common method of tranfacting bufinefs is as follows. The Chinefe merchant, having at Kiakta examined the merchandize he has occafion for in the warehoufe of the Ruffian trader, adjufts at the houfe of the latter the price over a difh of tea. Both parties next return to the magazine; and the goods in queftion are carefully fealed in the prefence of the Chinefe merchants. At the conclufion of this ceremony, they both repair to Maimatfchin; the Ruffian choofes the commodities he wants, not forgetting to guard againft fraud by a ftrict in-

---

they paid filver. This traffic brought fuch a profufion of that metal into Siberia, that its price was greatly reduced below its real value. A pound of filver was at that period occafionally fold at the frontiers for 8 or 9 roubles, which at prefent is worth 15 or 16. But fince the conclufion of thefe wars by the total reduction of the Calmucs under the Chinefe yoke, Ruffia receives a very fmall quantity of filver from the Chinefe. S. R. G. III. p. 593 & feq.

The filver imported to Kiakta is chiefly brought by the Bucharian merchants, who fell cattle to the Chinefe in exchange for that metal, which they afterwards difpofe of to the Ruffians for European manufactures. Gold-duft is alfo occafionally obtained from the fame merchants; the quantity however of thofe metals procured at Kiakta is fo inconfiderable, as fcarcely to deferve mention. The whole fum of gold and filver imported to Kiakta, in 1777, amounted to only 18,215 roubles. See p. 344.

fpection.

fpection. He then takes the precaution to leave behind a perſon of confidence, who remains in the warehouſe until the Ruſſian goods are delivered, when he returns to Kiakta with the Chineſe merchandize *.

The principal commodities which Ruſſia exports to China are as follow :

FURS and PELTRY. It would be uninterefting to enumerate all the furs and ſkins † brought for ſale to Kiakta, which form the moſt important article of exportation on the ſide of the Ruſſians. The moſt valuable are the ſkins of ſea-otters, beavers, foxes, wolves, bears, Bucharian lambs, Aſtracan ſheep, martens, ſables, ermines, grey-ſquirrels.

The greateſt part of theſe furs and ſkins are brought from Siberia and the New-diſcovered iſlands : a ſupply however not fully adequate to the demand of the market. Foreign furs are therefore imported to St. Peterſburg, and from thence ſent to Kiakta. England alone furniſhes a large quantity of beaver and

* Pallas Reiſe, P. III. p. 135.

† The liſt of all the furs and ſkins brought to Kiakta, with their ſeveral prices, is to be found in Pallas Reiſe, Part III. p. 136 to p. 142.

other

other ſkins, which ſhe procures from Hudſon's Bay and Canada *.

CLOTH. Cloth forms the ſecond article
of exportation which Ruſſia exports to China.
The coarſe ſort is manufactured in Ruſſia ;
the finer is foreign, chiefly Engliſh, Pruſſian,
and French. An arſhire of foreign cloth
fetches, according to its fineneſs, from 2 to 4
roubles. Camlets. Calimancoes. Druggets.
White flannels, both Ruſſian and foreign.

The remaining articles are, Rich ſtuffs.
Velvets. Coarſe linen, chiefly manufactured

* Liſt of furs ſent from England to Peterſburg in the
following years :

	Beaver-ſkins.	Otter-ſkins.
1775	46460	7143
1776	27700	12086
1777	27316	10703

The fineſt Hudſon's beavers have been ſold upon an ave-
rage at Peterſburg, from   70— 90 roubles per 10 skins.
Inferior ditto and beſt Ca-
    nada beavers from   50— 75
Young or cub-beavers from 20— 35
Beſt otter-skins from   90—100
Inferior ones from   60— 80
The qualities of theſe skins being very different occaſion
great variations in the prices.
At Kiakta, the beſt Hud-
ſon's Bay beaver is ſold from 7 to 20 roubles per skin.
Otter's ditto   —   6 — 35
Black foxes skins ftom Canada are alſo ſometimes ſent from
England to Peterſburg.
At Kiakta they fetch from 1 to 100 roubles per skin.

in

in Ruffia. Ruffia leather. Tanned hides.
Glafs ware and looking glaffes. Hardware,
namely knives, fciffars, locks, &c. Tin.
Ruffian talk. Cattle, chiefly camels, horfes,
and horned cattle. The Chinefe alfo pay
very dear for hounds, grey-hounds, barbets,
and dogs for hunting wild boars. Provifions *.
Meal. The Chinefe no longer import fuch
large quantities of meal as formerly ; fince
they have employed the Mongols to culti-
vate the lands lying near the river Orchon +,
&c. &c.

Lift of the moft valuable commodities
procured from China.

RAW AND MANUFACTURED SILK.
The exportation of raw filk is prohibited in
China under pain of death : large quantities
however are fmuggled every year into Kiakta,
but not fufficient to anfwer the demands of
the Ruffian merchants.

---

* In the year 1772, the Chinefe purchafed meat at Kiakta, at the following prices :
A pound of beef 3¾ copecs.
lamb 2½
Horfe-flefh for the Tartars ½. Pallas Reife, P. III.
† S. R. G. III. p. 495—571. Pallas Reife, P. III. p.
136—144.

A pood

A pood of the beft fort is eftimated at — 150 roubles ;
of the worft fort at 75

The manufactured filks are of various forts,
fafhions, and prices, viz. fattins, taffaties, da-
mafks, and gauzes, fcanes of filk died of all
colours, ribbands, &c. &c.

RAW AND MANUFACTURED COT-
TON. Raw cotton is imported in very large
quantities ; a great part of this commodity
being employed in packing up the china-ware
is conveyed into the inland part of Ruffia
without any additional expence of carriage.
A pood fells for—from 4 roubles, 80 cop.
to 12.

Of the manufactured cotton, that which
the Ruffians call Kitaika, and the Englifh
Nankeen, has the moft rapid fale. It is the
moft durable, and, in proportion to its goodnefs, the cheapeft of all the Chinefe ftuffs ;
it is ftained red, brown, green, and black.

TEAS. The teas which are brought into
Ruffia are much fuperior in flavour and quality to thofe which are fent to Europe from
Canton. The original goodnefs of the teas is
probably the fame in both cafes : but it is
con-

conjectured, that the transport by fea confiderably impairs the aromatic flavour of the
plant. This commodity, now become fo favourite an object of European luxury, is
efteemed by the Ruffian merchants the moft
profitable article of importation.

At Kiakta a pound of the beft tea * is
eftimated at   —   —   2 roubles.
Common ditto at   —   1
Inferior at   —   —   40 cop.

PORCELAIN OF ALL SORTS. For
fome years paft the Chinefe have brought to
Kiakta, parcels of porcelain, painted with
European figures, with copies of feveral fa-
vourite prints and images of the Grecian and
Roman deities.

Furniture, particularly Japan cabinets and
cafes, lackered and varnifhed tables and
chairs, boxes inlaid with mother-of-pearl,
&c. &c.

Fans, toys, and other fmall wares. Artificial flowers. Tiger and panther fkins. Rubies †, but neither in large quantities nor of

* At Peterfburg a pound of the beft green tea fetches 3
roubles.

† Rubies are generally procured by fmuggling; and by
the fame means pearls are occafionally difpofed of to the
Chinefe, at a very dear rate. Pearls are much fought for
by the Chinefe; and might be made a very profitable article.

great

great value. White lead, vermilion, and other colours. Canes. Tobacco. Rice. Sugar - candy. Preferved ginger, and other fweatmeats. Rhubarb *. Muſk, &c. &c.

It is very difficult to procure the genuine Thibet muſk, becauſe the Chineſe purchaſe a bad ſort, brought from Siberia, with which they adulterate that which is brought from Thibet †.

Ruſſia derives great advantages from the Chineſe trade. By this traffic, its natural productions, and particularly its furs and ſkins, are diſpoſed of in a very profitable manner. Many of theſe furs, procured from the moſt eaſterly parts of Siberia, are of ſuch little value that they would not anſwer the expence of carriage into Ruſſia ; while the richer furs, which are ſold to the Chineſe at a very high price, would, on account of their dearneſs, ſeldom meet with purchaſers in the Ruſſian dominions. In exchange for theſe commodities the Ruſſians receive from China ſeveral valuable articles of commerce, which they would otherwiſe be obliged to buy at a

* See Chap. VI. p. 351.
† S. R. G. III. p. 572—592. Pallas Reiſe, P. III. p. 144—153.

much

much dearer rate from the European powers, to the great difadvantage of the balance of their trade.

I have before obferved, that formerly the exportation and importation of the moft valuable goods were prohibited to individuals; at prefent only the following articles are prohibited. Among the exports, fire-arms and artillery; gun-powder and ball; gold and filver, coined and uncoined; ftallions and mares; fkins of deer, rein-deer, elks, and horfes; beaver's hair, potafh, rofin, thread, and * tinfel-lace: among the imports, falt, brandy, poifons, and copper-money.

The duties paid by the Ruffian merchants are very confiderable; great part of the merchandife is taxed at   25 per cent.

Furs, cattle, and provifions, pay

     a duty of   —   23.

Ruffian manufactures   18.

One per cent. is alfo deducted from the price of all goods for the expence of deepening the river Selenga; and 7 per cent. for the fupport of the cuftom-houfe.

* Tinfel-lace is fmuggled to the Chinefe, with confiderable profit; for they pay nearly as much for it as if it was folid filver. S. R. G. III. p. 588.

Some

Some articles, both of export and import, pay no duty. The exported are, writing, royal, and poſt paper; Ruſſian cloth of all ſorts and colours, excepting peaſants cloth. The imported are, ſattins, raw and ſtained cottons, porcelain, earthen-ware, glaſs corals, beads, fans, all muſical inſtruments, furniture, lackered and enamelled ornaments, needles, white-lead, rice, preſerved ginger, and other ſweet-meats *.

The importance of this trade will appear from the following table.

Table of exportation and importation at Kiakta, in the year 1777.

	Roubles.	Cop.
Cuſtom-houſe duties,	481,460.	$59\frac{1}{2}$.
Importation of Chineſe goods, to the value of	1,466,497.	$3\frac{3}{4}$.
Of gold and ſilver,	18,215.	
Total of importation	1,484,712.	$3\frac{3}{4}$.
Exportation of Ruſſian commodities	1,383,621.	35.

From this table it appears, that the total ſum of export and import amounts to 2,868,333.

* Pallas Reiſe, P. III. p. 154.

In

In this calculation however the contraband trade is not included, which is very large; and as the year 1777 was not fo favourable to this traffic as the preceding years *, we may venture to eftimate the grofs amount of the average trade to China at near 4,000,000 roubles.

CHAP. V.

Defcription of Zurukaitu—*and its trade—Tranfport of the merchandife through* Siberia.

AS almoft the whole intercourfe between Ruffia and China is confined to Kiakta, the general account of the traffic has been given in the preceding chapter. The defcription therefore of Zurukaitu, the other place fixed upon by the treaty of Kiakta for the

* In the years 1770, 1771, 1772, the cuftom-houfe duties at Kiakta (according to Mr. Pallas, P. III. p. 154.) produced 550,000 roubles. By taking therefore the medium between that fum and 481,460, the amount of the duties in 1777, the average fum of the duties will be 515,730; and, as the duties in 1777 make nearly a fixth of the whole fum of exportation and importation, by multiplying 515,730 by 6, we have the grofs amount of the average exports and imports at 3,094,380. But as feveral goods pay no duty; and as the contraband trade, according to the loweft valuation, is eftimated at the fifth part of the exports and imports, the grofs amount of the average trade to China may be fairly computed at near 4,000,000, the fum ftated above.

purpofe of carrying on the fame trade, will neceffarily be comprifed in a narrow compafs.

Zurukaitu is fituated in 137° longitude, and 49° 20′ N. latitude, upon the Weftern branch of the river Argoon, at a fmall diftance from its fource. It is provided with a fmall garrifon, and a few wretched barracks furrounded with chevaux de frife. No merchants are fettled at this place : a few traders come every fummer from Nerfhinfk, and other Ruffian towns, in order to meet two parties of Mongol troops, who are fent from the Chinefe towns Naun and Merghen, and arrive at the frontiers about July. Thefe troops encamp near Zurukaitu upon the other fide of the river Argoon, and barter with the Siberian merchants a few Chinefe commodities, which they bring with them.

Formerly the commerce carried on at Zurukaitu was more confiderable ; but at prefent it is fo trifling, that it fcarcely deferves to be mentioned. Thefe Mongols furnifh the diftrict of Nerfhinfk with bad tea and tobacco, bad filks, and fome tolerable cottons. They receive in return ordinary furs, cloth, cattle, and Ruffian leather. This trade lafts about a month

month or fix weeks ; and the annual duties
of the cuftoms amount upon an average to no
more than 500 roubles. About the middle of
Auguft the Mongols retire : part proceed immediately to China ; and the others defcend
the ftream of the Amoor as far as its mouth,
in order to obferve if there has been no ufur-
pation upon the limits. At the fame time the
Ruffian merchants return to Nerfhinfk, and,
were it not for a fmall garrifon, Zurukaitu
would be quite deferted *.

The Ruffian commodities are tranfported
by land from Peterfburg and Mofcow to Tobolfk. From thence the merchants fometimes embark upon the Irtifh down to its
junction with the Oby ; then they either tow
up their boats, or fail up the laft mentioned
river as far as Narym, where they enter the
Ket, which they afcend to Makofffkoi Oftrog.
At that place the merchandize is conveyed
about ninety verfts by land to the Yenifèi.
The merchants then afcend that river, the
Tungufka, and Angara, to Irkutfk ; crofs the
lake Baikal ; and go up the river Selenga almoft to Kiakta.

* S. R. G. III. p. 465. Pallas Reife, P. III. p. 428.

It

It is a work of fuch difficulty to afcend the ftreams of fo many rapid rivers, that this navigation Eaftwards can hardly be finifhed in one fummer* ; for which reafon the merchants commonly prefer the way by land. Their general rendezvous is the fair of Irbit near Tobolfk : from thence they go in fledges during winter to Kiakta, where they arrive about February, the feafon in which the chief commerce is carried on with the Chinefe. They buy in their route all the furs they find in the fmall towns, where they are brought from the adjacent countries. When the merchants return in fpring with the Chinefe goods, which are of greater bulk and weight than the Ruffian commodities, they proceed by water : they then defcend the ftreams of moft of the rivers, namely, the Selenga, Angara, Tungufka, Ket, and Oby to its junction with the Irtifh ; they afcend that river to Tobolfk, and continue by land to Mofcow and Peterfburg.

Before the paffage from Okotfk to Bolcherefk was difcovered in 1716, the only com-

---

* Some of thefe rivers are only navigable in fpring when the fnow water is melting ; in winter the rivers are in general frozen.

munication

munication between Kamtchatka and Siberia was by land; and the road lay by Anadirſk to Yakutſk. The furs * of Kamtchatka and of the Eaſtern Iſles are now conveyed from that peninſula by water to Okotſk; from thence to Yakutſk by land on horſe-back, or by rein deer: the roads are ſo very bad, lying either through a rugged mountainous country, or through marſhy foreſts, that the journey laſts at leaſt ſix weeks. Yakutſk is ſituated upon the Lena, and is the principal town, where the choiceſt furs are brought in their way to Kiakta, as well from Kamtchatka as from the Northern parts of Siberia, which lie upon the rivers Lena, Yana, and Indigirka. At Yakutſk the goods are embarked upon the Lena, towed up the ſtream of that river as far as Verkolenſk, or ſtill farther to Katſheg; from thence they are tranſported over a ſhort tract of land to the rivulet Buguldeika, down that ſtream to the lake Baikal, acroſs that lake to the mouth of the

* The furs, which are generally landed upon the Eaſtern coaſt of Kamtchatka, are either ſent by ſea to Bolcheretsk, or are tranſported acroſs the peninſula in ſledges drawn by dogs. The latter conveyance is only uſed in winter: it is the common mode of travelling in that country. In ſummer there is no conveyance, as the Peninſula contains neither oxen, horſes, or rein-deer. S. R. G. III. p. 478.

Se-

Selenga, and up that river to the neighbourhood of Kiakta.

In order to give the reader some notion of
that vaft tract of country, over which the
merchandize is frequently tranfported by
land-carriage, a lift of the diftances is here
fubjoined.

From Peterfburg to Mofcow   734 verfts.
        Mofcow to Tobolfk   2385
        Tobolfk to Irkutfk   2918
        Irkutfk to Kiakta   471

                               6508
            or 4338 miles and $\frac{2}{3}$.

From Irbit to Tobolfk   420
From Irkutfk to Nerfhinfk   1129
        Nerfhinfk to Zurukaitu   370

From Okotfk to Yakutfk   927
        Yakutfk to Irkutfk   2433

From Selenginfk to Zurukaitu 850
        Zurukaitu to Pekin   1588
        Kiakta to Pekin   1532

The Chinefe tranfport their goods to Kiakta
chiefly upon camels. It is four or five days
journey from Pekin to the wall of China, and
forty-fix from thence acrofs the Mongol defert
to Kiakta *.

* Pallas Reife, P. III. p. 134.

                                C H A P.

CHAP. VI.

Tartarian rhubarb *brought to* Kiakta *by the* Bucharian *Merchants—Method of examining and purchasing the roots—Different species of rheum which yield the finest rhubarb—Price of rhubarb in* Ruffia—Exportation—*Superiority of the* Tartarian *over the* Indian *rhubarb.*

EUROPE is fupplied with rhubarb from Ruffia and the Eaft-Indies. The former is generally known by the name of Turkey rhubarb, becaufe we ufed to import it from the Levant in our commerce with the Turks, who procured it through Perfia from the Bucharians; and it ftill retains its original name, although inftead of being carried, as before, to Conftantinople, it is now brought to Kiakta by the Bucharian merchants, and there difpofed of to the Ruffians. This appellation is indeed the moft general; but it is mentioned occafionally by feveral authors, under the different denominations of Ruffian, Tartarian, Bucharian, and Thibet Rhubarb. This fort is exported from Ruffia in large roundifh pieces, freed from the bark, with an hole through

through the middle : they are externally of a
yellow colour, and, when cut, appear va-
riegated with lively reddifh ftreaks.

The other fort is called by the Druggifts
Indian Rhubarb ; and is procured from Canton in longer, harder, heavier, more compact
pieces, than the former : it is more aftringent, and has fomewhat lefs of an aromatic
flavour ; but, on account of its cheapnefs, is
more generally ufed than the Tartarian or
Turkey Rhubarb.

The government of Ruffia has referved to
itfelf the exclufive privilege of purchafing
rhubarb ; it is brought to Kiakta by fome Bucharian merchants, who have entered into a
contract to fupply the crown with that drug
in exchange for furs.   Thefe merchants come
from the town of Selin, which lies South
Weftward of the Koko-Nor, or Blue Lake,
toward Thibet.   Selin, and all the towns of
Little Bucharia, viz. Kafhkar, Yerken, Atrar,
&c. are fubject to China.

The beft rhubarb purchafed at Kiakta is
produced upon a chain of rocks, which are
very high, and for the moft part deftitute of
wood : they lie North of Selin, and ftretch
as far as the Koko-Nor.   The good roots are
diftin-

diftinguifhed by large and thick ftems. The Tanguts, who are employed in digging up the roots, enter upon that bufinefs in April or May. As faft as they take them out of the earth, they cleanfe them from the foil, and hang them upon the neighbouring trees to dry, where they remain until a fufficient quantity is procured : after which they are delivered to the Bucharian merchants. The roots are wrapped up in woollen facks, carefully preferved from the leaft humidity ; and are in this manner tranfported to Kiakta upon camels.

The exportation of the beft rhubarb is prohibited by the Chinefe, under the fevereft penalties. It is procured however in fufficient quantities, fometimes by clandeftinely mixing it with inferior roots, and fometimes by means of a contraband trade. The College of Commerce at Peterfburg is folely * empowered to receive this drug, and appoints agents at Kiakta for that purpofe. Much care is taken in the choice ; for it is examined,

* The Emprefs has lately abolifhed this exclufive privilege vefted in the College of Commerce for the purchafe of rhubarb at Kiakta ; and now all perfons are indifcriminately permitted to buy that drug from the Bucharian merchants.

in

in the prefence of the Bucharian merchants, by an apothecary commiffioned by government, and refident at Kiakta. All the worm-eaten roots are rejected ; the remainder are bored through, in order to afcertain their foundnefs ; and all the parts which appear in the leaft damaged or decayed are cut away. By thefe means even the beft roots are diminifhed a fixth part ; and the refufe is burnt, in order to prevent its being brought another year *.

Linnæus has diftinguifhed the different fpecies of rhubarb by the names Rheum Palmatum, R. Rhaphonticum, † R. Rhabarbarum, R. Compactum, and R. Ribes.

Botanifts have long differed in their opinions, which of thefe feveral fpecies is the true rhubarb ; and that queftion does not appear to be as yet fatisfactorily determined. According to the moft general opinion, it is fup-

* Pallas Reife, P. III. p. 155—157. When Mr. Pallas was at Kiakta, the Bucharian merchant, who fupplies the crown with rhubarb, brought fome pieces of white rhubarb (von milchweiffen rhabarber) which had a fweet tafte, and was equal in its effects to the beft fort.

† See Murray's edition of Linnæus Syftema Vegetab. Gott. 1744. In the former edition of Linnæus Rheum Rhabarbarum is called R. Undulatum.

pofed

pofed to be the Rheum * Palmatum ; the
feeds of which were originally procured from
a Bucharian merchant, and diftributed to the
principal botanifts of Europe. Hence this
plant has been cultivated with great fuccefs ;
and is now very common in all our botanical
gardens. The learned doctor † Hope, profeffor of medicine and botany in the univer-
fity of Edinburgh, having made trials of the
powder of this root, in the fame dofes in
which the foreign rhubarb is given, found no
difference in its effects ; and from thence con-
clufions have been drawn; with great appearance of probability, that this is the plant
which produces the true rhubarb. But this
inference does not appear to be abfolutely
conclufive ; for the fame trials have been repeated, and with fimilar fuccefs, upon the
roots of the R. Rhaponticum and R. Rhabarbarum.

The leaves of the R. Rhaponticum are
round, and fometimes broader than they are
long. This fpecies is found abundantly in

* Mr. Pallas (to whom I am chiefly indebted for this
account of the Tartarian and Siberian Rhubarb) affured
me, that he never found the R. Palmatum. in any part of
Siberia.
† Phil. Tranf. for 1765, p. 290.

the loamy and dry deferts between the Volga
and the Yaik *, towards the Cafpian Sea. It
was probably from this fort that the name
Rha, which is the Tartarian appellation of
the river Volga, was firft applied by the Ara-
bian phyficians to the feveral fpecies of rheum.
The roots however which grow in thefe warm
plains are rather too aftringent; and therefore ought not to be ufed in cafes where
opening medicines are required. The Calmucs call it Badfhona, or a ftomachic. The
young fhoots of this plant, which appear in
March or April, are deemed a good anti-
fcorbutic; and are ufed as fuch by the Ruffians. The R. Rhaponticum is not to be
found to the Weft of the Volga. The feeds
of this fpecies produced at Peterfburg plants
of a much greater fize than the wild ones:
the leaves were large, and of a roundifh cor-
dated figure.

The R. Rhabarbarum grows in the crevices
of bare rocky mountains, and alfo upon gra-
velly foils: it is more particularly found in
the high vallies of the romantic country
fituated beyond Lake Baikal. Its buds do not

* The Yaik, now called the Ural, falls into the Cafpian
Sea, about four degrees to the Eaft of the Volga.

fhoot

fhoot before the end of April; and it continues in flower during the whole month of May. The ftalks of the leaves are eaten raw by the Tartars: they produce upon moft perfons, who are unaccuftomed to them, a kind of fpafmodic contraction of the throat, which goes off in a few hours; it returns however at every meal, until they become habituated to this kind of diet. The Ruffians make ufe of the leaves in their hodge-podge: accordingly, foups of this fort affect ftrangers in the manner above-mentioned. In Siberia the ftalk is fometimes preferved as a fweetmeat; and a cuftom prevails among the Germans of introducing at their tables the buds of this plant, as well as of the Rheum Palmatum, inftead of cauli-flower.

The R. Rhaponticum which commonly grows near the torrents has, as well as the R. Rhabarbarum of Siberia, the upper part of its roots generally rotten, from too much moifture: accordingly, a very fmall portion of the lower extremity is fit for ufe. The Ruffian College of Phyficians order, for the ufe of their military hofpital, large quantities of thefe roots to be dug up in Siberia, which are prefcribed under the name of rhapontic.

But

But the perfons employed in digging and preparing it are fo ill inftructed for that purpofe, that its beft juices are frequently loft.
Thefe roots ought to be drawn up in the
fpring, foon after the melting of the fnows,
when the plant retains all its fap and ftrength;
whereas they are not taken out of the ground
before Auguft, when they are wafted by the
increafe of the ftem, and the expanfion of the
leaves. Add to this, that the roots are no
fooner taken up, than they are immediately
fliced in fmall pieces, and thus dried: by
which means the medicinal qualities are fen-
fibly impaired.

But the fame roots, which in the inftance
laft-mentioned were of fuch little efficacy,
were, when dried with proper precaution,
found to yield a very excellent rhubarb. The
procefs obferved for this purpofe, by the ingenious Mr. Pallas, was as follows. The
roots, immediately after being drawn out,
were fufpended over a ftove, where being
gradually dried, they were cleanfed from the
earth: by thefe means, although they were
actually taken up in autumn, they fo nearly
refembled the beft Tartarian rhubarb in colour, texture, and purgative qualities, that
they

they anfwered, in every refpect, the fame medicinal purpofes.

A German apothecary, named Zukert, made fimilar trials with the fame fuccefs, both on the Rheum Rhabarbarum and R. Rhaponticum, which grow in great perfection on the mountains in the neighbourhood of Nerfhinfk. He formed plantations of thefe herbs on the declivity of a rock *, covered with one foot of good mould, mixed with an equal quantity of fand and gravel. If the fummer proved dry, the plants were left in the ground ; but if the feafon was rainy, after drawing out the roots, he left them for fome days in the fhade to dry, and then replanted them. By this method of cultivation he produced in feven or eight years very large and found roots, which the rock had prevented from penetrating too deep ; and when they were properly dried, one fcruple was as efficacious as half a drachm of Tartarian rhubarb.

From the foregoing obfervations it follows, that there are other plants, befides the Rheum

---

* In order to fucceed fully in the plantation of rhubarb, and to procure found and dry roots, a dry, light foil with a rocky foundation, where the moifture eafily filters off, is effentially neceffary.

Pal-

Palmatum, the roots whereof have been found to be fimilar, both in their appearance and effects, to what is called the beft rhubarb. And indeed, upon enquiries made at Kiakta concerning the form and leaves of the plant which produces that drug, it feems not to be the R. Palmatum, but a fpecies with roundifh fcalloped leaves, and moft probably the R. Rhaponticum : for Mr. Pallas, when he was at Kiakta, applied for information to a Bucharian merchant of Selin Chotton, who now fupplies the crown with rhubarb; and his defcription of that plant anfwered to the figure of the Rheum Rhaponticum. The truth of this defcription was ftill further confirmed by fome Mongol travellers who had been in the neighbourhood of the Koko-Nor and Thibet ; and had obferved the rhubarb growing wild upon thofe mountains.

The experiments alfo made by Zukert and others, upon the roots of the R. Rhabarbarum and R, Rhaponticum, fufficiently prove, that this valuable drug was procured from thofe roots in great perfection. But, as the feeds of the Rheum Palmatum were received from the father of the above-mentioned Bucharian merchant as taken from the plant which furnifhes

nifhes the true rhubarb, we have reafon to
conjecture, that thefe three fpecies, viz. R.
Palmatum, R. Rhaponticum, and R. Rhabarbarum, when found in a drier and milder
alpine climate, and in proper fituations, are
indifcriminately drawn up, whenever the fize
of the plant feems to promife a fine root. And
perhaps the remarkable difference of the rhubarb, imported to Kiakta, is occafioned by
this indifcriminate method of collecting them.
Moft certain it is, that thefe plants grow wild
upon the mountains, without the leaft cultivation ; and thofe are efteemed the beft which
are found near the Koko-Nor, and about the
fources of the river Koango.

Formerly the exportation of rhubarb was
confined to the crown of Ruffia : and no perfons but thofe employed by government enjoyed the permiffion of fending it to foreign
countries : this monopoly however has been
taken off by the prefent emprefs, and the
free exportation of it from St. Peterfburg
granted to all perfons upon paying the duty.
It is fold, in the firft inftance, by the College
of Commerce, for the profit of the Sovereign ;
and is preferved in their magazines at St. Peterfburg.

terſburg. The current price is ſettled every year by the College of Commerce.

It is received from the Bucharian merchants at Kiakta in exchange for furs; and the prime coſt is rated at 16 roubles per pood. By adding the pay of the commiſſioners who purchaſe it, and of the apothecary who examines it, and allowing for other neceſſary expences, the value of a pood at Kiakta amounts to 25 roubles; add to this the carriage from the frontiers to St. Pererſburg, and it is calculated that the price of a pood ſtands the crown at 30 roubles. The largeſt exportation of rhubarb from Ruſſia was made in the year 1765, when 1350 pood were exported, at 65 roubles per pood.

EXPORTATION of RHUBARB from St. PETERSBURG.

In 1777, 29 poods 13 pounds $\begin{cases} \text{at } 76\frac{1}{4} \text{ Dutch * dol-} \\ \text{lars, or 91 roubles,} \\ \text{30 copecs, per pood.} \end{cases}$

In 1778, 23 poods 7 pounds, at 80 ditto, or 96 roubles.

* If we reckon a Dutch dollar, upon an average, to be worth 1 rouble 20 copecs.

In

In 1779, 1055 poods were brought by the Bucharian merchants to Kiakta; of which 680 poods 19 pounds were felected. The interior confumption of the whole empire of Ruffia for 1777 amounted to only 6 poods 5 pounds *.

The fuperiority of this Tartarian rhubarb over that procured from Canton arifes probably from the following circumftances. 1. The fouthern parts of China are not fo proper for the growth of this plant, as the mountains of Little Bucharia. 2. There is not fo exact an examination in receiving it from the Chinefe at Canton, as from the Bucharians at Kiakta. For the merchants, who purchafe this drug at Canton, are obliged to accept it in the grofs, without feparating the bad roots, and cutting away the decayed parts, as is done at Kiakta. 3. It is alfo probable, that the long tranfport of this drug by fea is detrimental to it, from the humidity which it muft neceffarily contract during fo long a voyage.

* This calculation comprehends only the rhubarb purchafed at the different magazines belonging to the College of Commerce; for what was procured by contraband is of courfe not included.

APPENDIX.

APPENDIX, N° I.

Concerning the longitude of Kamtchatka, *and of the Eaftern extremity of* Afia, *as laid down by the* Ruffian Geographers.

THE important queftion concerning the longitude of the extreme parts of Afia has been fo differently ftated by the moft celebrated geographers, that it may not be amifs to refer the curious reader to the principal treatifes upon that fubject. The proofs by which Mr. Muller and the Ruffian geographers place the longitude of the Eaftern extremity of Afia beyond 200 degrees from the firft meridian of Fero, or 180° 6′ 15″ from Paris, are drawn from the obfervations of the fatellites of Jupiter, made by Kraffilnikof, as well at Kamtchatka, as in different parts of Siberia ; and from the expeditions of the Ruffians by land and fea towards Tfchukotfkoi Nofs.

Mr. Engel calls in queftion the exactnefs of thefe obfervations, and takes off twenty-nine degrees from the longitude of Kamtchatka, as

laid

laid down by the Ruffians. To this purpofe he has given to the public,

1. Memoires et obfervations geographiques et critiques fur la fituation des Pays Septentrionaux de l'Afie et de l'Amerique. A Laufanne, 1765. 2. Geographifche und Critifche Nachricht ueber die Lage der noerdlichen Gegenden von Afien und America. Mittau, 1772.

It appears to Monfieur de Vaugondy, that there are not fufficient grounds for fo extraordinary a diminution: accordingly he fhortens the continent of Afia only eleven degrees of longitude; and upon this fubject he has given the two following treatifes: 1. Lettre au fujet d'une carte fyftematique des Pays Septentrionaux de l'Afie et de l'Amerique. Paris, 1768. 2. Nouveau fyfteme geographique, par lequel on concilie les anciennes connoiffances fur les Pays au Nord Oueft de l'Amerique. Paris, 1774.

In oppofition to thefe authors, Monfieur Buache has publifhed an excellent treatife, entituled Memoires fur les Pays de l'Afie et de l'Amerique. Paris, 1775.

In this memoir he diffents from the opinions of Meffrs Engel and Vaugondy; and defends the

APPENDIX, N° I.   369

the fyftem of the Ruffian geographers in the following manner. Monfieur Maraldi, after comparing the obfervations of the fatellites of Jupiter, taken at Kamtchatka by Kraffilnikof, with the tables, has determined the longitude of Okotfk, Bolcheretfk, and the port of St. Peter and Paul, from the firft meridian of Paris as follows :

	h		
* Longitude of Okotfk	9	23	30
of Bolcheretfk	10	17	17
of the Port	10	25	5

Latitude of Okotfk 59° 22′, of Bolcheretfk 52° 55′, of the Port 53° 1′.   The

* Kraffilnikof compared his obfervations with correfponding ones taken at Peterfburg, which gave refults as follow :

From comparing an obfervation of an eclipfe of the firft fatellite, taken at Okotfk the 17th of January, 1743, with an obfervation of an eclipfe of the fame fatellite taken at Peterfburg on the 15th of January in the fame year, the difference of longitude between Peterfburg and Okotsk appeared to be 7ʰ 31′ 29″; from a comparifon of two other fimilar obfervations the difference of longitude was 7ʰ 31′ 34″, a mean of which (rejecting the ½ fecond) is 7ʰ 31′ 31″, being the true difference between the meridians of Peterfburg and Okotsk according to thefe obfervations. By adding the difference of the longitude between Petersburg and Paris, which is 1ʰ 52′ 25″, we have the longitude of Okotsk from Paris 7ʰ 23′ 56″, which differs only 26″ from the refult of Monf. Maraldi. Nov. Comm. Pet. III. p. 470.

In the fame manner the longitude of Bolcheretsk appears from the correfponding obfervations taken at that place and at Peterfburg to be 10ʰ 20′ 22″, differing from Mr. Maraldi about 2′ 5″. Nov. Com. p. 469.

But

The comparifon of the following refults, deduced from correfponding obfervations * of the eclipfes of Jupiter's fatellites taken at Bolcheretfk and at the port of Peter and Paul by Kraffilnikof, and at Pekin by the Jefuit miffionaries, will fhew from their near agreement the care and attention which muft have been given to the obfervations; and from hence there is reafon to fuppofe, that the fufpicions of inaccuracy imputed to Kraffilnikof are ill founded.

1741, Old Style.

Jan. 27, Em. 1 Sat. 12 9 25 at the port of St. Peter and Paul.

9 20 35 at Pekin.

Difference of the meridian at Pekin and the Port   2 48 50

Jan. 30, Imm. 111 Sat. 12 5 30 at the Port.

9 16 30 at Pekin.

2 49 0

But the longitude of the port of St. Peter and Paul, eftimated in the fame manner from correfponding obfervations, differs from the longitude as computed by Monf. Maraldi no more than 20 feconds ; p. 469.

* Obf. Aft. Ecc. Sat. Jovis, &c. Nov. Com. Petr. vol. III. p. 452, &c. Obf. Aft. Pekini factæ. Ant. Haller-ftein—Curante Max. Hell. Vindibonæ, 1768.

Feb.

	h		
Feb. 5, 1 Sat.	8	33	26 at the Port.
	5	43	45 at Pekin.

	h		
	2	49	41

	h		
Feb. 12, Em. 1 Sat.	10	28	49
	7	59	29

	h		
	2	49	20

And the longitude from Paris to Pekin being	7	36	23
The difference of the meridians of Paris and the Port will be	10	25	36

Which differs only 31 feconds from the determination of Mr. Maraldi.

1741.   Old Style.

	h		
March 23, Em. 11 Sat.	10	55	2 at Bolcheretſk.
	8	14	0 at Pekin.

	h		
	2	41	2

	h		
Dec. 31, Im. 1 Sat.	10	51	58 at Bolcheretſk.
	8	9	45 at Pekin.

Difference of the meridian at Pekin and Bolcheretſk	2	42	13

	h		
By taking the medium, the difference of the longitude between Bolcheretſk and Pekin will be found to be	2	41	37

Betwee

Between Bolcheretſk and Paris   10 18   0

Which differs only one minute and one ſecond from the determination of Mr. Maraldi.

In order to call in queſtion the concluſions drawn from the obſervations of Kraſſilnikof, Monſieur de Vaugondy pretends that the inſtruments and pendulums, which he uſed at Kamtchatka, were much damaged by the length of the journey; and that the perſon, who was ſent to repair them, was an unſkilful workman.   But this opinion ſeems to have been advanced without ſufficient foundation.   Indeed Kraſſilnikof * himſelf allows that his pendulum occaſionally ſtopt, even when neceſſary to aſcertain the true time of the obſervation.   He admits therefore that the obſervations which he took under theſe diſadvantages (when he could not correct them by preceding or ſubſequent obſervations of the ſun or ſtars) are not to be depended upon, and has accordingly diſtinguiſhed them by an aſteriſk : there are however a number of others, which were not liable to any exception of this kind ; and the obſervations already mentioned are compriſed under this claſs.

* Nov. Com. Pet. III. p. 444.

If

If the arguments which have been already produced fhould not appear fufficiently fatis-factory, we have the further teftimony of Mr. Muller, who was in thofe parts at the fame time with Kraffilnikof, and who is the only competent judge of this matter now alive. For that refpectable author has given me the moft pofitive affurances, that the in-ftruments were not damaged in fuch a manner as to affect the accuracy of the obfervations when in the hands of a fkilful obferver.

That the longitude of Kamtchatka is laid down with fufficient accuracy by the Ruffian geographers, will appear by comparing it with the longitude of Yakutfk; for as the latter has been clearly eftablifhed by a variety of obfervations, taken at different times and by different perfons, if there is any error in placing Kamtchatka fo far to the Eaft, it will be found in the longitude between Yakutfk and Bolcheretfk. A fhort comparifon there-fore of fome of the different obfervations made at Yakutfk will help to fettle the lon-gitude of Kamtchatka; and will ftill farther confirm the character of a fkilful obferver, which has been given to Kraffilnikof.

Kraf-

Kraffilnikof in returning from Kamtchatka obferved at Yakutfk feveral eclipfes of the fatellites of Jupiter, of which the following are mentioned by him as the moft exact.

1744, Old Style.

* Feb. 7. Imm. 1. Sat. 11 18 35
                       fomewhat doubtful.

    22. Imm. 11. Sat. 10 31 11 ⎫
    29. Imm. 11. Sat. 13 6 54 ⎪
Mar. 1. Imm. 1. Sat. 11 23 0 ⎬ all exact.
Apr. 9. Em. 1. Sat. 12 23 50 ⎭

The fame eclipfes, as calculated by the tables of Mr. Wargentin, for the Meridian of Paris, are as follow:

				h	′	″	Difference of the meridians of Paris and Yakutsk. h ′ ″
Feb.	7.	Imm.	1.	2	49	0	8 29 35
	27.	Imm.	11.	2	3	10	8 28 1
	29.	Imm.	11.	4	38	17	8 28 37
Mar.	1.	Imm.	1.	3	3	37	8 29 23
Apr.	9.	Em.	1.	3	54	12	8 29 46
The mean of which is							8 29 5

---

* Nov. Comm. Petr. T. III. p. 460.

The

The obfervations of Mr. Iflenief *, made
at Yakutfk in the year 1769, to which place
he was fent to obferve the tranfit of Venus,
have received the fanction of the Imperial
Academy. The longitude which he fixes for
Yakutfk is 8ʰ 29′ 34″; this correfponds, to a
fufficient degree of exactnefs, with the longitude inferred from the obfervations of
Kraffilnikof.

Thus the longitude of Yakutfk from Paris
being 8ʰ 29° 4″. or in degrees 127 16 0. and
of Bolcheretfk 10 17 17, or in degrees 150°
19′ 15. the difference of the longitude of thefe
two places, from aftronomical obfervations,
amounts to 1 48 8. or in degrees 27° 3′ 0″.
The latitude of Bolcheretfk is 52° 55′ 0″. and
that of Yakutfk 62° 1′ 50″; and the difference of their longitude being from the
preceding determination 27 3 0. the direct
diftance between the places meafured on a
great circle of the earth will appear by trigonometry to be 16° 57′. or about 1773 verfts,
reckoning 104½ verfts to a degree. This
diftance confifts partly of fea, and partly of
land; and a conftant intercourfe is kept up

* For Iflenief's obfervations at Yakutsk, fee Nov. Com.
Tom. XIV. Part III. p. 268 to 321.

be-

between the two places by means of Okotſk, which lies between them. The diſtance by ſea from Bolcheretſk to Okotſk is eſtimated by ſhips reckonings to be 1254 verſts, and the diſtance by land from Okotſk to Yakutſk is 927 verſts, making altogether 2118. The direct diſtance deduced by trigonometry (on a ſuppoſition that the difference of longitude between Bolcheretſk and Yakutſk is 27° 3ʹ.) is 1773, falling ſhort of 2181 by 408 ; a difference naturally to be expected from conſidering, that neither roads by land, nor the courſe of ſhips at ſea, are ever performed preciſely on a great circle of the earth, which is the ſhorteſt line that can be drawn on the earth's ſurface between two places.

By this agreement between the diſtance thus eſtimated, and that deduced by computation, on ſuppoſing the difference of longitude between Yakutſk and Bolcheretſk to be 27° 3ʹ. it ſeems very improbable, that there ſhould be an error of many degrees in the aſtronomical determination.

Since then the longitude between Fero and Peterſburg is acknowledged to be 48°—that between Peterſburg and Yakutſk 99° 21ʹ— and as the diſtance in longitude between Ya-

kutſk

kutfk and Bolcheretfk cannot be materially
lefs than 27° 3′; it follows that the longitude
of Bolcheretfk from Fero cannot be much
lefs than 174° 24′. Where then fhall we
find place for fo great an error as 27 degrees,
which, according to Mr. Engel, or even of
11°, which, according to Monf. Vaugondy, is
imputed to the Ruffian geographers in fixing
the longitude of Kamtchatka ?

From the ifle of Fero

Longitude of Yakutfk	—	147	0 0
of Okotfk	—	160	7 0
of Bolcheretfk	—	174	13 0
of the Port of St. Peter and Paul		176	10 0

As no aftronomical obfervations have been
made further to the Eaft than the Port of St.
Peter and Paul, it is impoffible to fix, with
any degree of certainty, the longitude of the
North-Eaftern promontory of Afia. It appears however from Beering's and Synd's
coafting voyages towards Tfchukotfkoi Nofs,
and from other expeditions to thofe parts by
land and fea, that the coaft of Afia in lat. 64.
ftretches at leaft 23° 2 30. from the Port, or
to about 200° longitude from the ifle of Fero.

APPEN-

APPENDIX, No II.

Lift of the principal charts reprefenting the Ruffian *difcoveries.*

THE following is an authentic lift of the principal charts of the Ruffian difcoveries hitherto publifhed. It is accompanied with a few explanatory remarks.

1. Carte des nouvelles dècouvertes au nord de la mer du fud, tant à l'Eft de la Siberie et du Kamtchatka, qu'à l'Oueft de la Nouvelle France dreflée fur les memoires de Mr. de l'Ifle, par Philippe Buache, 1750. A memoir relative to this chart was foon afterwards publifhed, with the fallowing title, Explication de la carte des nouvelles dècouvertes au Nord de la mer du fud par Mr. de l'Ifle ; Paris, 1752, 4to. This map is alluded to, p. 28 of this work. 2. Carte des nouvelles dècouvertes entre la partie orientale de l'Afie et l'Occidentale de l'Amerique, avec des vues fur la grande terre réconnue, par les Ruffes, en 1741, par Phil. Buache, 1752. 3. Nouvelle carte des dècouvertes faites par des vaiffeaux Ruffiens aux côtes inconnues de l'Amerique

l'Amerique feptentrionale avec les pais ad-
jacens, dreffée fur les memoires authentiques
de ceux qui ont affifté à ces découvertes, et
fur d'autres connoiffances ; dont on rend raifon dans un memoire feparé : à St. Peterfburg, à l'Academie Imperiale des fciences,
1754. 1758. This map was publifhed under
the infpeftion of Mr. Muller, and is ftill prefixed to his account of the Ruffian difcoveries *. The part which exhibits the New-
difcovered Ifles and the coaft of America was
chiefly taken from the chart of Beering's expedition. Accordingly that continent is reprefented as advancing, between 50 and 60
degrees of latitude, to within a fmall diftance
of Kamtchatka. Nor could there be any reafon to fufpeft, that fuch experienced failors
as Beering and Tfchirikof had miftaken a
chain of iflands for promontories belonging to
America, until fubfequent navigators had actually failed through that very part which was
fuppofed to be a continent.

* This map was publifhed by Jefferys under the following title : " A map of the Difcoveries made by the Ruffians
" on the North Weft coaft of America, publifhed by the
" Royal Academy of Sciences at Peterfburg. Repub-
" lifhed by Thomas Jefferys, Geographer to his Majefty,
" 1761."

4. A fe-

4. A fecond chart publifhed by the Academy, but not under the infpection of Mr. Muller, bears the fame title as the former. Nouvelle carte des découvertes faites par des vaiffeaux Ruffiens aux côtes inconnues de l'Amerique, &c. 1773.

It is for the moft part a copy of a manufcript chart known in Ruffia by the name of the chart of the *Promyfchlenics*, or merchant adventurers, and which was fketched from the mere reports of perfons who had failed to the New-difcovered Iflands. As to the fize and pofition of the New-difcovered Iflands, this chart of the Academy is extremely erroneous : it is however free from the abovementioned miftake, which runs through all the former charts, namely, the reprefenting of the coaft of America, between 50 and 60 degrees of latitude, as contiguous to Kamtchatka. It likewife removes that part of the fame continent lying in latitude 66, from 210° longitude to 224°, and in its ftead lays down a large ifland, which ftretches between latitude 64° and 71° 30′, from 207° longitude to 218°, to within a fmall diftance of both continents. But whether this latter alteration be equally juftifiable or not, is a queftion,

the

the decifion of which muft be left to future navigators *.

5. Carte du nouvel Archipel du Nord decouvert par les Ruffes dans la mer de Kamtchatka et d'Anadir. This chart is prefixed to Mr. Stæhlin's account of the New Northern Archipelago. In the Englifh tranflation it is called, A Map of the New Northern Archipelago, difcovered by the Ruffians in the feas of Kamtchatka and Anadyr. It differs from the laft-mentioned chart only in the fize and pofition of a few of the iflands, and in the addition of five or fix new ones; and is equally incorrect. The New-difcovered Iflands

---

* Mr. Muller has long ago acknowledged, in the moft candid and public manner, the incorrectnefs of the former chart, as far as it relates to the part which reprefents America as contiguous to Kamtchatka : but he ftill maintains his opinion concerning the actual vicinity of the two continents in an higher latitude. The following quotation is taken from a letter written by Mr. Muller in 1774, of which I have a copy in my poffeffion. " Pofterity muft judge if " the new chart of the Academy is to be preferred to the " former one for removing the continent of America " (which is reprefented as lying near the coaft of Tfchutfki) " to a greater difiance. Synd, who is more to be trufted " than the Promyfchlenics, perfifts in the old fyftem. He " places America as near as before to Tfchukotfkoi Nofs, " but knows nothing of a large ifland called Alafhka, " which takes up the place of the continent, and which " ought to be laid down much more to the South or South " Eaft."

are

are claffed in this chart into three groups,
which are called the Ifles of Anadyr *, the
Olutorian † Ifles, and the Aleütian Ifles.
The two laft-mentioned charts are alluded to,
p. 29 of this work.

6. An excellent map of the Empire of
Ruffia, publifhed by the geographical depart-
ment of the Academy of Sciences at St. Peterfburg in 1776, comprehends the greateft
part of the New-difcovered Iflands. A reduced copy of this chart being prefixed to this
work, I fhall only mention the authorities
from whence the compilers have laid down

* Monfieur Buffon has adopted the appellation and erroneous reprefentation of the ifles of Anadyr in his Carte
de deux regions Polaires, latcly publifhed. See Supplement
à l'Hift. Nat. vol. V. p. 615.

† The Olutorian Ifles are fo named from the fmall river
of Olutora, which flows into the fea at Kamtchatka, about
latitude 61°. The following remarks upon this group of
iflands are taken from Mr. Muller's letter mentioned in the
note, p. 381. " This appellation of Olutorian Ifles is not
" in ufe at Kamtchatka. Thefe iflands, called upon this
" chart Olutorians, lie according to the chart of the
" Promyfchlenics, and the chart of the Academy, very
" remote from the river Olutora: and it feems as if they
" were advanced upon this chart nearer to Kamtchatka
" only in favour of the name. They cannot be fituated
" fo near that coaft, becaufe they were neither feen by
" Beering in 1728, nor by the Promyfchlenics, Novikof and
" Baccof, when they failed in 1728 from the Anadyr to
" Beering's Ifland." See p. 46.

the

APPENDIX, N° II. 383

the New-difcovered Iflands. The Aleütian
ifles are partly taken from Beering's chart,
partly from * Otcheredin's, whofe voyage is
related in the eleventh chapter, and partly
from other MS. charts of different navigators.
The iflands near the coaft of the Tfchutfki
are copied from Synd's chart. The Fox
Iflands are laid down from the chart of Otcheredin. The reader will perceive, that the
pofition of the Fox Iflands, upon this general map of Ruffia, is materially different
from that affigned to them in the chart of
Krenitzin's and Levafhef's voyage. In the
former they are reprefented as ftretching between 56° 61′ North latitude, and 210° and
230° longitude from the ifle of Fero : in the

* I have a MS. copy of Otcheredin's chart in my poffeffion ; but as the Fox Iflands, in the general Map of
Ruffia, are copied from thence, the reader will find them
laid down upon the reduced map prefixed to this work. The
anonymous author of the account of the Ruffian Difcoveries, of whofe work I have given a tranflation in Part I.
feems to have rollowed, in moft particulars, Otcheredin's
chart and journal for the longitude, latitude, fize, and pofition of the New-difcovered Iflands. For this reafon, I
fhould have had his chart engraved if the Fox Iflands upon
the general map had not been taken from thence : there
feemed no occafion therefore for encreafing the expence of
this work, already too great from the number of charts, by
the addition of another not abfolutely neceffary.

latter

latter they are fituated between 51° 40′ and
55° 20′ latitude, and 199° 30′ and 207° 30′
longitude. According to the moſt recent accounts received from Peterſburg, the poſition
given to them upon this general map is conſiderably too much to the North and Eaſt;
conſequently that aſſigned to them upon Krenitzin's chart is probably the moſt to be de-
pended upon.

7. Carte des dècouvertes Ruſſes dans la
mer orientale et en Amerique, pour ſervir à
l'Eſſai * ſur le commerce de Ruſſie, 1778,
Amſter-

---

* The twelfth chapter of this Eſſay relates to the difcoveries and commerce of the Ruſſians in the Eaſtern
Ocean. The account of the Ruſſian difcoveries is a tranſlation of Mr. Stæhlin's Deſcription of the New Northern
Archipelago. In addition, he has ſubjoined an account of
Kamtchatka, and a ſhort ſketch of the Ruſſian commerce
to the New-diſcovered Iſlands, and to America. If we
may believe the author of this Eſſay, the Ruſſians have
not only difcovered America, but they alſo every year form
occaſional ſettlements upon that continent, ſimilar to thoſe
of the Europeans in Newfoundland. His words are: " Il
eſt donc certain, que les Ruſſes ont découvert le continent de l'Amérique ; mais on peut aſſurer qu'ils n'y ont
encore aucun port, aucun comptoir. Il en eſt des étab-
liſſements de cette nation dans la grande terre, comme de
ceux des nations Européennes dans l'iſle de Terre Neuve.
Ses vaiſſeaux ou frégates arrivent en Amérique ; leurs equi-
pages et les Coſaques chaſſeurs s'établiſſent ſur la côte; les
uns ſe retranchent, et les autres y font la chaſſe et la
pêche du chien marin et du narval. Ils reviennent enſuite
au

Amfterdam. It is natural to expect, that a chart fo recently publifhed fhould be fuperior to all the preceding ones ; whereas, on the contrary, it is by far the moft incorrect reprefentation of the New-difcovered Iflands which has yet appeared.

au Kamtchatka, après avoir été relevès par d'autres frégates fus les mêmes parages, ou à des diftances plus ou moins eloignés, &c. &c." See Effai fur le commerce de la Ruffie, p. 292, 293. Thus the public is impofed upon by fictious and exaggerated accounts.

APPEN-

APPENDIX, N° III.

Specimen of the Aleütian language.
(See Part II. Chap. VII. p. 241.)

Sun	Agaiya	One	Tagatak
Moon	Tughilag	Two	Alag
Wind	Katſhik	Three	Kankoos
Water	Tana	Four	Setſchi
Fire	Kighenag	Five	Tſhaw
Fearth hut	Oollae	Six	Atoo
Chief	Toigon	Seven	Ooloo
Man	Taiyaga	Eight	Kapoé
Wood	Yaga	Nine	Shifet
Shield	Kuyak	Ten	Aſok.
Sea-otter	Tſcholota		
Name of the nation.	Kanagiſt		

It is very remarkable, that none of theſe words bear the leaſt reſemblance to thoſe of the ſame ſignification, which are found in the different dialects ſpoken by the Koriacks, Kamtchadals, and the inhabitants of the Kuril Iſles.

APPENDIX, N° IV.

TABLE OF LONGITUDE AND LATITUDE.

For the convenience of the Reader, the following Table exhibits, in one point of view, the longitude and latitude of the principal places mentioned in this performance. Their longitudes are eftimated from the firft meridian of the Ifle of Fero, and from that of the Royal Obfervatory at Greenwich. The longitude of Greenwich from Fero is computed at 17° 34′ 45″. The longitude of the places marked * has been taken from aftronomical obfervations.

	Latitude			Longitude Fero			Greenwich	
	D.	M.	S.	D.	M.	S.	D.	M.
* Peterfburg —	59	56	23	48	0	0	30	25 †
* Mofcow —	55	45	45	55	6	30	37	31
* Archangel —	64	33	24	56	15	0	38	40
* Tobolfk —	58	12	22	85	40	0	68	26
* Tomfk —	56	30	0	102	50	0	85	15
* Irkutfk —	52	18	15	122	13	0	104	38
* Selenginfk —	51	6	0	124	18	30	106	44
Kiakta —	35	0	0	124	18	0	106	43
* Yakutfk —	62	1	50	147	0	0	129	25
* Okotfk —	59	22	0	160	7	0	142	32
* Bolcherefk —	52	55	0	174	13	0	156	38
* Port of St. Peter and Paul	35	1	0	176	10	0	158	36
Eaftern Extremity of Siberia	66	0	0	200	0	0	182	25
Unalafhka { According to the general map of Ruffia	58	0	0	223	0	0	205	25
According to the chart of Krenitzin and Levafheff	53	30	0	205	30	0	187	55

† I have omitted the feconds in the longitude from Greenwich.

INDEX.

A.

Spe-

I N D E X.

At-

INDEX.

C.

INDEX.

C.

D.

INDEX.

Efqui-

INDEX.

at-

INDEX.

INDEX.

INDEX.

Lyſſie

I N D E X.

INDEX.

Ple-

INDEX.

Ruffia

INDEX.

INDEX.

Siberia,

INDEX.

Stu-

INDEX.

Tfchi-

INDEX.

Uni-

INDEX.

FINIS.

SUPPLEMENT

TO THE

RUSSIAN DISCOVERIES.

A

COMPARATIVE VIEW

OF THE

RUSSIAN DISCOVERIES

WITH THOSE MADE BY

CAPTAINS COOK AND CLERKE;

AND A SKETCH OF

WHAT REMAINS TO BE ASCERTAINED
BY FUTURE NAVIGATORS.

BY WILLIAM COXE, A. M. F.R.S.

One of the Senior Fellows of King's College, Cambridge;
Member of the Imperial Œconomical Society at St. Peterſ-
burgh, of the Royal Academy of Sciences at Copenhagen; and
Chaplain to his Grace the Duke of MARLBOROUGH.

LONDON,

PRINTED BY J. NICHOLS,

FOR T. CADELL, IN THE STRAND.

MDCCLXXXVII.

T O

PETER SIMON PALLAS, M.D. F.R.S.

COUNSELLOR OF THE BOARD OF MINES

TO THE EMPRESS OF RUSSIA,

MEMBER OF THE IMPERIAL ACADEMY OF

SCIENCES AT ST. PETERSBURGH, &c.

THE FOLLOWING ATTEMPT TO

COMPARE THE DISCOVERIES

OF A NATION, WHOSE

CIVIL, TOPOGRAPHICAL, AND

NATURAL HISTORY

HE HAS AMPLY ELUCIDATED,

IS INSCRIBED,

B Y

HIS FAITHFUL AND OBEDIENT

HUMBLE SERVANT,

WILLIAM COXE.

Cambridge,
April 25, 1787.

ADVERTISEMENT.

THE author would have arranged, at a more early period, the following Comparative View, which seems necessarily connected with his former publication on the Ruffian Discoveries; if he had not been absent from England when Cook's Voyage first made its appearance; and if continued travels and avocations had not prevented him from consulting those books, charts, and manuscripts, which the examination of so intricate a subject required.

Mr. Pallas has lately favoured the public, in his *Neue Nordifche Beytraege*, with several curious particulars concerning the Tchutski, the two islands lying between East Cape and Cape Prince of Wales, and relative to the New-discovered islands. An extract of some of these particulars is given by Mr. Pennant in his Introduction to the Arctic Zoology, and more amply in his Supplement to that interesting work, in which the reader will find an excellent map of those parts, which are mentioned in this Comparative View.

[419]

CHAP I.

A comparative View of the Ruffian *Difcoveries,*
with thofe made by Cook *and* Clerke. 1. *On*
the Coaft of Afia. 2. *On that of* America.
3. *With refpect to the New-difcovered Iflands.*

AS my account of the Ruffian Difcoveries,
printed in 1780, contained the principal intelligence at that time known ; and
as, fince its publication, a new light has been
thrown upon that important fubject by Cook
and Clerke, I fhall, in this chapter, compare
the difcoveries of the Ruffians with the fubfequent obfervations of the Englifh navigators. 1. On the coaft of Afia, 2. on that of
America ; and 3. with refpect to the New-
difcovered Iflands.

1. The accuracy of Krafilnikof's obfervations,
at the Port of St. Peter and St. Paul, has
been confirmed by Captain Cook. The latter places that harbour in lat. 53′ 1′, long.
158′

158′ 36″ eaſt * ; the former in lat. 53′ 0″
38″, long. 176′ 10″ from Fero, or 158′ 35″
from Greenwich. The difference is only 22
feconds in the latitude, and 7 minutes in
the longitude. Hence the affertion of Vaugondy, that the Ruffians had advanced the
peninfula of Kamtchatka eleven degrees too
much to the eaſt, and of Engel, who fuppofed that error to be no lefs than 29 degrees, is evidently confuted; and the juſt-
nefs of the aſtronomical obfervations, made
by the Ruffian geographers, which I attempted
to prove in the firſt number of the Appendix to the Ruffian Difcoveries, p. 367, is now
incontrovertibly afcertained.

Though we cannot expect nearly the fame
accuracy in the longitude of thofe places,
which have not been laid down by aſtronomical obfervations; yet we fhall find, perhaps, that the errors of the Ruffians, even
under fuch difadvantages, have not always
been fo great, as might reafonably be fuppofed. Thus while the latitude of Kamt-

---

* It is neceffary to apprife the reader, that, in this Supplement, whenever the longitude given by Cook is mentioned, it is taken from the meridian of Greenwich. The
reader is alfo defired to confult the maps and charts which
accompany Cook's Voyage to the Pacific Ocean.

chatka

chatka Nofs, and of Kronotſkoi Nofs the moſt north-eaſterly point in the peninſula of Kamtchatka, agrees with the latitude of thoſe places, given by Captain Cook, their longitude is laid down 2′ 46″ too much to the weſt; and the fame error ſeems to prevail in the bearings of the Kamtchatka Coaſt, as traced on the Ruſſian charts.

Towards the north, the deficiency in the longitude is far more confiderable. The promontory of St. Thaddæus, the moſt north eaſterly point in the country of the Koriacs, lies, according to Cook, in lat. 62′ 50″, long. 180′; and is fituated, on the general map of Ruſſia, in lat. 63, long. 190, from Fero, or 172′ 25″ from Greenwich; which gives a difference of only 50′ in the latitude, but of 7′ 35″ in the longitude.

The next point of land obſerved by the Engliſh navigators, was that promontory called by Beering Tchukotſkoi Nofs, a name adopted by Captain Cook, but which is denominated by moſt of the Ruſſian geographers Anadirſkoi Nofs, from its poſition on the Bay of the Anadyr. The application of the term Tchukotſkoi Nofs to this promontory, may, perhaps, occafion ſome confuſion

to

to future navigators and geographers, as that
appellation has been ufually given, and ought
therefore to be appropriated, to the eaftern extremity of Afia, the Eaft Cape of Cook.
From Anadirfkoi Nofs, placed by the Englifh in lat. 64′ 13″, under the name of
Tchukotfkoi Nofs, to Cape Serdze Kamen, in
lat. 67. the utmoft extent of Beering's navigation to the north, Captain Cook, with great
candour, does juftice to the memory of Beering, by obferving, that " he has here de-
" lineated the coaft very well, and fixed the
" latitude and longitude of the places better
" than could be expected from the methods
" he had to go by *."

* Cook's Voyage, vol. II. p. 474. The reader is defired
to correct a paffage in the note, p. 263, of my Ruffian Difcoveries ; in which I afferted, upon the authority of Muller,
that Beering, in his expedition to the northern coafts of
Afia, did not double the north eaftern promontory of that
continent, properly called Tchukotskoi Nofs. Whereas it
appears, from a comparative view of Beering's and Cook's
difcoveries, that the former actually paffed that celebrated
point ; and that Cape Serdze Kamen, the utmoft extent
of his voyage, is fituated to the north, and not, according
to Muller, to the fouth of the faid promontory. Captain
Cook, who alone could afcertain thefe points, and whofe
judgment muft be confidered as decifive, informs us, that
Muller's account of Beering's expedition, and that part of
the chart prefixed to his Ruffian Difcoveries, which refers
to that expedition, are lefs accurate, than the relation of the
fame voyage, and the annexed map publifhed by Dr. Camp-
bell in the fecond edition of Harris's Collection of Voyages.

Within

Within this fpace our great navigator has corrected the errors of the Ruffian charts, and afcertained the pofition of the real Tchukotfkoi Nofs, which Muller had erroneoufly conjectured to lie above the 70th degree of latitude. He calls this great promontory of the Tchutfki Eaft Cape, proves it to be the moft eaftern extremity of Afia, and fixes its latitude in 66′ 6″, and long. 190′ 22″. Thus he has unqueftionably fhewn, that the Ruffians did not err in afferting, that the north eaftern extremity of Afia ftretched beyond the 200th degree of longitude from the Ifle of Fero, or 182 from Greenwich.

The earlieft and moft important of the Ruffian voyages in thefe parts, as it firft afcertained the feparation of the two continents, is that remarkable expedition of Defhnef, in which, according to Muller, he failed from the mouth of the Kovyma, doubled Tchukotfkoi Nofs, or the Eaft Cape of Cook, and was fhipwrecked in the Sea of Kamtchatka. An account of this expedition is given in my Ruffian Difcoveries *. But as from want of circumftantial evidence, many

* See p. 252.

per-

perfons ftill doubt, whether Defhnef faiied round this celebrated promontory; it may not, perhaps, be uninterefting to ftate a few particulars in Cook's narrative, which may feem to corroborate the authenticity of Defhnef's voyage.

Defhnef's defcription of the North Eaftern Cape correfponds in feveral material circumftances with that of the fame promontory given by Cook. According to Defhnef, it " *confifts almoft entirely of rocks* *." Cook fays, that " it fhews a fteep *rocky* cliff next " the fea; and at the very point are *fome* " *rocks like fpires.* The land about this pro " montory is compofed of hills and vallies: " the former terminate at the fea in *fteep rocky* " *points,* and the latter in low fhores. The " hills feemed to be *naked rocks* †."

Defhnef adds, that, on the coaft near the promontory, the natives had reared a *pile like a tower, with the bones of whales.* Cook likewife noticed thefe piles as very common on the coaft of the Tchutfki. " Over the " dwelling ftands a kind of fentry box, *com-* " *fofed of the large bones of large fifh* ;" and

---

* " Aus lauter Felfen beftunde." S. R. G. III. p. 17.
† Cook's Voyage, Vol. II. p. 472.

again,

again, " near the dwellings were erected ftages " of *bones*, fuch as before defcribed *." Cook alfo agrees with Defhnef in placing two fmall iflands directly oppofite to the promontory ; and Captain King confirms another affertion of the Ruffian navigator, that the paffage from the fame promontory to the mouth of the Anadyr may, with a fair wind, be per-formed in feventy-two hours †.

To thofe perfons who object to Defhnef's narrative, becaufe Cook and Clerke were, in two fucceffive years, prevented by the ice from penetrating into the frozen ocean ; it may be replied, that Defhnef paffed in a fmall veffel, which might more eafily be worked through than the Englifh fhips ; and that the year, in which he failed round, is re-prefented as more free from ice than ufual. The feafon alfo, in which Defhnef probably doubled the great Siberian promontory, was more.favourable to navigation in the Frozen Sea, than the times of the year employed by the Englifh. For although he failed on

* Vol. II. p. 451, 472.
† The reader will find thefe two laft-mentioned points more fully difcuffed by Captain King, Vol. II¹. p. 264.

the

the firft of July *, yet he does not appear to have arrived in the Eaftern Ocean until the latter end of September. Soon after Ankunidof's veffel was fhipwrecked on Tchukotfkoi Nofs, Defhnef mentions, that he landed on the firft of October †, and fkirmifhed with the Tchutfki. It follows therefore, from the length of the interval between the day of his departure from the mouth of the Kovyma to his arrival in the Eaftern Ocean, that he probably waited for an opportunity of getting through the ice, which he at length effected. Whereas Cook quitted that dreary region on the 29th of Auguft; and Clerke, fo early as the month of July. The middle and the latter end of September are generally efteemed the moft proper periods for navigating the Frozen Ocean.

The fole aim of Defhnef being to fail from the Kovyma to the Anadýr, it was not incompatible with his plan to continue on the coaft, and to perfevere in expecting a favourable occafion for executing his purpofe, without expofing himfelf to thofe difficulties and dangers, which feamen from more diftant quar-

* June 20, O. S.   † Sept. 20, O. S.

ters

ters muft neceffarily experience. On the contrary, the grand defign of the Englifh navigators being to afcertain the practicability of a North Eaftern paffage, and having incontrovertibly determined that important queftion in the negative, they accomplifhed the primary object of their expedition. They could not therefore, confiftently with their views and inftructions, by delaying their departure from thofe frozen regions, hazard the danger of being hemmed in by the ice, in order merely to fhow the poffibility of getting round to the Kovyma.

Should all thefe circumftances be confidered as proofs, that Defhnef performed this much-difputed voyage ; yet, as he neither made any aftronomical obfervations, nor traced a chart of the coaft, his expedition, though it decided the long-agitated difpute concerning the feparation of the two continents, did not, however, contribute to an accurate knowledge of the north-eaftern extremity of Afia, for which we are indebted to Cook alone.

2. The difcoveries of the Ruffians on the Continent of America come next under confideration. Several of thofe coafts, vifited by

the

the Ruffians, which they fuppofed, though on very uncertain grounds, to be parts of America, and which they had imperfectly defcribed, have been afcertained by Cook to belong to that Continent.

Thus Cook * difcovered a great mountain on the Coaft of America, in latitude 58′ 53″, longitude 220′ 52″, which he allows to be the fame as Eeering's Mount St. Elias, lying, according to his eftimation, in latitude 58′ 28″, longitude 236′, from Fero, or 218′ 25″ from Greenwich. The difference in latitude is merely 28 feconds, and of longitude only 2′ 27″; and the defcriptions of it, given by Cook and Beering, exactly agree.

Cook † likewife explored the fame Continent, fituated in latitude 54′ 43″ and 55′ 20″, in longitude 224′ 44″, which makes it probable, that the land vifited by Tchirikof, and placed by him in latitude 56′, longitude 241′ from Fero, or 223′ 25″ from Greenwich, was really a part of America.

Alaxa, called fometimes Alaxfu, Alach-fnak and Alafhka, reached by many Ruf-

* Vol. II. p. 346.　　† Ib. p. 343.

fians,

fians *, particularly by Krenitzin and Levatchef, and fuppofed to be a great ifland in the vicinity of America, was found by Cook to be a promontory of that Continent. Its fouth-weftern point, reprefented on Krenitzin's chart, in latitude 54′ 42″, longitude 206′ 50″, from Fero, or 189′ 15″ from Greenwich, is laid down by Cook in latitude 54′ 10″, longitude 195′, which gives only a difference of 32 minutes in latitude, and 5′ 45″ in longitude.

That promontory lying oppofite to the country of the Tchutfki, which, according to Muller †, was firft feen by Gvofdef in 1730, and the moft weftern point of which is reprefented on the chart that accompanies his Ruffian Difcoveries, as lying in the 66th degree of latitude, and in the 211th of longitude from the Ifle of Fero, or 193′ 25″ from Greenwich. This point of land is probably the fame as that touched at by Synd, and placed by him in latitude 64′ 40″, and longitude 38′ 15″ from Okotfk ; or 181° 25′ from Greenwich.

* See Ruf. Dif. p. 72, 76, 77, 208.
† S. R. G. III. p. 131.

This

This promontory, named Cape Prince of Wales, Cook found to be the moſt weſtern point of America hitherto explored, lying in latitude 65′ 46′, in longitude 191′ 45″, which gives a difference of latitude from Muller of only 14 minutes, from Synd of 1′ 20″; and of longitude from Muller of only 1′ 40″, but from Synd of 10 degrees. It is diſtant from the eaſtern cape of Siberia only thirteen leagues. Thus Cook has the glory of aſcertaining the vicinity of the two continents, which had only been conjectured from the reports of the Tchutſki, and from the imperfect obſervations of the Ruſſian naⲧ vigators.

It reflects the higheſt honour on the Britiſh name, that even our great navigator extended his diſcoveries much further in one expedition, and at ſo great a diſtance from the point of his departure, than the Ruſſians accompliſhed in a long ſeries of years, and in parts belonging, or contiguous, to their own empire. But although we aſcribe this tribute of applauſe to the man whoſe claim is indiſputably founded; yet we ought not to withhold that portion of praiſe due to the Ruſſians, for having firſt navigated thoſe ſeas, and made
thoſe

thofe difcoveries which the Englifh have confirmed and greatly exceeded.

It muft indeed be confeffed, that Cook cenfures with juftice Staehlin's chart of the New Archipelago *; and ftrongly condemns it as an impofition on the public; fuch fictions in a work fo refpectably vouched, as the moft accurate reprefentation of the New-difcovered Iflands, being calculated only to miflead future navigators. In fact, Muller alfo, and the beft-informed Ruffians, had previoufly pronounced Mr. Staehling's account, and the annexed map, to be extremely erroneous †.

But our great navigator feems to have been too rigid in cenfuring Muller for placing Tchukotfkoi Nofs in too high a latitude; and for " his very imperfect knowledge of " the geography of thefe parts ‡." He did not fufficiently appreciate the merits of an author, who, though he unavoidably erred in fome particulars, yet deferves great approbation for his fagacity in uniformly fupporting the exiftence of Beering's Straits,

* Vol. II. p. 475. 486. 506. particularly.
† Ruf. Dif. p. 29, 380, 381.
‡ Vol. II. 470, 471. See alfo p. 503.

and the vicinity of the two continents; when thofe opinions had been treated as chimerical. If Cook had been able to read Muller's account of the Ruffian Difcoveries in the original German, and not in inaccurate tranflations *; if he had fairly weighed the extreme difficulty of drawing intelligence from imperfect journals of ignorant adventurers, from vague accounts, or uncertain tradition; if he had diftinguifhed what Muller advances as conjectural †, from what he lays down as fact; if he had known that Muller had candidly acknowledged and rectified feveral miftakes; if he had compared his trifling fources of information with his own pofitive proofs; he would not have been offended by thofe inaccuracies, which muft neceffarily arife from fuch complicated and multifarious queftions: he would probably have been lefs fevere in

* The Englifh tranflation of that work is the moft inaccurate.

† Mr. Muller's map of the north eaftern coaft of Siberia is allowed, by Captain King, "to bear a confiderable re-" femblance to the furvey of the Englifh navigators, as far " as the latter extended ‡;" and it is to be obferved, that the great promontory, which Muller lays down in latitude 75. as Tchukotfkoi Nofs, is reprefented in his map as very uncertain; and as a country, the extent of which is wholly unknown. *Pays des Tfchutfki dont on ne connoit pas l'etendue.*

‡ Vol. III. p. 263.

his

his judgement of a writer, who firſt excited the curioſity of the public towards thoſe diſcoveries, which occaſioned his own glorious expedition, under the auſpices of the ſovereign who now fits upon the Britiſh throne.

3. The new-diſcovered iſlands between Aſia and America form the third part of the preſent inquiry.

As my former account of the Ruſſian Diſcoveries renders it unneceſſary to particularize all the iſlands viſited by the Ruſſians, and laid down in their charts, I ſhall only ſelect the principal iſlands which were either aſcertained, or appear to have been obſerved by the Engliſh navigators.

Kadyak, or Kodiak, one of the moſt diſtant iſlands reached by the Ruſſians, is fully deſcribed from Glottof's journal in the tenth chapter of my Ruſſian Diſcoveries. It is placed by Glottof in the 230th degree of longitude from Fero, or 212′ 25″ from Greenwich; and is ſuppoſed to be not far diſtant from the coaſt of a wide extended woody continent, or from that part of America which Beering formerly touched at. This conjecture is confirmed by Cook, who mentions it as contiguous to America, and forming one of an extenſive group,

which

which he imagines to comprife thofe called by Beering Shumagin's Iflands *. Its true pofition is determined by Cook to be in latitude 55′ 18″, and longitude 199. The difference of longitude will not appear fo remarkably erroneous, when it is confidered that Glottof's account was computed merely from fhips reckonings, and that of Cook is founded on aftronomical obfervations.

This group is part of that chain, called the Fox Iflands; the longitude of which is very erroneoufly given upon all the Ruffian maps, and the latitude faithfully reprefented only on Krenitzin's chart; as will be more fully fhewn in the comparative account of Unalafka.

The next ifland which Cook accurately defcribes is that named Halibut, probably the fame as the ifland called Sannaga by Sóloviof, in his journal, a manufcript extract of which I have in my poffeffion. This ifland, termed Senagak by the Aleutian chief †, is flightly mentioned in my account of the Ruffian Difcoveries ‡, but is not laid down in

* Vol. II. p. 413. † Ruff. Dif. p. 238.
‡ It is not improbable, that this ifland is the fame as Kita Managan, which is reprefented on Krenitzin's chart, as lying near to Alaxa, and which has nearly the fame pofition as Halibut's Ifland in Cook's chart.

any

any of their charts under that name; it will probably appear to be Halibut's Ifland, by a comparative examination of the two defcriptions given by Cook and Soloviof.

" Halibut's Ifland lies near to the pro-
" montory of Alafka, is feven or eight leagues
" in circuit, and, except the *head, which is a*
" *round hill, the land of it is very low and bar-*
" *ren.* There are feveral fmall iflands near
" it of a fimilar appearance; but there feemed
" to be a paffage between them and the main,
" two or three leagues broad *."

Soloviof †, who anchored in a bay of Sannaga, Auguft 19, 1771, thus defcribes it:

" Sannaga is fituated not far from Unimak
" and Alaxa, and is feparated from the latter
" by a channel of about twenty leagues. It
" appeared to be about eight leagues in length,
" and about a league and three quarters in
" breadth. On the northern fide of the wef-
" tern point is a *fmall peak, joined to a low*

---

* Vol. II. p. 416.

† I have only printed a fmall part of his journal, as it contains no material information, in additional to thofe journals already publifhed in my Account of the Ruffian Difcoveries. Soloviof failed from Okotfk on this expedition to the Fox Iflands on the 6th of September, 1770; and returned on the 16th of July, 1775.

" *ridge*

" *ridge of hills extending* to the eaft and weft,
" about a verft, or three quarters of a mile.
" *Except this rifing ground, the whole ifland is*
" *low and marfhy.* It is watered by many
" fprings and lakes, containing fifh fimilar to
" thofe of Okotfk. *The ifland produces neither*
" *trees nor berries.* It is furrounded by many
" fmall iflands. It is feparated from a little
" ifland fituated near its fouthern point by a
" ftrait, about a league broad, which is fome-
" times dry. In reconnoitring this ifland,
" Soloviof obferved feveral deferted huts, but
" met with no inhabitants."

Unalafka, or Oonalafka, the largeft ifland,
next to Unimak, in the whole chain of the
Fox Iflands, and which has been frequently
vifited and defcribed by the Ruffians, was
alfo particularly obferved by Cook, who anchored in a fine bay on the north fide, called
by the natives Sanganoodha, and of which
he has given a chart. Unalafka is placed by
Cook in latitude 53′ 55″, longitude 193′ 30″;
by Krenitzin in latitude 53′ 30″, longitude
205′ 30″ from Fero; or 187′ 55″ from
Greenwich; on the general map of Ruffia
in latitude 58′, longitude 225′ from Fero; or
205′ 25″ from Greenwich. Thus it appears,
that

that in latitude Krenitzin only differs from Cook 25 minutes; and in longitude 5′ 35″.; whereas the general map of Ruffia varies 4′ 5″ even in latitude, and in longitude 11′ 55″. The fame error alfo prevails in the pofition of Unimak, Umnak, Amughta, and the other ifles adjacent to Unalafka, the fituations of which are corrected and determined by Cook *. Here it may be remarked, that the relative pofition of that part of the Fox Iflands, which ftretches fouth eaft from the head-land Alaxa, is well laid down in Kre-nitzin's chart; and that in all refpects it de-ferves the preference over the reprefentation of thofe iflands on the general Map of Ruffia.

The defcription of Unalafka and of the contiguous iflands, their extent, productions, and the manners of the natives, as given by Cook, correfponds entirely with the account of the fame iflands in the Ruffian Difco-veries; and ferves to prove, that the jour-nals, from which my account was drawn, are in thefe refpects faithful and accurate. No iflands in the chain of the Fox Iflands were obferved by Cook to the weft of

* See Cook's Voyage, Vol. II.

Amughta:

Amughta: a few fcattered Iflands are indeed reprefented on the chart which accompanies his journal, not from his own obfervation, but from a map communicated by a Ruffian, named Ifmailof, which I fhall hereafter confider *.

Whether the ifland, called by Cook Gore's Ifland, lying in latitude 60′ 10″, in longitude 187′, may be confidered as the ifland of St. Matthew, placed on Synd's chart in latitude 59′ 30″, longitude 34′ 10″ from Okotfk; or 176′ 42″ from Greenwich; is a conjecture which may deferve inquiry. The difference of latitude is only 40 minutes; and the deficiency in the longitude of 10′ 18″ nearly coincides with Synd's error of longitude obfervable in other inftances, while the general outline of its coaft, its relative fize and bearings to the head-lands of the two continents, fufficiently agree in the two charts.

The exiftence of the ifland St. Laurence, obferved by Beering near the Coaft of Siberia, was alfo confirmed by Cook; and it is not without probability, that thofe called Clerke's,

* Vol. II. p. 497, &c. See alfo Vol. III. p. 193, 194.

Anderſon's, and King's Iſlands, may perhaps form part of that group obſerved by Synd, and repreſented, on his chart, as lying near the head-lands of the Tchutſki.

The moſt eaſtern part of Copper Iſland is laid down, in the Ruſſian charts, in latitude 55′, longitude 184′ from Fero; or 166′ 25″ from Greenwich; and, after the obſervations of the Engliſh, is determined to lie in latitude 54′ 28″, longitude 167′ 52″, which gives a difference of but 32′ in the latitude, and of only 1′ 27″ in the longitude.

CHAP. II.

Sketch of what remains to be aſcertained.—1. On the coaſt of Aſia.*—2. On that of* America.*— 3. And in relation to the New-diſcovered Iſlands.—Expedition of Captain* Billings.

HAVING now reviewed and compared the Ruſſian Diſcoveries with thoſe made by Cook and Clerke, it is the deſign of this ſecond chapter to lay before the reader what remains to be aſcertained in thoſe remote quarters of the globe. In treating this

ſub-

subject, I shall follow the same order which I adopted in the first; and endeavour to explain the *desiderata* towards completing the geography, 1. of the Asiatic coast; 2. of the American Continent; 3. of the New-discovered Islands.

1. What principally remains to be examined on the Asiatic coast, is that region of Siberia stretching from Cape North in latitude 68′ 56″, longitude 180′ 51″, the utmost extent of Cook's discoveries, to the mouth of the Kovyma in the Frozen Ocean.

Cook conjectures, and the conjectures of so great a man deserve to be weighed with the utmost attention, that the northern coast of Asia, from the Indigirka eastwards, has been laid down by the Russian geographers more than two degrees too much to the northward: and Captain King no less ingeniously conceives, that nearly the same error of longitude prevails in the bearings of the Asiatic coast in the Frozen Ocean, which is proved to exist in the eastern coast of Siberia *. If therefore it should be deemed probable, that the Kovyma is represented

* See these questions fully and ably discussed by Captain King, Vol. III.

too much to the north and weſt, the diſtance between the mouth of that river and Cape North muſt be conſiderably leſs than is uſually imagined *.

It now remains to determine the unknown coaſt between Cape North and Shelatſkoi Noſs, the moſt eaſtern point traced by the Ruſſians in the Frozen Ocean, to take a more accurate delineation of the ſhore between Shelatſkoi Noſs and the Kovyma than has been effected by Shalaurof †, and to fix, by aſtronomical obſervations, the longitude and latitude of the mouth of the Kovyma.

2. The principal objects of examination on the American coaſt are the following parts of that continent, which Cook was prevented from exploring. That ſpace reaching from Woody Point in latitude 50′ 1″, and longitude 229′ 26″, to latitude 53′ 22″, longitude 225′ 14″, comprizes 3′ 22″ of latitude, and 4′ 12″ of longitude; and is the more remarkable, as it contains the place where geographers have aſcribed the ſtrait of Admiral de Fonte. "And although there is little rea-

* Cook's Voyage, Vol. II. p. 263—270.
† See Shalaurof's Voyage and Chart in my Ruſſian Diſcoveries.

" ſon

" fon to give credit," as Cook expreffes himfelf, " to fuch vague and improbable ftories,
" as carry their own confutation * ;" yet
it is to be regretted, that he was prevented
from entirely difproving thofe pretended difcoveries which fome perfons ftill confider as
authentic.

The fhore between Shoal-Nefs, in latitude
60′, longitude 198′ 10″, and Point Shallow
Water, in latitude 63′, longitude 198′, is
alfo entirely undefcribed ; and what renders
this coaft an interefting fubject of inquiry,
is the inference of Captain Cook, that here
runs a confiderable river from the continent
into the fea †.

Perhaps it would well deferve the attention
of fome future navigator, to explore Cook's
river ftill further than the Englifh navigator was able to penetrate : he traced it as
high as latitude 61′ 30″, longitude 210′,
feventy leagues or more from its mouth,
without feeing the leaft appearance of its
fource. Perhaps this great river, which, to
ufe Cook's expreffion ‡, " promifes to vie
" with the moft confiderable ones already

* Vol. II. p. 343.   † Ib. p. 491.   ‡ Ib. p. 396.

" known

" known to be capable of extenfive inland
" navigation," may nearly join thofe waters
and lakes which Hearne difcovered in his
curious expedition from Hudfon's Bay to the
Arapathefcow Indians, recorded in Dr.
Douglas's learned Introduction to Cook's
Voyage * ; and may thus help to eftablifh
an inland communication between the Pacific
and Atlantic Oceans.

To the north of Beering's Straits, the land
of America from Point † Mufgrave in latitude 67′ 45″, longitude 194′ 51″, to Icy
Cape, in latitude 70′ 29″, longitude 198′
20″, where Cook was totally ftopped by the
ice, was not, excepting a fmall portion near
Cape Lifburne, and another to the fouth of
that promontory, obferved either by Cook or
Clerke ; and its true bearings muft be afcertained by future navigators.

But the moft important point of further
inquiry is to trace the direction of the American continent from Icy Cape, whether it
again trends to the north weft, and, according to the reports of the Tchutfki, approaches
the coafts of Northern Siberia, or verges directly to the eaft towards Baffin's Bay.

* P. xlvii.   † Vol. II. p. 454. 461.

The

The execution of fuch an undertaking, in fuch diftant regions, and in fo high a latitude, muft neceffarily be attended with extreme difficulty and hazard. For the points of diftance between Icy Cape and the north weftern extremity of Baffin's Bay, include a fpace of no lefs than feventy-one degrees longitude : of which nearly the central point has been explored by Hearne alone *.

It muft be neverthelefs admitted, that fuch inquiries, however interefting to increafe our knowledge of the globe, do not tend to throw any new light on the practicability of a north-eaft paffage; which has been difproved by the obftacles and difficulties encountered by the Ruffians in navigating the Frozen Ocean †, and more particularly by the undoubted teftimony of Cook himfelf.

3. The new-difcovered iflands remain to be confidered. We have already remarked, that, as Cook obferved only a few of thofe numerous iflands which lie fcattered in the Eaftern Ocean between Afia and America, the pofition and defcription of the remainder are to be drawn from the Ruffian accounts. It

---

* See the Introduction to Cook's Voyage.
† See Ruffian Difcoveries, p. 271.

can-

cannot be denied that the Ruffians have frequently corrupted their names, increafed their
number, and miftaken their fituation. It is probable, indeed, that Synd may have aug-
mented the number of iflands which lie near
the coafts of the Tchutfki; that St. Theodore,
Imyak, and Tzetchina, which are laid down
among the Aleutian Ifles in the general map
of Ruffia, do not exift ; and that the Andrea-
noffki Ifles, which are confidered as a feparate group, form the moft wefterly part of
that extenfive chain termed the Fox Iflands,
of which Unalafhka, fo amply defcribed by
Cook and the Ruffians, is nearly the center.

It may be urged, however, that, if the inaccuracy of the Ruffian charts, in general, be
admitted, and their accounts are juftly deemed
imperfect, what advantages can be derived
from their publication ?

To this it may be replied, that confiderable
information may be obtained even from imperfect accounts, and that many points have,
in effect, been afcertained, as the reader has
already perceived in this Comparative View.
We find even Cook himfelf anxious to procure intelligence from a Ruffian named Ifmailof, from whom he received a chart of the
Ruffian

Ruffian Difcoveries. This chart, however, was not founded on the obfervations of a fingle navigator, but feems to have been a compilation from different charts and journals, and, confequently, extremely erroneous.

Nor does it appear that Ifmailof either pof-feffed, or had feen, Krenitzin's chart of the Fox Iflands, which, according to the ob-fervations of the Englifh, is proved to be the moft accurate reprefentation of the Fox Iflands given by the Ruffians. The correction of this erroneous chart from Ifmailof's own ex-perience, and additional remarks, muft have been ftill doubtful. For, as Captain Cook could not fpeak the Ruffian language, and as he had no Ruffian interpreter on board, the imperfect knowledge of this illiterate man was rendered ftill more imperfect by the only mode of communication they could adopt, that of converfing by figns.

And yet, under all thefe difadvantages, Cook gained fome information relative to the pofition and number of the iflands which he had not explored; an information which he has thought worthy to be laid before the public.

He

He particularly informs us, that " a paf-
" fage was marked in Ifmailof's chart, com-
" municating with Briftol Bay, which covers
" about fifteen leagues on the coaft, that I
" had fuppofed to belong to the continent,
" into an ifland diftinguifhed by the name of
" Oonemak. This paffage might eafily
" efcape us, as we were informed that it is
" very narrow, fhallow, and only to be navi-
" gated through with boats, or very fmall
" veffels *."

The exiftence of this ftrait, which Cook
has adopted in his chart, from Ifmailof's obfervations, might likewife have been collected from Krenitzin's chart, and the feveral
journals in my Account of the Ruffian Difcoveries, wherein Unimak or Oonemak is
fhewn to be an ifland feparated from Alaxa,
fince proved to be the continent of America,
by a narrow ftrait.

It muft not be thought furprifing, that
a collection of voyages, performed by ignorant traders merely for the fake of obtaining
furs, and not with a view of difcovery, fhould
be defective in determining the pofition and

* Vol. II. p. 505.

number of so many islands. We ought rather to wonder that the descriptions, in general, are tolerably accurate, and afford that degree of information which they are found to contain. Nor must it be forgotten that Beering's and Krenitzin's expedition, which alone were undertaken by Imperial authority, reflect considerable honour on the Ruffian name.

The particulars which remain to be afcer_tained with refpect to the new-difcovered iflands, are, to remove the uncertainty arifing from the confufion of names, to determine the true number, and to fix the longitude and latitude. And when it is confidered that the fea, unexplored by Cook, includes a fpace of at leaft ten degrees of latitude, and twenty of longitude, much, in this inftance, remains to be effected by the labours of future adventurers.

Thefe are the principal objects of examination on the coafts of Afia and America, and in refpect to the new-difcovered iflands. In order to forward thefe great ends, the Emprefs of Ruffia, with that boundlefs liberality and enlightened fpirit which characterifes her actions, has planned and commanded a voyage of of difcovery. The care of this expedition, which was agitated and determined during my fecond vifit to Peterfburgh in 1785, is committed to Captain Billings, an Englifh naval officer in the Ruffian fervice, who is well qualified to conduct fuch an undertaking, as he accompanied Captain Cook in his laft celebrated voyage to the Pacific Ocean. I fhall briefly ftate the plan and purport of this expedition.

According to its firft object, Captain Billings is to proceed by Irkutfk, Yakutfk, and Okotfk, to Kovimfkoi Oftrog : having traced the courfe of the Kovyma, and fettled by aftronomical obfervations the exact pofition of its mouth, he will endeavour to delineate the coafts extending from that point to Cape North, the utmoft period of Cook's navigation on the North-eaftern fhores of Siberia. For this purpofe he will embark in fuch veffels as are ufually employed for coafting voyages in the Frozen Ocean ; fix the longitude and latitude of the principal parts by aftronomical obfervations ; form exact charts of the bays and inlets which he may have occafion to explore ; and caufe views to be taken of the bearings, head-lands, and remarkable

markable objects on the coaft. If he fhould
be prevented by the ice, or any other ob-
ftacle, from getting round by fea to Tchukotfkoi Nofs, he muft difembark, and endeavour to proceed by land or over the ice,
furveying the coaft and diftrict of the Tchutfki,
and obtaining an accurate knowledge of their
manners, population, and country. In both
cafes, and in all inftances, he is enjoined to
abftain from the leaft degree of violence; is
directed to ufe every effort towards concili-
ating the affection of the natives; to obtain
information and affiftance by the gentleft treat-
ment, and a proper diftribution of prefents;
and to confirm them in their dependence and
favourable opinion of the Ruffian government, to which they have recently fubmitted.

While he continues in thefe parts, he will
not neglect an opportunity of exploring the
iflands and coafts of America, that may be
fituated in the Frozen Ocean, or to the north
of Beering's ftraits.

Having attempted to execute thefe defigns,
he is to return to Okotfk, where two fhips,
of a proper burden for a voyage of difcovery,
will be prepared for his further embarkation.
He

He is then to fail and follow the numerous chain of iflands which extend to the continent of America; determining their refpective longitudes and latitudes by a feries of aftronomical obfervations; taking an exact chart of their pofitions, and particularly noticing thofe roads and harbours which appear to be moft fecure. He is alfo to extend his refearches towards fuch parts of the American coaft, which bad weather and other impediments prevented preceding navigators from furveying. And, in cafe his former attempts to determine the coaft of the Tchutfki from the mouth of the Kovyma to Cape North, and to gain an accurate information of the country, fhould be ineffectual; he is again ordered to fail towards Tchukotfkoi-Nofs, and endeavour to penetrate by fea from Beering's Straits to the mouth of the Kovyma, and to make thofe obfervations, and obtain that intelligence of thofe regions which he could not procure on the former occafion.

Six years will be requifite for the accomplifhment of thefe various purpofes. In order to enfure its fuccefs, every poffible en-
courage-

couragement, in regard to promotion and
rank, as the refpective objects are fulfilled,
is given to the commander and his followers.
No expence has been fpared towards procuring fuch an apparatus and inftruments as
are neeeffary for this expedition.

For the purpofe alfo of elucidating the
natural hiftory of thofe diftant regions, at
prefent fo imperfectly known, the commander is accompanied by Monfieur Patrin,
an eminent French naturalift, fome time refident at Irkutfk, who is furnifhed with fuch
excellent inftructions as are moft calculated
to forward the object of his miffion.

Captain Billings fet out from St. Peterfburgh on this expedition in the latter end of
1785. He arrived at Irkutfk in March, 1786;
and at Okotfk in July of the fame year,
from whence he propofed inftantly to take
his departure for the Kovyma. It is not indeed improbable, that, before the prefent
period, he may have afcertained the longitude
and latitude of the mouth of the Kovyma;
and thus have determined one important fact,
relative to the precife diftance between the
Kovyma and Cape North. The length of
time

time requifite for the conveying of intelligence from thofe diftant regions to St. Peterfburgh, and the difficulty of obtaining certain information from that capital, renders it impoffible to gratify the further curiofity of the reader.

[454]

POSTSCRIPT.

THE reader is requested to correct the longitude of Kamtchatka, mentioned p. 5 of my Ruſſian Diſcoveries, as lying between 173 and 182 degrees from the iſle of Fero; or 155 and 165 from Greenwich. Whereas, by the obſervations of the Engliſh, it is ſituated between 155 and 169 from Greenwich; or 172 and 186 from Fero; the Ruſſian geographers having laid down the North-eaſtern part of the peninſula near three degrees too much to the weſt.

ERRATA.

P. 420. l. 4. for *ſeven* minutes read *one* minute.
421. l. 17. for 50′. read 10″.
428. l. 13. for 28. read 25.

I N D E X.

A.

Anadirſkoi Noſs. See *Tchukotſkoi-Noſss.*

B.

Beering. Juſtice done to his memory by Captain Cook, 422. A miſtake concerning him rectified, *ibid.* note.

Billings (Capt.) an Engliſh naval officer in the Ruſſian ſervice, appointed on an expedition planned by the Empreſs for new diſcoveries, 449. Plan and purport of this expedition, 442—453.

C.

Charts (Ruſſian,) erroneous with reſpect to the bearings of the Kamtchatka coaſt, 421. Conſiderable information, however, to be gathered from them relative to the new-diſcovered iſlands, 444—448.

Cook (Capt.) his diſcoveries on the continent of America compared with the Ruſſian accounts, 427—433. between Aſia and America, 433—439. He conjectures that the Ruſſian geographers are erroneous reſpecting the Northern coaſt of Aſia, 440. Parts of the American continent which he was prevented from exploring, 441—444.

D.

I N D E X.

D.

F I N I S.